Uncertain Demographics and Fiscal Sustainability

There is widespread acceptance that much of the developed world faces a potential pensions and welfare crisis as a result of declining birth rates and an ageing population. However, there is considerable uncertainty about the specifics of demographic forecasting and this has significant implications for public finances. *Uncertain Demographics and Fiscal Sustainability* addresses the economic consequences of uncertainty and, with particular reference to European economies, explores the impact of demographic risks on public finances, including pension systems, health care and old-age care expenditures. Covering a spectrum of theoretical and empirical approaches, different types of computational models are used to demonstrate not only the magnitudes of the uncertainties involved but also how these can be addressed through policy initiatives. The book is divided into four parts covering demographic, measurement, policy and methodological issues. Each part is followed by a discussion essay that draws out key elements and identifies common themes.

JUHA M. ALHO is Professor of Statistics at the University of Joensuu, Finland. He is the author (with Bruce D. Spencer) of *Statistical Demography and Forecasting* (2005) and a former president of the Finnish Society of Biostatistics.

SVEND E. HOUGAARD JENSEN is Managing Director of the Copenhagen-based Centre for Economic and Business Research (CEBR), Professor of Economics at Copenhagen Business School and a member of the Danish Council for Research Policy.

JUKKA LASSILA is Research Director at the Research Institute of the Finnish Economy (ETLA) in Helsinki. He has co-ordinated several international research projects concerning population ageing and was scientific co-ordinator in the EU Fifth Framework research project 'Demographic Uncertainty and the Sustainability of Social Welfare Systems'.

Uncertain Demographics and Fiscal Sustainability

Edited by

Juha M. Alho, Svend E. Hougaard Jensen and
Jukka Lassila

CAMBRIDGE
UNIVERSITY PRESS

CAMBRIDGE UNIVERSITY PRESS
Cambridge, New York, Melbourne, Madrid, Cape Town,
Singapore, São Paulo, Delhi, Mexico City

Cambridge University Press
The Edinburgh Building, Cambridge CB2 8RU, UK

Published in the United States of America by Cambridge University Press, New York

www.cambridge.org
Information on this title: www.cambridge.org/9781107405059

First published 2008
First paperback edition 2011

A catalogue record for this publication is available from the British Library

ISBN 978-0-521-87740-4 Hardback
ISBN 978-1-107-40505-9 Paperback

Contents

Figures

Tables

Contributors

NAMKEE AHN Fundacion de Estudios de Economia Aplicada (FEDEA), Spain

JUHA M. ALHO University of Joensuu, Finland

PABLO ANTOLIN OECD

ALEX ARMSTRONG Netherlands Bureau for Economic Policy Analysis (CPB), The Netherlands

VLADIMIR BORGY Centre d'Etudes Prospectives et d'Informations Internationales (CEPII), France

D. PETER BROER Netherlands Bureau for Economic Policy Analysis (CPB), The Netherlands

HARRI CRUIJSEN Democast, The Netherlands

NICK DRAPER Netherlands Bureau for Economic Policy Analysis (CPB), The Netherlands

HANS FEHR University of Würzburg, Germany

MARTIN FLODÉN Stockholm School of Economics, Sweden

CHRISTIAN HABERMANN University of Würzburg, Germany

SVEND E. HOUGAARD JENSEN Centre for Economic and Business Research (CEBR), Denmark

OLE HAGEN JØRGENSEN Centre for Economic and Business Research (CEBR), Denmark

NICO KEILMAN University of Oslo, Norway

JUKKA LASSILA Research Institute of the Finnish Economy (ETLA), Finland

NIKU MÄÄTTÄNEN Research Institute of the Finnish Economy (ETLA), Finland

ANDRÉ NIBBELINK Netherlands Bureau for Economic Policy Analysis (CPB), The Netherlands

SHRIPAD TULJAPURKAR Stanford University, USA

TARMO VALKONEN Research Institute of the Finnish Economy (ETLA), Finland

JUSTIN VAN DE VEN National Institute of Economic and Social Research (NIESR), UK

MARTIN WEALE National Institute of Economic and Social Research (NIESR), UK

ED WESTERHOUT Netherlands Bureau for Economic Policy Analysis (CPB), The Netherlands

Preface

This book arose from two research projects, 'Demographic Uncertainty and the Sustainability of Social Welfare Systems' (DEMWEL) and 'Uncertain Population of Europe' (UPE).

DEMWEL was carried out between January 2003 and March 2006 by research teams from the following nine institutes: CEBR, the Centre for Economic and Business Research, Copenhagen, Denmark; CEPII, Centre d'Etudes Prospectives et d'Informations Internationales, Paris, France; CEPS, the Centre for European Policy Studies, Brussels, Belgium; CPB, the Netherlands Bureau for Economic Policy Analysis, The Hague, The Netherlands; ETLA, the Research Institute of the Finnish Economy, Helsinki, Finland; FEDEA, Fundacion de Estudios de Economia Aplicada, Madrid, Spain; FPB, the Belgian Federal Planning Bureau, Brussels, Belgium; NIESR, the National Institute for Economic and Social Research, London, UK; and the University of Würzburg, Germany.

DEMWEL utilized results produced in UPE. The latter ran from September 2001 to August 2004 and was carried out by researchers from the Central Bureau of Statistics, The Netherlands; the Central Bureau of Statistics, Norway; NIDI, The Netherlands; Statistics Finland; and the University of Joensuu, Finland.

Both DEMWEL and UPE were funded by the EU's Fifth Framework Programme. A grant from the Yrjö Jahnsson Foundation for editing this book is also gratefully acknowledged.

1   Introduction

*Juha M. Alho, Svend E. Hougaard Jensen and
Jukka Lassila*

It is a widely held perception that future population paths can be projected with a fairly high degree of certainty. For example, as an input to assessments of the future stance of public finances following population ageing, most countries now routinely report old-age dependency ratios and other demographic indicators. However, by concentrating on one (or a few) selected population path(s), this practice fails to recognize that population forecasts are, in fact, highly uncertain.

Uncertainty in demographics has traditionally been accounted for by considering 'high' and 'low' scenarios in addition to a 'medium' assumption. However, it has long been known that this approach has serious shortcomings. For example, the scenarios assume a perfect (positive or negative) correlation not only between the vital processes of fertility, mortality and migration but also across age and time for each vital process. Moreover, the method is intrinsically unable to assign probabilities to its 'high–low' ranges.

While the flaws associated with the traditional approach in themselves warrant an alternative approach, what matters from an economic perspective is the extent to which the application of stochastic forecasting techniques modifies outcomes obtained using traditional techniques. Despite the different methodologies used in the production of stochastic forecasts, it turns out as an empirical regularity that the level of uncertainty in demographic forecasts is much higher than generally believed. We would clearly expect this finding to translate into economic variables, by making the variability in health- and pension-related as well as in broader macroeconomic outcomes much larger than often recognized.

This volume focuses on these and other important unresolved issues concerning uncertain demographics. We have a collection of twelve chapters, with four discussion essays, which focus on the impact of demographic risks on public finances in general and pension systems and health and old-age care expenditures in particular, and it is discussed how policy strategies and specific policies may be designed in order to reduce the threats caused by such uncertainties. The chapters cover a spectrum

1

of theoretical and empirical approaches, and different types of computational models are used to demonstrate not only the magnitudes of the
uncertainties involved but also how these can be addressed through policy
initiatives. We have grouped the chapters into four main parts, each with a
particular focus: demographic issues; measurement issues; policy issues;
and methodological issues. Each part contains original and self-contained
contributions on a specific topic, and concludes with a Discussion draw-
ing out key elements from each contribution and identifying common
themes.

Demographic issues

The first part of the book, on demographic issues, has two interrelated
contributions. In Chapter 2, Nico Keilman, Harri Cruijsen and Juha Alho
discuss problems in official population projections prepared by the UN
and Eurostat. These forecasts are widely used to provide a demographic
foundation for analyses of likely future economic developments. It was
recently concluded by the US National Academy of Sciences Panel on
Population Projections that the UN forecasts represent, in many respects,
the state of the art. Yet, the authors show that the forecasts appear to suffer
from systematic biases. Mortality has declined faster than the official forecasters expected, so in forecast revisions the future number of the elderly
has been continuously revised upwards. Similarly, net migration has been
typically underestimated, which shows up in forecasts as a gradual revision towards higher numbers, especially in the working-age populations.
The authors argue that methods that rely more closely on empirical data
on past trends and past levels of the demographic processes should be
used. These lead to higher numbers of the elderly – and higher numbers
of workers – than anticipated in the official forecasts. Both aspects have
important implications for research on ageing.

In Chapter 3, Juha Alho, Harri Cruijsen and Nico Keilman take up the
problem of uncertainty in demographic forecasting. Even if biases could
be reduced in future forecasts by statistical techniques, the application of
the same techniques suggests that considerable uncertainty remains. In
the past, demographic forecasters have produced alternative (high and
low) variants, in addition to the most likely forecast, to provide forecast
users with an indication of the uncertainty one might reasonably expect.
The authors argue that the alternative variants are inherently defective as
descriptors of uncertainty. In essence, this is due to the fact that forecast
errors across sex, age, vital processes (of fertility, mortality and migration), and future year have complex correlations that cannot be coher-
ently approximated by deterministic methods. In contrast, a stochastic

formulation allows the representation of such dependency structures in a flexible manner. The authors emphasize the need to provide an empirical foundation for uncertainty estimates, and provide examples from recent work with European data. In particular, it is shown that the volatility of fertility, life expectancy and net migration is much higher than suggested by the official high and low variants. The chapter contains an appendix that systematically compares traditional forecasts and stochastic forecasts.

Measurement issues

The second part of the book is devoted to measurement issues in relation to the consequences of demographic uncertainty. The basic question is: given the estimates of demographic uncertainty, how uncertain are the projections of ageing costs? By combining economic models and stochastic population simulations, the chapters provide estimates for several European countries.

In Chapter 4, Martin Weale assesses the implications of demographic uncertainty for the budgetary position in Belgium, Denmark, Finland, Germany, the Netherlands, Spain and the United Kingdom. More specifically, Weale evaluates the frequency distribution of the increase in taxes needed to deliver fiscal solvency. The projections reported in this chapter, taken at face value, imply a substantial amount of variation in the tax adjustment needed to restore fiscal balance in the countries examined. The considerable amount of variation in the means is not surprising, since it is well known that different countries are affected by demographic change in different ways. However, there is also a lot of variability in the standard deviations, which may have a less intuitive explanation. Weale argues that this, to a large extent, should be attributed to the nature of the simulations, not simply the structure of the model used to carry out the simulations.

In Chapter 5, Jukka Lassila and Tarmo Valkonen summarize quantitative estimates of the uncertainty in long-term pension expenditure projections caused by demographic factors for Belgium, Denmark, Finland, Germany, the Netherlands, Spain and the UK. The estimates are obtained from model-based country studies which use stochastic population simulations as inputs. The results show a great deal of uncertainty in pension projections. There are significant differences between the uncertainty estimates in these countries. One reason is that the critical demographic feature, the ratio of people in old age to those of working age, appears more predictable in some countries than others. The differences also reflect differences in pension systems, especially whether there are automatic demographically based adjustment mechanisms as in Finland and Germany. The properties of the models that were used also have effects. The chapter also relates the uncertainty estimates of the country studies to the uncertainty considerations in recent administrative projections that rely on sensitivity analysis as a method to describe uncertainties. The range of the resulting, judgemental quantifications of uncertainty turns out to be small, as compared to those obtained in the country studies that rely on empirical estimates of demographic uncertainty.

Chapter 6, by Namkee Ahn, tries to improve upon the existing literature on the projection of future health expenditure by incorporating probabilistic handling of uncertainties in future population. The impact of uncertainties in fertility, mortality and immigration rates on the age profile of health expenditure is detailed. Ahn also compares the effect of different scenarios of price/preference changes to the range of outcomes that reflect only demographic uncertainty. According to the median prediction, public health expenditure will increase by 33 per cent (or 2 to 5 percentage points as a share of GDP) during the period 2004–2050 purely due to changes in population age-structure, under the hypothesis of constant real age-specific health expenditure. Taking into account demographic uncertainty, one can say that chances are four out of five that the increase is between 28 per cent and 39 per cent. However, even a slightly higher growth rate of per-capita health expenditure (due to price or preference change), relative to that of per-capita GDP, results in a much more substantial increase in total expenditure.

Policy issues

Policies with important linkages to demographics are currently being considered in many European countries. For example, longevity adjustment of pension benefits has been introduced in Finland, Latvia and Sweden, and an indexation scheme which takes demographics into account has been introduced in Germany. Other, new instruments for managing economic risks caused by uncertain demographics have become of interest. Such policy measures may have substantial income and risk-bearing consequences for the citizens, but the magnitude of the effects depend on demographic development. Combining current economic simulation models with stochastic population paths allows us to analyse and quantify the effects. The insights obtained may be important, because the most rapid phase in population ageing (arising from the retirement of the baby-boomers) is just around the corner, and the time for making structural changes is quickly running out.

In Chapter 7, Hans Fehr and Christian Habermann compare the effects of two adjustment mechanisms of the German pension system under demographic uncertainty. The first instrument is an increase of the statutory retirement age, which would reduce future benefits and contribution rates. As an alternative, they consider an increase in the weight of the indexation scheme that links future pensions to changes in the dependency ratio. Both reforms redistribute income from the elderly to the young, and to future generations. They have exactly the same consequences for the intertemporal budget constraint of the government. By taking into account the uncertainty of future population projections, the authors illustrate variations in the intergenerational risk-sharing consequences of the two reforms. They show that increasing the weight of the indexation scheme creates a much larger risk for the current elderly than the increase in the retirement age. The conclusion is that the latter is to be preferred, since it avoids a double burden for the elderly.

Jukka Lassila and Tarmo Valkonen, in Chapter 8, study the effects of longevity adjustment in the context of Finland's earnings-related pension system. If longevity increases, new old-age pensions are automatically reduced and pension contribution rates will be lower. Moreover, the higher the contribution rate would have been without the reform, the bigger the reduction. On the receiving side, longevity adjustment increases uncertainty about the level of pensions. Lassila and Valkonen conclude that longevity adjustment significantly weakens the defined-benefit nature of the Finnish pension system, in effect introducing a strong defined-contribution flavour. With longevity adjustment, demographic uncertainty actually makes future benefits more uncertain than future contributions when measured in comparable units. Without longevity adjustment almost all of the uncertainty would be in contributions. The authors note that the relative timing of longevity and fertility risks is important. For the next twenty to thirty years the effects of future fertility changes on pension outcomes are small, and the longevity adjustment decreases the dominant uncertainty effect of demographics. After thirty years, future fertility starts to affect labour supply more, and longevity adjustment alone is inadequate for controlling the effects of demographic risks.

Chapter 9, by Alex Armstrong, Nick Draper, André Nibbelink and Ed Westerhout, focuses on the implications of demographic uncertainty on public debt policies. The idea is that uncertainty causes households to save for precautionary purposes to the government sector. A computational general equilibrium model for the Netherlands (GAMMA) is combined with stochastic population paths to compare alternative fiscal policy rules. The comparison shows that in an uncertain demographic environment, setting the short-term tax rates higher than the expected long-term tax rates implies a higher level of social welfare than a tax-smoothing strategy. Interestingly, this result is due not only to the risk aversion of households but also to the concavity of the government's revenue function. The effects are non-trivial. In the two-period setting applied, the first-period labour income tax rate that corresponds to optimal policies is about four percentage points higher than the level that corresponds to a tax-smoothing strategy. This tax increase is particularly painful if it comes on top of the tax increase that is needed to finance the implicit debt that is due to the expected ageing of the population. Yet, even if adopted, precautionary savings policies appear to do little to mitigate the expected aggregate utility loss from demographic uncertainty.

Methodological issues

The combined use of economic and demographic tools in a stochastic setting is still in its infancy, and using the current models leaves much to be desired. An obvious question concerns promising directions to extend the economic models. In addition, how should stochastic population simulations be refined to better serve economic analysis? Attempts to answer these questions are made in the contributions to the final part of the book.

In Chapter 10, Vladimir Borgy and Juha Alho extend existing methods tailored for national economies (which the earlier chapters illustrated) to the multi-regional case. Their model builds on a deterministic model of the world economy (INGENUE) that divides the world into ten regions. Because of data problems, demographic analyses comparable to those available for Europe do not exist for the other major regions of the world at the required, age-specific level. However, the authors use existing analyses regarding uncertainty in the total populations of world regions to extend and calibrate what are essentially models of the type discussed in Chapter 3 to the ten regions. In this manner a full stochastic multi-regional model of world population is created. Sample paths from the ten regions are used as inputs in INGENUE. The authors consider the induced uncertainty in such macro-economic variables as GDP growth and world interest rate.

The remaining chapters embark on an entirely different, theoretical path to extending the models of earlier chapters. In Chapter 11, Juha Alho and Niku Määttänen consider a simple life-cycle savings problem in the presence of both idiosyncratic and aggregate uncertainty concerning mortality. In other words, not only is the decision-maker's own survival random, but so is the future trend of mortality of her cohort. A simplified Markovian mortality model is built that allows a full rational-expectations solution to the life-cycle savings plan. This is used as a benchmark to assess the nature of other types of decision-makers that have either more (as in the case of perfect foresight) or less information concerning future mortality. In particular, the authors show that in the setting they consider, a decision-maker who revises her savings decisions periodically can achieve nearly as high a lifetime utility as that obtained under rational expectations. As the former decision strategy is considerably easier to compute, this finding points to the potential usefulness of considering a similar updating approach in the context of the more complex overlapping-generations models, for which rational-expectations analyses are, at least currently, beyond our computational capacities.

In Chapter 12, Svend E. Hougaard Jensen and Ole Hagen Jørgensen analyse some macro-economic and distributional effects of stochastic fertility and longevity using a three-period model with overlapping generations. A new solution technique is adopted that solves the model in terms of analytical elasticities. The novelty of this contribution is an analysis of longevity adjustment of the retirement age as a policy instrument to generate efficient risk-sharing in an economy faced by demographic shocks. Jensen and Jørgensen find that a rise in the retirement age following an increase in expected longevity may leave both workers and retirees better off. However, this is not the case within an alternative setting where taxes on wage incomes are adjusted to share risks efficiently across generations. So, the retirement age outperforms taxes as a policy instrument. Recognizing a number of limitations in their proposed analytical framework (including an assumption of an inelastic labour supply), the authors suggest extensions for future research.

In Chapter 13, by Justin van de Ven and Martin Weale, the implications for the annuities market of aggregate mortality uncertainty (risk) are explored. Any cohort can insure itself against individual mortality risk, but insurance against aggregate mortality risk can be provided only by means of a transaction between different cohorts. Van de Ven and Weale consequently study the pricing of aggregate mortality risk using an overlapping-generations model. In their model, the old and the young have different attitudes to the mortality risk of the old because the young can adjust their future consumption to the mortality out-turn of the old in a way that the old cannot. Annuity rates are calculated that balance the willingness of the young to purchase the aggregate mortality risk of the old. The authors find that moderate rates of aggregate mortality risk are likely to imply market-clearing annuity rates, which are between 1 per cent and 7 per cent below actuarially fair rates, depending upon the extent of risk aversion.

Part I

Uncertain demographics

2　Changing views of future demographic trends

Nico Keilman, Harri Cruijsen and Juha M. Alho

Introduction

Are population processes easy to predict? The relative inertia of population stocks suggests that this is the case. Indeed, errors in population forecasts five to ten years into the future are often smaller than the errors of economic forecasts over a similar period (Ascher, 1978). However, population flows are much harder to predict (Keilman, 1990), so in the long run, population processes are much more uncertain than generally recognized. Yet, many tasks of social policy, such as planning of schools and health care require information about the likely developments of population variables for twenty or thirty years into the future. Analyses of the sustainability of pension systems require that we take an even longer view, so the US Office of the Actuary routinely prepares forecasts seventy-five years into the future (Andrews and Beekman, 1987), for example.

One way the uncertainty in population variables manifests itself is through changing views, over time, of the demographic future. For instance, a forecast of a particular population made in 2000 may be different from one made ten years earlier. New data for the period 1990–2000, different interpretations of historical developments before 1990, refined techniques of analysis and prediction – all these shape different conditions for the forecast made in 2000, compared to the one made in 1990. As an example, consider Table 2.1. It shows UN forecasts of the 2050 old-age dependency ratio (OADR), i.e. the ratio of the elderly population (aged 65+) to the working age population (aged 20–64). We show forecasts that were made in 1994 (the so-called '1994 Revision'), and compare them with forecasts computed ten years later ('2004 Revision').

We see that the UN changed its view towards greater ageing in four of the five countries. Leaving out Germany, we find that the average increase in the forecasted OADR was 18 per cent over a decade! From the perspective of analysing the sustainability of pension systems, this is of major importance. Below we shall see that the UN has indeed become more optimistic concerning life expectancy. It so happens that life expectancy

11

Table 2.1. *Predictions of the old-age dependency ratio in 2050: selected countries.*

	1994 Revision	2004 Revision
Austria	0.517	0.599
Finland	0.402	0.504
France	0.471	0.524
Germany	0.585	0.550
Norway	0.385	0.453

predictions for Germany are also higher for the 2004 Revision than for the 1994 Revision. However, its effect on the German OADR is compensated by an increase in expected immigration levels, which primarily affects the population of working age.

It is not surprising that the UN has changed its views concerning population variables in European countries in 2050. After all, we cannot know the future with certainty, and updates are necessary. However, the changes from one forecast round to the next are far from random. Instead, they display rather *characteristic* patterns. Our purpose in this chapter is to document systematic changes that characterize population forecasts prepared by the UN and Eurostat. In the case of fertility and migration, there are also important differences between the two organizations. Moreover, we shall see that the changes are directly relevant for research on ageing, which frequently relies on official forecasts as a guide for what to expect.

Indicators such as the OADR in Table 2.1 summarize a population's age-structure. The age-structure can be deduced once one assumes certain levels for future fertility, mortality and international migration. We will analyse how the assumptions concerning these flows have changed. We consider a group of eighteen European countries. The group consists of the fifteen members of the European Union prior to the joining of the new member states in 2004 (i.e. Austria, Belgium, Denmark, Finland, France, Germany, Greece, Italy, Ireland, Luxembourg, the Netherlands, Portugal, Spain, Sweden and the United Kingdom) plus Iceland, Norway and Switzerland. Except for Switzerland, these countries made up the so-called European Economic Area, hence we call the area 'EEA+'.[1] These countries were also included in our own UPE forecasts,[2] with which we will make comparisons throughout.

The data used in this chapter stem partly from the World Population Prospects of 1994, 1996, 1998, 2000, 2002 and 2004, forecasted by the UN and partly from Eurostat forecasts. Cruijsen and Eding (1997), De Jong and Visser (1997), De Jong (1998) and Van Hoorn and De

Beer (1998) document the assumptions for the Eurostat forecasts of 1994, while Economic Policy Committee (2001) contains information about the Eurostat forecast of 1999. Eurostat's 2004-based forecast is described in Eurostat (2005) and Lanzieri (2006). The UPE website (www.stat.fi/tup/euupe/) gives information about the UPE forecasts.

After an introductory section on the cohort-component method of population forecasting, we will study UN forecasts prepared every second year between 1994 and 2004. Eurostat computes its forecasts less frequently, and we will use those with base years 1995, 1999 and 2004. An important finding is that the UN and Eurostat have systematically adjusted their views with respect to life expectancy and net migration towards higher levels. Yet, based on UPE work, we also explain why we believe that these levels still fall short of what one should expect.

Conventional and stochastic population forecasts based on the cohort-component method

The UN and Eurostat (and most statistical agencies) produce population forecasts using the cohort-component approach (Shryock and Siegel, 1976; Keilman and Cruijsen, 1992). In this method one starts from the observed population numbers broken down by age and sex, called the base population or jump-off population. The year for which this population is observed is the base year or jump-off year. The method predicts the numbers for future years by repeatedly applying assumed death rates for each combination of age and sex, and birth rates for women of childbearing age (e.g. 15–49). The simplest way to handle migration is to add to the projected survivors, for every year in the future, net migration numbers broken down by age and sex.

Stochastic (or probabilistic) forecasts are carried out similarly, but now future vital rates and numbers for net migration are considered as random variables that reflect the uncertainty of future population developments (e.g. Alho and Spencer, 2005). Their distribution can be specified in alternate ways. The scaled model of error, which we used in the UPE forecasts, assumes that the vital rates are normal in the log scale, and that net migration numbers are normal in the original scale. The normal distribution requires that one specify the mean of the distribution as a measure of location, and the standard deviation as a measure of spread (or scale) around the mean, to reflect forecast uncertainty. Below we give details about the mean values of the distributions of fertility and mortality rates, and net migration numbers. Alho, Cruijsen and Keilman (this volume, chap. 3) describe the scaled model in more detail and explain how the standard deviations around the means were specified using empirical data. Their appendix also provides a schematic comparison of conventional and stochastic forecasts.

Changes in forecast assumptions of the UN and Eurostat

A forecast for a given future year may change over subsequent forecast rounds either because of updates of the starting population, or because assumptions for the flows have been changed, or both. Consider the updates. Imagine a forecast for 2050 with base year 1994. Because of the recursive nature of the cohort-component bookkeeping, the forecast for 2050 also includes a forecast for 1996 as an intermediate step. However, an update with base year 1996 starts from a *known* population for 1996. This will generally be different from the *predicted* numbers for 1996 as computed in 1994. Even if assumptions concerning post-1996 fertility, mortality and migration were to remain unchanged, this would lead to a different forecast for the population in 2050. Thus, a comparison of subsequent forecasts of population size does not necessarily reflect changing views on flows only. However, by computing annual *growth rates* for future population size, as implied by the various forecast rounds, we can control for changes in the base data.

In this section, we examine the extent to which the UN and Eurostat have changed their views, over time, regarding the population growth rate, fertility, mortality and migration in population forecasts for European countries for the year 2050. We limit ourselves to the medium variant (UN terminology), or baseline scenario (Eurostat terminology), of each forecast, as it is generally considered to be the most plausible one. We also give point predictions from the UPE forecast.

Annual population growth

Figure 2.1 illustrates how the average annual growth rate to 2050 for the population in the EEA+ countries changed over subsequent forecast rounds. We see that until recently the UN and Eurostat expected *negative* population growth for the eighteen EEA+ countries to 2050. However, the 2004 forecasts of both organizations predict a small *positive* growth after jump-off time. In comparison, the UPE forecast expects even more growth, albeit at an annual rate not exceeding 1.8 per thousand.[3]

Fertility

We have examined the total fertility rate (TFR). The TFR for a certain year tells us how many children a woman would have on average

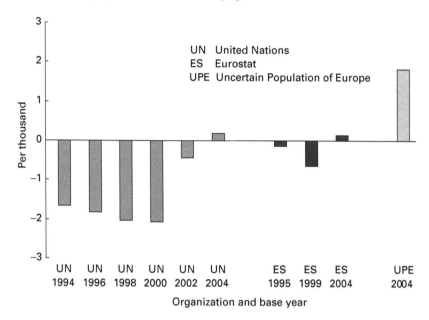

Figure 2.1. Forecasts of average annual rate of population growth in EEA+ countries to 2050. Averages across eighteen EEA+ countries (UN, UPE) and fifteen EU-15 countries (Eurostat).

if age-specific fertility rates in that year were constant for a long time. Figure 2.2 shows a decrease in the 2050 TFR over successive rounds of both the UN and Eurostat forecasts.[4] Table 2.2 gives country-specific values. The TFRs in the 1994 round and 1996 round of the UN are at or close to replacement level (2.1 children per woman) in 2050. Yet, Figure 2.1 indicated negative population growth for those forecasts. The reason is that the TFR was below replacement level in the starting years 1994 and 1996 (see Figure 2.3). Thus the interpolated path from the low 1994/1996 values to the 2050 value had several years with fertility below replacement. Table 2.2 also shows country-specific Eurostat numbers for 2049 (all three rounds) and the UPE point predictions for 2049. A comparison with Figure 2.3 shows that the UPE numbers (with average 1.66) and the most recent Eurostat numbers (with average 1.69) are reasonable extrapolations of historical fertility trends. The UN extrapolations seem high, particularly for Mediterranean and German-speaking populations.

The 1994 and 1996 Revisions of the UN forecasts assumed that countries with below-replacement fertility at jump-off time, would eventually experience an increase towards replacement level. This was the case

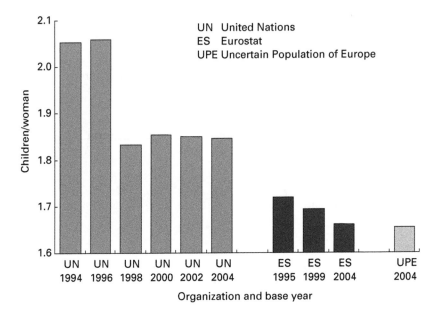

Figure 2.2. Total fertility rate assumptions in EEA+ countries, 2045–2049. Averages across eighteen EEA+ countries (UN, UPE) and fifteen EU-15 countries (Eurostat).

for all EEA+ countries except Iceland during the first half of the 1990s (Figure 2.3). Most of these countries were assumed to reach the replacement level in 2050 or earlier, but a few countries would reach it after 2050 (Table 2.2).

The earliest UN forecasts did not document reasons why particular future levels were chosen. Methodological sections in the projection reports outlined the extrapolation methods, but there was little or no interpretation of historical or future trends. Starting with the 1998 Revision the situation improved somewhat with the publication of an Analytical Report for each revision, but still few arguments are given for the assumptions.[5]

In the documentation of the 1994 and 1996 Revisions, the UN does not give reasons for the target level of 2.1 children per woman. Earlier forecasts (e.g. Revisions of 1973 and 1984) also assumed replacement-level fertility. Arguments in favour of this assumption include the belief that the demographic 'system' has an in-built tendency to maintain itself ('homeostasis'), and that sustained low fertility will inevitably lead to policy reactions (O'Neill *et al.*, 2001). However, there is no empirical evidence that the population in a low-fertility country necessarily returns

Table 2.2. *Country-specific predictions for the total fertility rate in 2050: UN, Eurostat and UPE forecasts.*

Period	UN Revision of …						Eurostat forecast of …			UPE
	1994 2040–50	1996 2045–50	1998 2040–50	2000 2045–50	2002 2045–50	2004 2045–50	1995 2049	1999 2049	2004 2049	2004 2049
Austria	2.10	2.07	1.68	1.65	1.85	1.85	1.60	1.50	1.45	1.40
Belgium	2.10	2.10	1.86	1.82	1.85	1.85	1.80	1.80	1.70	1.80
Denmark	2.10	2.10	1.87	1.90	1.85	1.85	1.80	1.80	1.80	1.80
Finland	2.10	2.10	1.90	1.94	1.85	1.85	1.80	1.70	1.80	1.80
France	2.10	2.10	1.96	1.90	1.85	1.85	1.80	1.80	1.85	1.80
Germany	1.89	1.93	1.64	1.61	1.85	1.85	1.50	1.50	1.45	1.40
Greece	1.99	2.08	1.75	1.85	1.85	1.78	1.70	1.60	1.50	1.40
Iceland	2.10	2.10	1.90	2.10	1.85	1.85	2.10	–	–	1.80
Ireland	2.10	2.10	2.10	2.10	1.85	1.85	1.80	1.80	1.80	1.80
Italy	1.86	1.82	1.66	1.61	1.85	1.85	1.50	1.50	1.40	1.40
Luxembourg	2.10	2.10	1.78	1.90	1.85	1.85	1.80	1.80	1.80	1.80
Netherlands	2.10	2.10	1.86	1.81	1.85	1.85	1.80	1.80	1.75	1.80
Norway	2.10	2.10	1.98	2.07	1.85	1.85	1.90	–	–	1.80
Portugal	2.10	2.10	1.76	1.83	1.85	1.85	1.70	1.70	1.60	1.60
Spain	1.82	1.85	1.68	1.64	1.85	1.85	1.50	1.50	1.40	1.40
Sweden	2.10	2.10	1.99	2.01	1.85	1.85	1.90	1.80	1.85	1.80
Switzerland	2.10	2.10	1.72	1.72	1.85	1.85	–	–	–	1.40
United Kingdom	2.10	2.10	1.90	1.91	1.85	1.85	1.80	1.80	1.75	1.80
Average[1]	2.05	2.06	1.83	1.85	1.85	1.85	1.77	1.73	1.69	1.66
Standard deviation[1]	0.095	0.091	0.131	0.160	0	0.016	0.174	0.159	0.173	0.192

Note: [1] Averages and standard deviations across eighteen countries. In computing these summary measures for the Eurostat forecasts, we imputed UN values for Iceland, Norway and Switzerland.

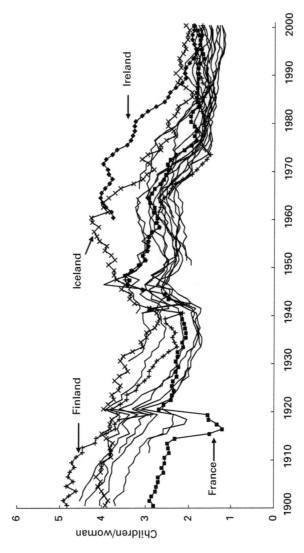

Figure 2.3. Total fertility rate in eighteen EEA+ countries, 1900–2000. (*Source:* Council of Europe, 2002.)

to replacement level. Moreover, policies that aim to promote high fertility involve substantial economic transfers, and they may have an effect only in the short run (Gauthier and Hatzius, 1997). Finally, the theories of childbearing behaviour point to a variety of reasons why individuals prefer fewer children (Van de Kaa, 1987). These include less adherence to strict norms; less religiosity and increased individual freedom on ethical issues; female education, which has led to women having greater economic independence and facilitates divorce; and more assertiveness in favour of symmetrical gender roles. Thus, lower fertility is thought to be the result of processes that cannot be reversed (such as modern contraception) or that we value for various reasons (such as women's emancipation). These theories of childbearing behaviour in low-fertility countries gained acceptance in the 1980s, but they had no impact on the UN for a decade or so. Starting with the 1998 Revision, the UN no longer assumed convergence towards replacement level.

Mortality

The most widely used measure of mortality is life expectancy: the number of years an individual could expect to live if age-specific death rates were to remain constant over a long period. We have examined life expectancy for men and women separately. Table 2.3 gives results by country, whereas Figure 2.4 plots average values (across countries) for the UN, Eurostat and UPE forecasts.

Between 1994 and 2004, the UN has become more optimistic regarding the life expectancy in EEA+ countries in 2050: on average, life expectancy predictions went up by 2.4 years for men and by 1.6 years for women; see Figure 2.4. To put these numbers into perspective: in the latter part of the twentieth century *actual* life expectancy has increased by roughly one to two years per decade in developed countries (National Research Council, 2000); see Figure 2.5. Record (or 'best practice') life expectancy has increased by 2.2 years per decade (Oeppen and Vaupel, 2002). Thus, the increases are only of the same order of magnitude as the actual improvement in 1994–2004. In consequence, the assumed levels remain lower than corresponding UPE figures. Note that the spread across the eighteen UN or the fifteen Eurostat countries for the 2004 forecasts is much larger than the spread in earlier forecasts, or that in the UPE forecast. One gets the impression that national (as opposed to average international) trends have been given a higher weight than before.

The notion of a maximum life expectancy seems to underlie UN forecasts for low-mortality countries. For instance, the 1994 Revision and

Table 2.3. *Country-specific predictions for life expectancy in 2050: UN, Eurostat and UPE forecasts.*

	UN Revision of . . .						Eurostat forecast of . . .			UPE
	1994	1996	1998	2000	2002	2004	1995	1999	2004	2004
Period	2040–50	2045–50	2040–50	2045–50	2045–50	2045–50	2049	2049	2049	2049
a. Men										
Austria	79.8	78.9	78.8	80.8	80.8	82.7	80.0	81.0	83.5	84.4
Belgium	79.8	79.1	78.9	81.1	81.1	81.1	80.0	80.5	82.3	84.2
Denmark	77.7	77.7	77.7	79.0	79.0	80.0	79.0	79.4	80.8	83.2
Finland	78.2	78.7	79.3	79.8	79.8	82.1	79.0	80.0	81.8	84.7
France	78.9	79.5	78.9	80.6	80.6	81.5	80.0	80.0	82.6	85.5
Germany	78.6	78.7	78.9	80.7	80.6	80.9	79.0	80.0	81.9	84.9
Greece	79.8	80.0	79.8	79.9	79.7	79.6	81.0	81.0	80.2	82.8
Iceland	80.4	81.6	81.0	80.8	81.2	84.3	82.0	–	–	85.9
Ireland	78.5	79.1	79.8	78.9	78.9	81.0	79.0	79.0	82.3	84.7
Italy	80.5	80.7	79.6	79.5	79.5	82.2	80.0	81.0	83.5	85.7
Luxembourg	78.3	78.7	78.7	80.0	80.8	80.8	80.0	80.0	81.5	85.2
Netherlands	79.4	79.7	79.3	79.6	79.6	80.6	80.0	80.0	80.2	82.5
Norway	78.1	78.7	80.5	80.8	80.8	82.7	81.0	–	–	83.7
Portugal	77.7	78.1	77.9	77.9	77.9	79.4	78.0	78.0	80.3	84.2
Spain	79.6	79.4	79.2	79.4	81.0	81.4	79.0	79.0	81.3	85.9
Sweden	81.0	81.3	81.1	82.1	82.1	83.4	82.0	82.0	83.3	84.7
Switzerland	79.5	79.8	79.7	79.9	79.9	82.8	–	–	–	85.3
United Kingdom	79.1	79.4	79.2	80.6	80.6	81.5	80.0	80.0	82.8	83.4
Average[1]	79.1	79.3	79.1	80.0	80.1	81.2	79.9	80.1	82.1	84.5
Standard deviation[1]	0.98	1.02	0.90	0.97	1.01	1.31	1.06	0.93	1.22	1.04

b. *Women*

Austria	85.3	85.4	84.5	86.6	86.6	87.1	85.0	86.0	87.6	88.7
Belgium	85.6	85.0	84.8	86.7	86.7	86.7	85.0	85.5	88.2	88.3
Denmark	83.3	82.9	82.9	83.9	83.9	84.6	83.0	83.1	83.7	87.3
Finland	84.5	84.7	85.8	86.1	86.1	87.1	85.0	85.0	86.5	88.7
France	85.4	86.9	86.0	87.3	87.3	88.0	87.0	87.0	89.0	89.7
Germany	84.4	84.7	84.5	86.2	86.3	86.5	84.0	85.0	86.8	89.1
Greece	84.8	85.1	84.8	85.1	84.9	84.5	85.0	85.0	85.1	86.9
Iceland	85.4	85.5	85.4	85.5	85.7	87.8	87.0	85.0	–	89.9
Ireland	83.9	84.4	84.9	84.0	84.0	86.1	84.0	84.0	86.9	89.9
Italy	86.2	86.4	85.3	85.6	85.6	88.1	85.0	86.0	88.7	89.8
Luxembourg	85.4	84.7	84.5	85.5	86.5	86.5	85.0	85.0	86.6	89.4
Netherlands	85.0	85.1	84.9	84.9	84.9	85.8	85.0	85.0	83.6	86.4
Norway	83.9	84.1	86.4	86.7	86.7	87.2	85.0	–	–	87.9
Portugal	83.9	84.2	83.9	84.1	84.1	85.4	84.0	84.0	86.6	88.4
Spain	85.2	85.7	85.5	85.9	87.3	88.3	85.0	85.0	87.9	90.1
Sweden	86.5	85.9	85.7	87.1	87.1	87.6	86.0	86.0	86.5	88.7
Switzerland	85.7	86.0	85.8	86.0	86.0	88.3	–	–	–	89.4
United Kingdom	84.2	84.6	84.4	85.6	85.6	85.4	85.0	85.0	86.5	87.5
Average[1]	84.9	85.1	85.0	85.7	85.9	86.7	85.0	85.3	86.9	88.7
Standard deviation[1]	0.87	0.93	0.84	1.02	1.10	1.22	0.99	0.94	1.51	1.11

Note: [1] See Table 2.2, note 1.

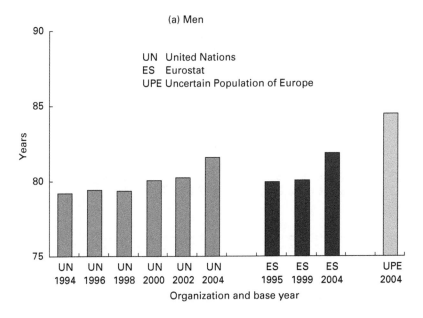

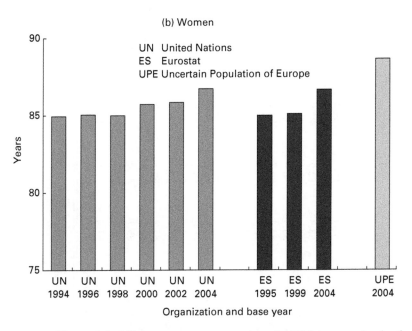

Figure 2.4. Life expectancy assumptions in EEA+ countries in the period 2045–2049. Averages across eighteen EEA+ countries (UN, UPE) and fifteen EU-15 countries (Eurostat).

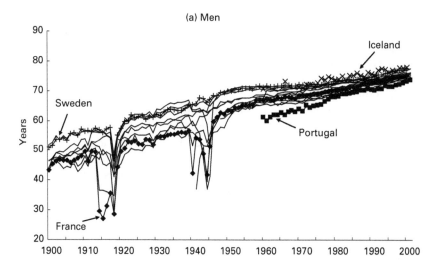

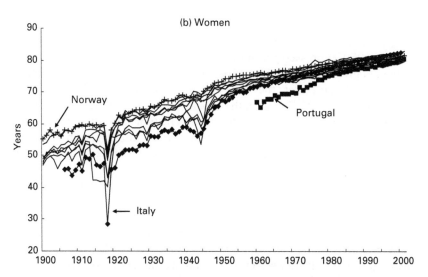

Figure 2.5. Life expectancy at birth in eighteen EEA+ countries, 1900–2000. (*Source:* Council of Europe, 2002.)

the 1996 Revision mention a maximum of 87.5 years for women and 82.5 years for men. Life tables used in the 2004 Revision assume a maximum life span of 92.5 years for women and 87.5 years for men. As countries approach the maximum values, the UN assumes that annual improvements in life expectancy become smaller.[6]

The UN has continuously adjusted the maximum life span upwards (National Research Council, 2000, p. 129). For instance, the 1973 Revision, with the year 2000 as the forecast horizon, uses 77.5 and 72.6 years, respectively. Men and women in Japan and Iceland had already attained these values in the early 1970s. The UN is not alone in using maximum life span values that have to be updated continuously (Oeppen and Vaupel, 2002). However, a panel of the US National Research Council (2000) carried out a broad assessment of UN mortality forecasts and concluded that the existence of a maximum life span is conceivable but that it is unlikely that the possible maximum would be reached within near decades.

Migration

Migration is analysed here in terms of the level of net immigration around 2050, expressed per thousand of the population in the year 2000.[7] Table 2.4 gives the assumed numbers by 2050 according to the UN Revisions of 1998 and later, the three Eurostat forecasts and the UPE forecast. Up to the 1996 Revision, the UN assumed that migration would be zero by 2050 in the countries concerned. The table also includes average net migration levels for the whole of the EEA+ countries. In addition, Figure 2.6 plots simple averages (across countries) of net migration per thousand of population.

Since the middle of the 1990s, both the UN and Eurostat have assumed ever higher levels of net migration to European countries around 2050. Large immigration flows into Germany dominate the pattern. Nevertheless, compared to the UPE assumptions, migration currently assumed by the UN and Eurostat seems low. The UN gives very little justification for the migration levels they select. For instance, the reports of the Revisions of 2000, 2002 and 2004 just state that 'The future path of international migration is set on the basis of past international migration estimates and an assessment of the policy stance of countries with regards to future international migration.'

The UPE assumptions

Figures 2.2, 2.4 and 2.6 suggest that the UN has been somewhat reluctant to acknowledge new levels or trends for demographic developments.[8]

Table 2.4. *Country-specific predictions for net migration (per thousand of the population in 2000) in 2050: UN, Eurostat and UPE forecasts.*

Period	UN Revision of . . .				Eurostat forecast of . . .			UPE
	1998 2040–50	2000 2045–50	2002 2045–50	2004 2045–50	1995 2049	1999 2049	2004 2049	2004 2049
Austria	0	0.62	1.75	2.50	2.78	2.48	2.51	3.5
Belgium	0	1.29	1.29	1.29	1.46	1.46	1.81	2
Denmark	0	1.91	1.91	2.30	1.88	1.88	1.24	2
Finland	0	0.78	0.78	1.57	0.97	0.97	1.17	1.5
France	0	0.69	1.29	1.03	0.84	0.84	0.99	1.5
Germany	2.45	2.20	2.58	2.45	2.44	2.44	2.18	3.5
Greece	0	1.91	2.86	3.34	2.36	2.36	3.29	4.5
Iceland	0	0	0	0	0.72	–	–	1.5
Ireland	0	2.77	2.77	5.54	−0.71	1.31	3.26	3.5
Italy	0	1.05	1.08	2.09	1.39	1.39	1.98	4.5
Luxembourg	0	9.83	9.83	9.83	4.58	4.58	6.35	6
Netherlands	0	1.94	1.94	1.94	2.21	2.21	1.96	3
Norway	0	2.30	2.30	2.76	1.79	–	–	3.5
Portugal	0	1.01	1.01	3.55	2.50	2.50	1.49	4.5
Spain	0	0.76	1.42	1.52	1.50	1.50	2.55	4.5
Sweden	1.14	1.14	1.14	2.27	2.26	2.26	2.42	3
Switzerland	0	0.56	0.56	1.12	–	–	–	3.5
United Kingdom	0	1.63	2.32	2.23	0.76	1.18	1.66	3.5
EEA+	0.56	1.40	1.81	2.06	–	–	–	3.38
Average[1]	0.20	1.80	2.05	2.63	1.75	1.71	2.15	3.31
Standard deviation[1]	0.62	2.13	2.10	2.15	1.14	1.04	1.34	1.25

Note: [1] See Table 2.2, note 1.

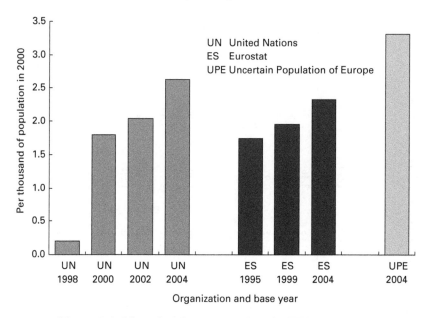

Figure 2.6. Net migration assumptions in EEA+ countries, 2045–2049. Averages across eighteen EEA+ countries (UN, UPE) and fifteen EU-15 countries (Eurostat).

This phenomenon is sometimes called 'assumption drag' (Ascher, 1978), and it has also been noted in demographic forecasts prepared by national statistical agencies (Keilman, 1990, 1997). For instance, the sharp decline in birth rates in the 1970s or improved life expectancies of men in the 1970s, after a period of stagnation, were only gradually accommodated in forecasts. To a degree, this is to be expected. We do not have behavioural models of sufficient explanatory power for predicting fertility, mortality or migration accurately. Therefore, we have to rely on long-term trends to an extent that might seem, in retrospect, too heavy. Moreover, examples of hasty changes and subsequent reversals also exist. These observations are a major motivation for considering forecast uncertainty seriously. However, if the same type of forecast error appears repeatedly, or the forecasts appear to be systematically *biased*, then corrections should be made.

In the UPE project, assumptions were derived from three sources:
1. time-series analyses of age-specific and total fertility; age- and sex-specific mortality and life expectancy; and net migration by age and sex, relative to total population size;
2. analyses of historical forecast errors for total fertility, life expectancies and net migration; and
3. interviews with experts on fertility, mortality and migration.

This section summarizes the UPE assumptions and provides motivation. We limit ourselves to point predictions of the predictive distributions. Alho, Cruijsen and Keilman (this volume, chap. 3) discuss uncertainty measures and predictive intervals. More information can also be found in Alders, Keilman and Cruijsen (2007) and the references therein, including the UPE website, www.stat.fi/tup/euupe/.

In practice, a starting point for specifying values for country-specific point predictions of the total fertility rate, the life expectancy at birth and the level of net migration was time-series analysis. Estimates obtained from the analyses were adjusted, sometimes considerably, to reflect expert views on whether current levels or current trends would persist. Below, we discuss qualitative considerations that were taken into account in this process.

Fertility

Past trends, contemporary levels and recent explanatory research indicate that there is a clear geographic division in fertility levels in Europe. Factors that are thought to have an impact on future fertility include:

- increased female education and female economic autonomy;
- rising consumption aspirations;
- increased investments in career development by both sexes;
- rising 'post-materialist' traits such as self-actualization, ethical autonomy, freedom of choice and tolerance of the non-conventional;
- a stronger focus on the quality of life with rising taste for leisure as well;
- a retreat from irreversible commitments and a desire for maintaining an 'open future';
- rising probabilities of separation and divorce, and hence a more cautious 'investment in identity'.

The Northern and Western EEA+ countries are experiencing levels of completed fertility rate (CFR) and total fertility rate (TFR) of about 1.8 children per woman, whereas the Mediterranean and German-speaking countries are at the historically low levels of around 1.4 children per woman. For the period 2003–2049, it was assumed that these clusters will remain essentially at their current levels (Table 2.2).

The Northern and Western cluster of countries comprises Belgium, Denmark, Finland, France, Iceland, Ireland, Luxembourg, the Netherlands, Norway, Sweden and the United Kingdom. The Mediterranean and German-speaking cluster consists of Austria, Germany, Greece, Italy, Spain and Switzerland. Portugal does not fall easily into either class. Its fertility is somewhere in the middle. The TFR in Portugal will rise to a level of 1.6 children per woman.

In addition to the factors mentioned above, it was pointed out to us that the Northern and Western countries were the first to postpone child-bearing, and the first to recuperate. In the Mediterranean and German-speaking countries, there was also postponement but much less recuperation. In the latter countries, one-child families became quite popular, and we expect that this will persist on account of relatively weak childcare and housing facilities. Thus, postponement was not seen as a reason to alter the specification above.

Our specification is in line with the 2004 fertility forecast of Eurostat, but very different from the UN assumption of perfect convergence to a level of 1.85 children per woman. These are the simple correlation coefficients across countries of assumed TFR values by 2050 for the three organizations:

	UN 2004	Eurostat 2004	UPE 2004
UN 2004	1		
Eurostat 2004	0.255	1	
UPE 2004	0.333	0.969	1

Mortality

The assumptions for mortality were made in terms of age-specific mortality rates and their rate of decline. For each of the eighteen countries we assumed that the rate of decline starts from recent country-specific values, and changes linearly over time towards the common rate of decline, which is to occur by the year 2030. The eventual rate of decline was empirically estimated from data for Austria, Denmark, Finland, France, Germany, Italy, the Netherlands, Norway, Sweden, Switzerland and the United Kingdom during the latest thirty-year period observed. In some countries, the extrapolation procedure would imply diverging developments of male and female life expectancies. This is in contrast with observations in the last two or three decades. It seems plausible to assume that the gender gap in life expectancy will continue to decline as differences between men and women in life style (e.g. smoking) are becoming smaller. For this reason, we made a proportional adjustment such that the gender gap equals four years in the target year. In the case of Ireland, however, the gender gap was assumed to equal five years on account of strongly diverging trends in the recent past.

The basic assumption of ongoing international convergence means that in countries with an exceptionally fast rate of decline in the past, the rate of decline would be expected to slow down to some extent. In countries with a modest rate of improvement in the past, the decline would be expected to catch up. This takes into account the fact that recent developments differ strongly among the European countries. We saw no reason why they would reverse in the near future. On the other hand, it is hard to see why, in the long term, countries would diverge from each other and from the average European trend. These assumptions imply that especially for males the differences between countries are becoming smaller. In 2002, the difference between the lowest male life expectancy (Portugal) and the highest (Iceland) was about 4.7 years. This difference is assumed to decrease to 3.3 years (lowest for the Netherlands and highest for Spain). For females, differences are decreasing only slightly.

The resulting expected gains in life expectancy at birth for men during the period 2002–2049 vary between 6.5 (Netherlands) and well over 10 years (Luxembourg, Portugal and Spain). For women, slightly smaller improvements are expected, varying from 5.7 (Netherlands) to 9.6 (Ireland). Table 2.3 gives the resulting levels of the life expectancy in 2049. Alders, Keilman and Cruijsen (2007) note that the relative variation in life expectancies in 2049 is in line with international trends since the beginning of the twentieth century. In contrast, the UN and Eurostat assume a larger spread across countries in life expectancies in their more recent forecasts than in their earlier ones.

Compared to the UN and Eurostat forecasts, the UPE forecast assumes higher levels for life expectancy. This is primarily motivated by the fact that past forecasts of national statistical agencies in European countries have systematically underpredicted life expectancy. Life expectancies were too low by more than 2 years for European forecasts fifteen years ahead, and by 4.5 years twenty-five years ahead (Keilman 1997; Keilman and Pham 2004).

The disagreement between UPE assumptions for life expectancy in 2049 on the one hand, and corresponding UN and Eurostat assumptions on the other, is larger for men than for women. As a descriptive statistic, we give the simple correlations across countries:

	UN 2004	Eurostat 2004 *Men*	UPE 2004	UN 2004	Eurostat 2004 *Women*	UPE 2004
UN 2004	1			1		
Eurostat 2004	0.858	1		0.765	1	
UPE 2004	0.518	0.521	1	0.743	0.799	1

Migration

As to migration, the following principal factors are thought likely to influence migration developments in the coming fifty years:

- economic developments will induce fluctuations in the demand for labour and people will come from other EEA+ countries, but also from the outside to fill existing opportunities;
- the ageing of the EEA population will induce demand for labour, in particular in the health sector;
- developments in the South and East will put pressures on the gates of the wealthy EEA.

The starting point for the UPE point forecasts was a linear trend model. We detected a significant upward linear trend in net migration for many countries. However, it is very uncertain whether these rising trends will persist. For one thing, in many countries they would lead to high levels that have no precedent in history. Yet, the assumption of a break in the trend is equally problematic. As a compromise, values were sought between the linear trend and the current level. Eventually it was assumed that for the EEA+ countries as a whole, net migration per thousand of population in 2000, will rise to a level of around 3.5 in 2049. This is considerably less than the 5 per thousand according to the linear trend model, but higher than the current value of approximately 2.7. Next, we made long-term country-specific assumptions on net migration, that varied from 1.5 (Finland, France and Iceland) to 6 per thousand (Luxembourg); see Table 2.4.

As in the case of life expectancy, past official forecasts have systematically underpredicted levels of immigration in Europe. Net migration forecasts were too low, either because international migration was simply set to zero (the UN Revisions of 1994 and 1996) or because the levels assumed were too low. Also, similarly to life expectancy, the last row of Table 2.4 reflects a stronger belief in the convergence of levels of migration in the UPE forecast than in the most recent forecasts of UN or Eurostat.

Conclusions

Since the middle of the 1990s, the UN and Eurostat have changed their views about the likely demographic outlook in the eighteen countries of the EEA+ region. The surprise is that changes from one forecast round to the next display a very characteristic pattern. The UN and Eurostat have systematically adjusted their views on life expectancy and net migration towards higher levels. Moreover, since 1998 the UN no longer considers replacement-level fertility as the most probable long-term level, but it still assumes higher levels than Eurostat.

We have contrasted the UN and Eurostat forecasts with our own views that form the basis of the probabilistic UPE forecasts. On fertility we essentially agree with Eurostat, but the UN assumes convergence to a level that is about 10 per cent higher. However, the UPE assumptions on life expectancy and net migration are higher than those of the UN and Eurostat. This difference can be traced back to the realization that, in the past, official forecasts have been systematically too low for both life expectancy and net migration. However, a more detailed comparison between UPE assumptions and those of the UN and Eurostat is hampered by the lack of argument-based justifications for the assumptions of the latter two.

The high UPE assumptions for life expectancy and international migration imply larger working-age populations and larger numbers of the elderly than do the UN and Eurostat forecasts. Overall, UPE expects a monotonic increase in the population of EEA+ from the current level of 392 million to 427 million in 2050 (corresponding to an average annual growth rate of 0.2 per cent). In contrast, the 2004 Revision of the UN predicts a decline from 407 million in 2030 to 400 million in 2050. Eurostat predicts that the fifteen member countries of the former EU will have a population of 384 million in 2050, 7 per cent less than the UPE prediction for these countries.

How important are these differences? In Table 3.1 it is shown that the standard deviation of predictive distribution for the 2050 total populations in EEA+ countries is 15 per cent of the point forecast. However, as the countries are not perfectly correlated, the relative standard deviation for the EEA+ is smaller. Alho and Nikander (2004) present an 80 per cent prediction interval for the total population in 2050. Under a normal approximation one can deduce that the standard deviation for the EEA+ is about 8.4 per cent. Thus, the UN, Eurostat and UPE forecasts for the total population are within one standard deviation. The differences are non-trivial, but probably not qualitatively important in economic applications.

Yet, from the perspective of ageing research, the assumption of higher life expectancies (and, to a lesser extent, higher net migration) implies that the number of persons aged 65+ has fast become outdated in the official forecasts. For example, consider France, Germany and Italy in 2050. In the 1998 Revision, the UN expected populations of 15.28, 20.79 and 14.38 million, respectively. Six years later, in the 2004 Revision the expected populations were 17.11, 22.38 and 18.09 million, respectively. Corresponding median values (80 per cent prediction intervals in parentheses) from Alho and Nikander (2004) for France, Germany and Italy are 18.20 ([15.13, 21.13]), 25.03 ([20.26, 29.70]) and 19.29 ([15.54, 22.67]) million, respectively. Although the most recent revision is not radically different from the UPE medians, a forecast made six years earlier is so low that by current estimates the chance of such low values is only one in ten. Since economic analyses of the type considered in this volume are intended for strategic planning, they should not become outdated in five to ten years' time. Instead of concentrating on minor differences in forecasts made by different agencies at a given time, it seems more fruitful to recognize that they are all likely to be in error. This is the motivation for handling forecast uncertainty in probabilistic terms.

NOTES

1 For practical reasons, we excluded EEA-member Liechtenstein.
2 UPE stands for 'Uncertain Population of Europe'. This was an EU-funded research project that produced the first stochastic forecasts for all EEA+ countries.
3 The higher growth rate is partly explained by stronger population growth in France (2.6 per thousand in UPE; 0.9 according to the UN), in Spain (1.5 rather than −0.3 per thousand) and the UK (3.0 rather than 2.6 per thousand). There is also some effect caused by a *lower* starting population in the UPE forecasts, by 4.7 million. If the UPE forecast had started from the same population as the UN, the average growth rate to 2050 would have been 1.6 per thousand instead of 1.8.
4 These are simple averages across countries. When weighted with country-specific numbers for the 2050 population, the trend is similar but the values are between 0.3 and 0.6 children per woman lower.
5 At the time of writing (September 2006), there is still very little publicly available documentation for the 2004 Eurostat forecast.
6 Countries do not necessarily reach the maximum life expectancy by 2050. In fact, in the 2004 Revision, only Japanese women do so.
7 Numbers for the 2000 population in each country were taken from UN data. Using statistics from the Council of Europe or from Eurostat would have resulted in slightly different values. The patterns, however, would have been the same.
8 To a smaller extent, this is also the case for Eurostat.

REFERENCES

Alders, M., Keilman, N. and Cruijsen, H. (2007). 'Assumptions for Long-term Stochastic Population Forecasts in 18 European Countries'. *European Journal of Population*, 23: 33–69.
Alho, J. M. and Nikander, T. (2004). 'Uncertain Population of Europe. Summary Results from a Stochastic Forecast'. Available at www.stat.fi/tup/euupe/del12.pdf.
Alho, J. M. and Spencer, B. (2005). *Statistical Demography and Forecasting*. New York: Springer.
Andrews, G. H. and Beekman, J. A. (1987). *Actuarial Projections for the Old-Age, Survivors, and Disability Insurance Program of Social Security in the United States of America*. Itasca, IL: Actuarial Education and Research Fund.

Ascher, W. (1978). *Forecasting: An Appraisal for Policy-makers and Planners.* Baltimore: Johns Hopkins University Press.

Council of Europe (2002). *Recent Demographic Developments in Europe 2002.* Strasbourg: Council of Europe Publishing.

Cruijsen, H. and Eding, H. (1997). 'Beyond the Predictable: Demographic Changes in the EU up to 2050'. *Statistics in Focus,* no. 7. Luxembourg: Eurostat.

De Jong, A. (1998). 'Long-term Fertility Scenarios for the Countries of the European Economic Area'. Eurostat Working Paper E4/1998-17, Luxembourg.

De Jong, A. and Visser, H. (1997). 'Long-term International Migration Scenarios for the Countries of the European Economic Area'. Eurostat Working Paper E4/1997-6, Luxembourg.

Economic Policy Committee (2001). *Budgetary Challenges Posed by Ageing Populations: the Impact on Public Spending on Pensions, Health and Long-term Care for the Elderly and Possible Indicators of the Long-term Sustainability of Public Finances* (EPC/ECFIN/655/01-EN final). Brussels.

Eurostat (2005). 'EUROPOP2004, Population Projections: EU25 Population Rises Until 2025, Then Falls'. News Release 448/2005, 8 April.

Gauthier, A. and Hatzius, J. (1997). 'Family Benefits and Fertility: An Econometric Analysis'. *Population Studies,* 51: 295–306.

Keilman, N. (1990). *Uncertainty in National Population Forecasting: Issues, Backgrounds, Analyses, Recommendations.* Amsterdam: Swets and Zeitlinger.

(1997). 'Ex-post Errors in Official Population Forecasts in Industrialized Countries'. *Journal of Official Statistics,* 13: 245–77.

Keilman, N. and Cruijsen, H. (1992), eds. *National Population Forecasting in Industrialized Countries.* Amsterdam: Swets and Zeitlinger.

Keilman, N. and Pham, D. Q. (2004). *Empirical Errors and Predicted Errors in Fertility, Mortality and Migration Forecasts in the European Economic Area.* Discussion Paper no. 386. Oslo: Statistics Norway.

Lanzieri, G. (2006). 'Long-term Population Projections at National Level'. *Statistics in Focus* 3/2006.

National Research Council (2000). *Beyond Six Billion: Forecasting the World's Population.* Panel on Population Projections. Washington, DC: National Academy Press.

Oeppen, J. and Vaupel, J. (2002). 'Broken Limits to Life Expectancy'. *Science,* 296(5570): 1029–31.

O'Neill, B., Balk, D., Brickman, M. and Ezra, M. (2001). 'A Guide to Global Population Projections'. *Demographic Research,* 4, 13 June.

Shryock, H. S., Siegel, J. S. and associates (1976). *The Methods and Materials of Demography,* condensed edn by E. G. Stockwell. New York: Academic Press.

United Nations (various years) *World Population Prospects.* New York: United Nations.

Van de Kaa, D. (1987). 'Europe's Second Demographic Transition'. *Population Bulletin,* 42: 1–59.

Van Hoorn, W. and de Beer, J. (1998). 'Long-term Mortality Scenarios for the Countries of the European Economic Area'. Eurostat Working Paper E4/1998-8, Luxembourg.

3   Empirically based specification of forecast uncertainty

Juha M. Alho, Harri Cruijsen and Nico Keilman

Introduction

To make a conventional population forecast one needs to specify age-specific fertility rates for women, and mortality rates for women and men, for all future years of interest. These are used to generate births and deaths. The simplest way to handle migration is to specify net migration in absolute numbers that are added to population each year. Starting from a jump-off population, the so-called cohort-component bookkeeping (e.g. Shryock, Siegel and associates, 1976) is used recursively to keep track of the resulting changes in population, by age and sex. These methods were first used by Cannan (1895) for England and Wales, and since the 1920s and 1930s they have been widely used in Europe (DeGans, 1999). The early forecasters were aware that calculations based on the cohort-component method are only as reliable as the assumptions that go into making them. Alternative variants were offered from early on, but even the forecast producers themselves were uneasy about the methods that were used to prepare them (e.g. Modeen, 1934).

Stochastic (or probabilistic) cohort-component forecasts are similar, but in this case future fertility and mortality rates and net migration are considered as random variables (e.g. Alho and Spencer, 2005). Their distributions can be specified in various ways. Perhaps the simplest is to give first the location of the distribution, and then to specify the spread (or scale) around it to reflect forecast uncertainty. Under a normal (Gaussian) assumption for the rate (or, for example, its log transform), the measure of location is the mean (or median) and the measure of spread is the standard deviation, for example. An advantage of the normal model is that the dependency structure of the various random variables can be given in terms of correlations in an interpretable way.

From the perspective of random vital rates, cohort-component book-keeping is a non-linear operation. Simulation is frequently used to carry out the propagation of uncertainty, from the rates to future population numbers. A joint distribution derived in this manner for the future demographic variables can be called a *predictive distribution*. In other words, it is the probability distribution of the future demographic variables, conditional on what is known as the jump-off time, or the time when a forecast is made.

Complementing Keilman, Cruijsen and Alho (this volume, chap. 2), who discuss the specification of the most likely future values of the vital rates, or the location of the predictive distributions, we illustrate in this chapter how the second-order characteristics (scales and correlations) of the predictive distributions can be specified. We carry out our analyses in a multi-country setting, i.e. we use information from other countries to stabilize error estimates that would otherwise be expected to be highly autocorrelated, and, as such, hard to estimate (Alho and Spencer, 2005).

The specification of locations is essentially equivalent to the preparation of the 'medium' variant of a conventional population forecast. The novel task of specifying the scales and correlations is important, however. It has been demonstrated that, in the past, official forecasts have had much larger errors than one would have anticipated by looking at the alternatives ('high' and 'low') that are often provided (e.g. Keilman, 1990; National Research Council, 2000). In applications involving the sustainability of public finances (e.g. pensions), too narrow a view of future contingencies can lead to erroneous policy decisions (e.g. Auerbach and Lee, 2001).

The interpretation of a predictive distribution depends on the way the location and scale are specified. The statistical outlook allows for a combination of modelling of vital processes, analysis of past forecast errors and judgement concerning factors that may not have fully manifested themselves yet (Alho and Spencer, 2005). We know from elementary statistics that probability statements always depend on a model (e.g. Freedman, Pisani and Purves, 1978), so we need to be able to construct a model that is capable of incorporating the various sources of information available. As a starting point we will *specify scales and correlations in such a way that, had they been used in the past, the prediction intervals of demographic variables would have had the specified level of coverage*. In this chapter we try to give enough detail so the reader can critically examine our assessment of uncertainty.

We begin by evaluating the spread provided by Eurostat's and the UN's high and low forecasts for eighteen European countries against probabilistic estimates produced by the project UPE, and others. This shows to what extent the past underestimation of uncertainty persists. We then review approaches to specifying past uncertainty and present details of the scaled model for error that was applied in the economic work considered in this volume. We consider prediction intervals for the basic demographic variables and compare them to the official high–low intervals, in order to see what might explain the differences. We conclude by discussing the implications of the findings for ageing research.

For readers who are not familiar with the stochastic approach to population forecasting we include, in an appendix, a schematic comparison of conventional and stochastic forecasts.

Uncertainty in official forecasts of total population

A practical finding from experiments with stochastic population forecasting in the 1980s was that the 'plausible ranges' formed by official high and low projections, or scenarios, for the total population were usually too narrow to give a realistic indication of the uncertainty to be expected. Stoto (1983) found, for example, that in the United States the high–low intervals were somewhat narrower than the 'one-sigma intervals' that one would expect, based on the normal distribution, to capture the future population about two-thirds of the time. This came as a surprise, since the primary motivation for the development of stochastic approaches was to enhance the logical coherence of alternative forecasts rather than the level of uncertainty *per se*. Yet, since we now know that the high–low intervals were too narrow, we also know that their use has had the potential to mislead decision-makers by encouraging a concentration on too narrow a range of alternative future paths.

Using Table 3.1 we can investigate to what extent the most recent official forecasts of the population of eighteen European countries (consisting of 'EU-15' plus Iceland, Norway and Switzerland) continue to provide narrow ranges. We consider year 2050.

In order to produce comparable measures we calculate the following measure from the UN and Eurostat forecasts. Define M = middle forecast, H = high forecast and L = low forecast. The measures under columns 'UN' and 'ES', are of the form $100 \times (H - L)/2M$, i.e. it is the half-width of the relative difference between the high and the low, expressed in percentage terms. The column 'UPE' has been derived from summary data for a predictive distribution for each of the countries. The values used are available at www.stat.fi/tup/euupe/de112.pdf, where for each country there is a table comparable to our Table 3.1 giving the median of the predictive distribution, M', together with the upper end-point of the 80 per cent prediction interval, H', and the lower end-point of the 80 per cent prediction interval, L', up to year 2050. The entry given in Table 3.1 is calculated as $100 \times (H' - L')/2 \times 1.2816 \times M'$, where 1.2816 is the 0.9 fractile of the standard normal distribution. This approximates the coefficient of variation of the predictive distribution of the total

Table 3.1. *Relative uncertainty as expressed by high and low forecasts of the United Nations (2004) and Eurostat (2005), the relative standard deviation derived by the UPE project (UPE) and as estimated from the empirical errors of the UN forecasts in the period 1970–1990 (EMP), for the total population in 2050.*

	UN	ES	UPE	EMP
Austria	14.0	16.4	14.2	19.3
Belgium	9.8	13.1	13.2	8.8
Denmark	14.7	12.7	12.4	9.6
Finland	14.5	11.2	13.4	12.4
France	14.6	11.4	14.9	9.3
Germany	14.5	17.8	15.0	17.0
Greece	14.4	15.0	16.0	16.2
Iceland	15.1	–	15.1	9.9
Ireland	14.0	13.7	16.5	34.6
Italy	13.8	12.3	17.6	9.0
Luxembourg	9.0	16.4	16.8	45.4
Netherlands	12.0	15.2	12.8	9.3
Norway	14.3	–	13.2	10.3
Portugal	14.2	16.7	16.5	27.8
Spain	14.4	13.9	17.0	23.2
Sweden	14.3	13.2	15.3	20.0
Switzerland	15.0	–	11.8	30.8
United Kingdom	15.0	15.6	13.5	11.6
Median	14.6	13.9	15.0	14.3
Standard deviation	1.7	2.0	1.8	10.6

population in 2050.[1] Finally, the column 'EMP' is the estimated coefficient of variation (of the true population about the forecast) obtained from an empirical analysis of errors in the UN forecasts made in the period 1970–1990, as given in Table 2 of Chapter 8 in Alho and Spencer (2005).

Two findings are important. First, by using the median values across countries as a measure, we find that *all* four approaches lead to almost the same value of slightly under 15 per cent. This indicates that the high–low intervals of official forecasts for these countries are comparable to 'one-sigma intervals'; or, the probability is about two-thirds that the high–low intervals capture the total population in 2050. This agrees with Stoto's finding from the United States that there is a large probability that total population will be outside the range deemed 'plausible'.[2]

Second, the standard deviations across countries are almost the same, at about 2 percentage points, for the two official forecasts and the UPE values. As we will see below, it is likely that this is by deliberate design: forecasters, both official and those of the UPE project, have found it difficult to defend values that differ considerably across countries. The contrast with column 'EMP' is striking. The standard deviation is quite large compared to the median. This is caused by a number of countries with very large values.

We note also that although the EMP values are based on an analysis of past errors of the UN forecasts, their correlation with the UN values is negative (with P-value $= 0.2$ for the hypothesis of zero correlation). Their correlation with both the ES and UPE values is positive (P-values $= 0.1$). Although the observation that future developments have turned out to be different from what was anticipated has been a frequent motive for updating forecasts, the lack of correlation is consonant with the fact that official forecast assumptions have rarely been based on a systematic evaluation of past forecast errors.

Prudence would seem to dictate that a *higher* level of uncertainty should be specified than that given in the column UPE. As discussed by Keilman, Cruijsen and Alho (this volume, chap. 2), there have been systematic problems in the past forecasts. Eliminating those is one reason for preferring somewhat lower estimates of uncertainty. We note also that there is evidence that small countries typically have somewhat larger errors than larger countries (e.g. Alho and Spencer, 2005). No attempt was made to induce such regularity into the UPE specifications, however.

Modelling and estimating uncertainty

Problems of coherence in conventional forecasts

In the preceding section, we limited ourselves to total population. However, in many applications one is interested in sub-populations. For example, in ageing research one studies the old-age dependency ratio D. Defining W as the size of the population of working age (say, 20–64), and defining E as the size of the elderly population (65+), then $D = E/W$. Define, further, Y as the number of young (0–19) and the total population as $P = Y + W + E$.

The nature of uncertainty depends on lead time, so for the following discussion let us assume that we are looking about twenty years into the future. Then, the uncertainty in Y depends primarily on fertility, the uncertainty in W on migration and the uncertainty in E on mortality. The reasons why we make errors in forecasting different components are typically unrelated. (To be sure, higher-than-expected immigration may cause an underestimation of fertility and mortality, but the level of migration is rarely high enough, relative to variations of fertility and mortality caused by other factors, for this to matter.) Thus, it is a realistic approximation to assume the three error sources are statistically independent. It follows that errors in forecasts of P from Y, W and E *partly cancel.*

In conventional forecasts this is not taken into account. Instead, a high forecast for P, say $H(P)$, is obtained from the high forecasts of the components, $H(P) = H(Y) + H(W) + H(E)$, and similarly for the low forecasts, $L(P) = L(Y) + L(W) + L(E)$. It follows that if we view, in accordance with the medians of Table 3.1, $[L(P), H(P)]$ roughly as a two-thirds level prediction interval for P, then $[L(Y), H(Y)]$, $[L(W), H(W)]$ and $[L(E), H(E)]$ must have *lower* levels of coverage. How much lower? The precise answer depends on many details but note that if Y, W and E have the same expectation and the same coefficient of variation, say C, then the coefficient of variation of P is $C \times \sqrt{3}/3$, or 58 per cent of those of its components. Or, under a normal approximation, the intervals for the three components would each have only a 44 per cent probability of covering the true population, instead of 67 per cent.

Things get worse with the old-age dependency ratio D. How could one get an upper and lower interval for it at all? There is no guarantee that $H(E)/H(W)$ is bigger than $L(E)/L(W)$. It could be smaller! It is certainly true that $H(E)/L(W) > L(E)/H(W)$, but forming an interval from these two is not 'plausible', since it only makes sense if there were a perfect negative association between W and E. Of course, one could separately produce upper and lower values for E and W such that the resulting interval for D would be 'reasonable'. Unfortunately, such values would typically be unusable for P.

Compounding the logical difficulties, there are even more basic problems. For example, if $[L(E), H(E)]$ is specified, based on mortality, to be of a 'plausible' width, how can one guarantee that the width of $[L(W), H(W)]$ is of a similar 'plausibility' when it is based on migration? If one of these has a coverage probability of 30 per cent and the other 70 per cent, both are 'plausible' values, but combining them does not seem sensible. The same problem for determining comparable scales arises even for a single vital process, when different lead times, different ages or the two sexes are considered jointly.

Scaled model for uncertainty

In the program PEP[3] that was used to carry out the demographic analyses in this volume, the variances of the logarithms of the future age-specific fertility and mortality rates are represented in terms of the following model (Alho and Spencer, 1997, 2005; Alho, 1998).

Suppose the true age-specific rate for age j during forecast year ($t > 0$) is of the form $R(j, t) = F(j, t) \exp(X(j, t))$, where $F(j, t)$ is the point forecast and $X(j, t)$ is the relative error. Suppose that the error processes are of the form $X(j, t) = \varepsilon(j, 1) + \ldots + \varepsilon(j, t)$, where the error increments are of the form

$$\varepsilon(j, t) = S(j, t)(\eta_j + \delta(j, t)). \tag{1}$$

Here, the $S(j, t)(> 0)$ are (non-random) scales to be specified, whence the name *scaled model*. The model assumes that for each j, the random variables $\delta(j, t)$ are independent over time $t = 1, 2, \ldots$ In addition, the variables $\{\delta(j, t) | j = 1, \ldots, \mathcal{J}; t = 1, 2, \ldots\}$ are independent of the random variables $\{\eta_j | j = 1, \ldots, \mathcal{J}\}$, and

$$\eta_j \sim N(0, \kappa), \delta(i, t) \sim N(0, 1 - \kappa), \tag{2}$$

where $0 < \kappa < 1$ is a parameter to be specified. We see that $\mathrm{Var}(\varepsilon(j, t)) = S(j, t)^2$.

In the UPE applications it was assumed that $\mathrm{Corr}(\eta_i, \eta_j) = \rho^{|i-j|}$, or $\mathrm{Corr}(\eta_i, \eta_j) = \mathrm{Corr}(\delta(i, t), \delta(j, t)) = \rho^{|i-j|}$, for some $0 < \rho < 1$. This allows for less than perfect correlation in age-specific mortality and fertility, across age.

Since $\kappa = \mathrm{Corr}(\varepsilon(j, t), \varepsilon(j, t + h))$ for all $h \neq 0$, we can interpret κ as a constant autocorrelation between the error increments. Under a random walk model the error increments would be uncorrelated with $\kappa = 0$, for example. Together, the autocorrelation κ and the scales determine the variance of the relative error $X(j, t)$.

Example 3.1. Consider the special case of constant scales, or $S(j, t) = S(j)$ for all t. It follows that

$$\mathrm{Var}(X(j, t)) = a(j)t + b(j)t^2, \tag{3}$$

where $a(j) = S(j)^2(1 - \kappa)$ and $b(j) = S(j)^2\kappa$. If $a(j)(> 0)$ and $b(j)(\geq 0)$ can be estimated from the data, then the corresponding values of $S(j)^2$ and κ can be deduced as $S(j)^2 = a(j) + b(j)$ and $\kappa = b(j)/(a(j) + b(j))$. For intuition, note that the model with constant scales can be interpreted as a random walk with a random drift. The relative importance of the two components is determined by κ.   □

The key properties of the scaled model are:
- Since the choice of the scales $S(j, t)$ is unrestricted, any sequence of non-decreasing error variances can be matched. In particular, heteroscedasticity can be allowed.

- Any sequence of cross-correlations over ages can be majorized using the AR(1) models of correlation.
- Any sequence of autocorrelations for the error increments can be majorized. This means that we can always find a conservative approximation to any covariance structure using the model.

As discussed by Alho and Spencer (2005) the scaled model can be used to replicate prediction intervals of the mortality forecasts with the method of Lee and Carter (1992), for example.

The representation of error in net migration in PEP is done in absolute terms, using variables of the same type as $\varepsilon(j, t)$, above, but now j takes only two values and refers to *sex*. Dependence on age is not stochastic, and assumed to be deterministic, and it is given by a fixed distribution $g(j, x)$ over age x for each $j(= 1, 2)$, i.e. the error of net migration in age x, for sex j, during year $t(> 0)$, is additive and of the form

$$Y(j, x, t) = S(j, t)g(j, x)(\eta_j + \delta(j, t)). \tag{4}$$

The assumption of perfect dependence is not motivated by a belief that there would not be any cancellation of error across age in migration. Surely there is. Instead, the quality of migration data is too poor in most countries to merit a more refined approach.

An advantage we had over earlier national analyses in this field was that we had eighteen countries under scrutiny simultaneously. This allowed us to discount idiosyncrasies (evident, for example, in column 'EMP' of Table 3.1) that could dominate the forecast results of an individual country. This is one of the traditional methods of 'borrowing strength' from similar units of observation that is widely used in small-domain estimation (e.g. Rao, 2003).

Approaches to assessing forecast uncertainty

The presence of autocorrelation distinguishes time-series analysis from the more standard statistical theory that assumes statistical independence among observations. For example, even though one can estimate the mean of a stationary sequence simply by averaging the observations, the calculation of the corresponding standard error presumes that the autocorrelation structure has been identified and estimated. In general, positive autocorrelation leads to *higher* standard errors than one would expect under independent sampling of otherwise similar data (e.g. Alho and Spencer, 2005). Intuitively, autocorrelation reduces the amount of information which a sample of given size contains.

Even if one abstracts from technicalities, it is clear that in a time-series context one is typically interested in forecasting a future value (i.e. a random variable) rather than a parameter of the process, so additional complexities arise that are related to the handling of possible non-stationarity, and to other aspects of the identification of model type.

Nevertheless, for a wide range of models (such as linear stochastic processes (Box and Jenkins, 1976; Alho and Spencer, 2005)) the results are well known. Thus, if demographic forecasts are carried out using a formal statistical model, both optimal predictions and prediction intervals can typically be produced once the model has been identified and its parameters have been estimated. Accounting for uncertainty related to the standard errors of the parameters has long been neglected in ARIMA modelling for example, but Markov chain Monte Carlo techniques have overcome many of the technical obstacles (Chib and Greenberg, 1994; Alho and Spencer 2005). These can be used 'off the shelf', but the question remains of how the choice of models and their validity over time can be included as part of the assessment of uncertainty.

Errors in past forecasts provide an obvious source of information on the level of error one might expect in the future (Keilman, 1990, 1997). It is not necessary to believe that future errors will be similar to those in the past, but if one does not believe that they will be, it is necessary to provide argumentation as to why the future is expected to be different from the past.

A difficulty in the use of past errors as a guide is that of obtaining estimates that are statistically stable. We have seen in Table 3.1 that empirical forecast errors can vary considerably from one country to another. Other analyses indicate that there can also be large variations over time (Alho and Spencer, 2005). One would expect this to be the case given the high autocorrelation of forecast errors.

Another problem in the use of past errors as a guide is that the number of observations (i.e. the number of available past forecasts) diminishes rapidly when lead time is increased. There is no country in the world for which there would be more than a handful of forecasts with lead time exceeding fifty years, whose error can be assessed. Yet, for pension problems, even longer lead times must be considered (Lee and Tuljapurkar, 1998).

As a way out, it was proposed by Alho (1990) that one should resort to so-called naïve, or baseline, forecasts. It had been noted that official forecasts of fertility, in industrialized countries, typically assume little change from the current level (Lee, 1974). Thus, one can approximate past forecasts by assuming no change. This forecast is easily computed for any point in the past, even if no forecast was actually carried out at that time. Its empirical error can similarly be computed with ease, as long into the future as there are data points. In the case of mortality an assumption of a constant rate of change has been shown to be competitive with official forecasts (Alho, 1990), so it can serve as a baseline forecast.

Example 3.2. Suppose we have data for years $t = 1, 2, \ldots, T$. Suppose a baseline forecast, made at t with lead time $k = 1, 2, \ldots$ for $R(j, t + k)$ is denoted by $F(j, t, k)$. The absolute value of its relative error is then $e(j, t, k) = |\log(F(j, t, k)) - \log(R(j, t + k))|$. It follows that we have a collection of values $Z(j, k) = \{e(j, t, k) \,|\, t = 1, 2, \ldots, t - k\}$ available. These can be used to estimate the parameters $a(j)$ and $b(j)$ of (3) in various ways. In order to discount the values of outliers caused, for example, by wars, a robust procedure is to determine first the medians $M^*(j, k) =$ median over t of the set of values $Z(j, k)$, for every $k = 1, 2, \ldots$ of interest. Then, since the 0.75 fractile of a standard normal distribution is 0.6745, we can find a standard deviation for a normal distribution whose absolute value has the same median, as $M(j, k) = M^*(j, k)/0.6745$. These $M(j, k)$ values can serve as our basic data. Returning to the case of Example 3.1, we note that by minimizing the sum of squares,

$$\Sigma_t (M(j, t)^2 - a(j)t - b(j)t^2)^2, \tag{5}$$

we can find values $a(j)$ and $b(j)$ that fit as closely as possible. If the values satisfy the necessary positiveness conditions, we can deduce the parameters of the scaled model. □

The example given above is by no means the only approach available. First, in the case of fertility and mortality we consider *relative* error $X(j, t)$. Absolute error could also be used, but given the large variations in the level of the processes, relative error is a more comparable measure. Second, in assessing the magnitude of error we do not subtract the mean. This means that *we are including the possible forecast bias* in the error estimate. This is motivated by the fact that we do not believe that biases can be avoided in the future either. Third, the added twist of using the medians rather than *averages* typically reduces the estimated uncertainty. This is relevant if the intended use of the predictive distribution is to give an indication of how much variability one should expect under normal, peacetime conditions. For analyses with other background assumptions, one might resort directly to root-mean-squared error or other measures of spread.

In general, error estimates based on naïve forecasts should be conservative in the sense of providing intervals that are potentially too wide. Indeed, it is possible to find countries and periods during which naïve forecasts have been very bad. However, this is also true of official forecasts, and as discussed in Alho (1990), official US forecasts of mortality have not been better than naïve forecasts in the post-World War II period. Note also that like error estimates based on past forecasts, error estimates based on naïve forecasts are 'self-validating' in that they are correct if volatility does not change. In this respect they are superior to purely model-based estimates.

Practical specification of uncertainty

Variance of total fertility and age-specific fertility

Based on empirical estimates from six countries with long data series (Denmark, Finland, Iceland, the Netherlands, Norway and Sweden) one could determine that the (logarithm of the) total fertility rate behaves essentially like a process of independent increments, so we took $\kappa = 0$ for all countries. The same analysis led to an approximate formulation with a scale appropriate for the total fertility 0.06 (Alho and Spencer, 2005). However, during the most recent decade, fertility has been less volatile than in the past, on average. To account for the recent decreases in volatility we estimated a starting level of scale for each country based on data from 1990–2000. These were assumed to increase linearly to 0.06 in twenty years time.

The initial scales determined in this manner were scaled up by a factor of 1.25 (or, we took $S(j, t) = 1.25 \times 0.06$ for $t > 20$) to account for the fact that the correlation of the relative error over age was not perfect, but 0.95. This cross-correlation has an empirical basis in the work of Alho (1998) in Finland. The same scale was used in all ages.

The relative standard deviations of error for the total fertility rate are given in Table 3.2.[4]

For comparison, by defining M = middle forecast, H = high forecast, and L = low forecast, the measures under columns 'UN' and 'ES', are of the form $100 \times (H - L)/2M$. For the United Nations forecasts, it is assumed that all countries except Greece have $M = 1.85$, $H = 2.35$, and $L = 1.35$, but that Greece has $M = 1.78$. In contrast, Eurostat has both different point forecasts for different countries and, in some cases, assymmetric high–low intervals. The difference between the UN and Eurostat assumptions is striking. The Eurostat values are almost exactly one-half of the UN ones. Presumably both attempt to cover a 'reasonable range', but the message given to the forecast users is quite different.

The UPE values are based on an empirical analysis, and a UPE–UN comparison shows that UN values are approximately three-quarters of the empirically estimated UPE values that yield the 'one-sigma intervals'; or, the probability content of the UN high–low intervals is about 55 per cent. The implication is that the high–low intervals for the young (Y) have a

Table 3.2. *The standard deviation of the relative error of total fertility during first and last forecast years as specified by the UPE project, and relative uncertainty as expressed by high and low forecasts of the United Nations (2004) and Eurostat (2005).*

Source Year	2003	UPE 2049	UN 2050	ES 2050
Austria	2.2	36.6	27.0	17.2
Belgium	2.6	36.9	27.0	13.2
Denmark	1.9	36.3	27.0	13.9
Finland	2.0	36.3	27.0	13.9
France	2.3	36.7	27.0	13.5
Germany	2.9	37.2	27.0	17.2
Greece	1.6	36.0	28.1	18.3
Iceland	2.8	37.2	27.0	–
Ireland	2.2	36.6	27.0	11.1
Italy	2.5	36.8	27.0	17.9
Luxembourg	2.6	37.0	27.0	13.9
Netherlands	1.9	36.3	27.0	14.3
Norway	2.2	35.8	27.0	–
Portugal	2.2	36.6	27.0	15.6
Spain	2.6	36.9	27.0	17.9
Sweden	3.9	38.4	27.0	13.5
Switzerland	1.5	36.0	27.0	–
United Kingdom	1.5	35.9	27.0	14.3
Median	2.2	36.6	27.0	14.3
Standard deviation	0.6	0.6	0.3	2.2

clearly lower level of coverage than the resulting intervals for the total population (P).

Variance and autocorrelation of age-specific mortality

In the case of mortality the UPE project had available direct estimates of relative uncertainty in naïve forecasts of age-specific mortality. However, we were also urged by the expert we interviewed[5] not to underestimate the potential effect of unforeseen developments in medical technology on mortality. This is especially relevant in the oldest ages for which past improvements had the least effect. Also, given that conditions influencing future mortality may be quite different for young ages than for older ones it was decided to make estimates of uncertainty by age. Thus, for mortality, the scales we used depended on age. On the other hand, we

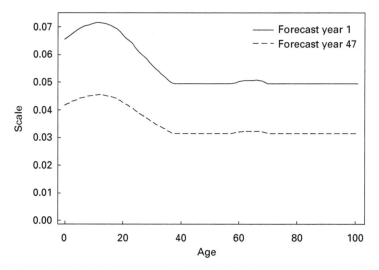

Figure 3.1. Scales for age-specific mortality in forecast year 1 and forecast year 47.

could not see a good reason to make separate estimates for males and females, or for the different countries. This enhances statistical stability. Finally, as we were also urged to consider the possibility of changing trends in the future, we used a value $\kappa = 0.05$ for the autocorrelation of the error increments. Purely empirical estimates from the eighteen countries would have led to an average value close to zero, whereas an empirical analysis of Finland alone (Alho, 1998) gave as high a value as 0.15. Judgement was brought to bear.

Contemporaneous correlation of (the logarithm of) age-specific mortality, in a given age, was taken to be 0.85 between males and females. In Alho (1998) an average correlation of 0.80 was obtained. This was increased, on judgemental grounds, to maintain a smaller male–female gap.

Figure 3.1 gives the scales in forecast years 1 and 47. We see that in the past, volatility has been highest in the youngest ages. For those ages where the curves are flat, empirical estimates were adjusted upwards to the level of the overall average on judgemental grounds.

Figure 3.2 summarizes the effect of scales and autocorrelation into a standard deviation of the relative forecast error. The curves are all parallel, and the one shown in Figure 3.2 represents the lowest level of uncertainty that obtains in the middle and oldest ages (the flat regions in Figure 3.1). The shape of the curve is based on an analysis of errors of naïve forecasts

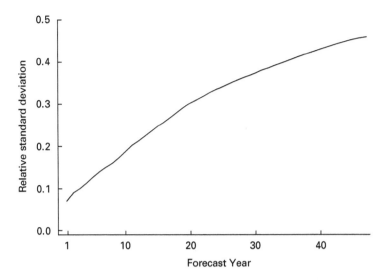

Figure 3.2. Relative standard deviation of age-specific mortality for ages 40+.

from Austria, Denmark, France, Italy, the Netherlands, Norway, Sweden, Switzerland and the UK. The scales were deduced from these estimates. The concavity explains why the later curve is lower than the earlier one in Figure 3.1.

Table 3.3 presents a comparison between the one-sigma intervals of the UPE project and the half-width of Eurostat (2005) high–low intervals for life expectancy at birth, both expressed in years. The UPE intervals are based on Table 8 (p. 64) of the final report that is available at www.stat.fi/tup/euupe/upe_final_report.pdf. The width of the 80 per cent intervals given there has been divided by 2 × 1.2816 (as in the case of Table 3.1) to arrive at the values of Table 3.3. Remarkably, the United Nations (2004) provides one mortality variant only, and is therefore omitted. The finding is that uncertainty in life expectancy as expressed by Eurostat has a width of two-fifths of a one-sigma interval. Under a normal assumption such an interval would have a probability of less than 31 per cent of covering the true value.

In substantive terms this means that should a user of the Eurostat forecast take the high–low intervals for the elderly as a 'reasonable range' (or, *a fortiori*, the lack of any range on the part of the UN), then the true uncertainty to be expected would be grossly underestimated.

Table 3.3. *The half-width of one-sigma intervals for life expectancy at birth as specified by the UPE project for the year 2049, and the half-width of the high–low interval of Eurostat (2005) for the year 2050.*

Source	UPE		ES	
Sex	Females	Males	Females	Males
Austria	2.9	3.3	1.2	1.4
Belgium	3.4	3.8	1.3	1.5
Denmark	3.9	3.9	1.4	1.5
Finland	3.3	3.7	1.2	1.4
France	3.4	3.9	1.3	1.5
Germany	3.6	4.2	1.4	1.6
Greece	3.1	3.5	1.3	1.6
Iceland	4.1	3.3	–	–
Ireland	3.7	3.7	1.6	1.8
Italy	3.3	3.5	1.2	1.4
Luxembourg	4.1	4.6	1.5	1.5
Netherlands	3.4	3.5	1.4	1.4
Norway	3.3	3.5	–	–
Portugal	3.6	4.1	1.6	1.9
Spain	3.5	4.0	1.1	1.6
Sweden	3.9	3.6	1.2	1.2
Switzerland	3.2	3.3	–	–
United Kingdom	3.5	3.7	1.8	1.2
Median	3.5	3.7	1.3	1.5
Standard deviation	0.33	0.35	0.19	0.18

Variance and autocorrelation of net migration

As discussed above, the uncertainty of net migration was formulated in terms of a model where cross-correlation over age was taken to be 1.0. The functions $g(j, x)$ are given in Figure 3.3 separately for males ($j = 1$, solid) and females ($j = 2$, dashed). As discussed by Alho and Spencer (2005) it makes sense to specify the distributions as proportional to gross migration. The estimates given were obtained from the years 1998–2002 for Sweden, Denmark and Norway, which have reliable data on gross migration.[6] The values for both sexes sum to 1.0, or $\Sigma_x g(j, x) = 1$, $j = 1, 2$.

The scales for total migration were assumed to be the same for both females and males. They start from an initial level for year 2003 and rise linearly to a final level ten years later. The initial level represents recent past volatility, but the final level is primarily judgemental: estimates

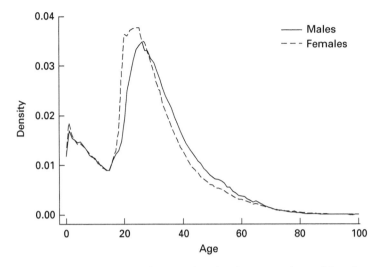

Figure 3.3. Distribution of gross migration by age: males and females.

obtained using time-series models were adjusted mostly downwards, but in some cases upwards, to reach an interpretable order of uncertainty among the countries. The cross-correlation of the sexes was assumed to be 0.90, based on empirical analyses by Alho (1998) of Finland and by Keilman, Pham and Hetland (2002) of Norway. An adjustment was made to the scales of both sexes to allow for less than perfect correlation.

Finally, the values for autocorrelations κ were determined for each country by a three-step procedure. First, time-series models estimated by Keilman and Pham (2004) were used to deduce the standard deviation of the predictive distribution of the cumulative net migration by the year 2050. Second, judgemental estimates of the same standard deviation were derived based on the assumption that the probability would be 2.5 per cent that the cumulative net migration would be negative by the year 2050. This calculation is based on the point forecasts of net migration as discussed by Keilman, Cruijsen and Alho (this volume, chap. 2); see also www.stat.fi/tup/euupe/. The former estimates were slightly higher but both were of the same order of magnitude, on average. However, there were some countries for which the time-series based estimates were implausibly high. These were first adjusted, and then the two estimates were averaged. This produced a set of candidates for standard deviations from which those values of κ could be deduced that would lead exactly to these standard deviations. We noted, however, that the estimates of κ arrived at in this way varied significantly across countries. Therefore, as the third step, we used a synthetic estimator (Rao, 2003) to pull the

Table 3.4. *Scale of total net migration in 2003 and 2049 per thousand of population in year 2000, the estimated autocorrelation κ as specified by the UPE project and the half-width of the high–low interval of Eurostat (2005), per population in year 2005.*

| Year | Scale | | κ | ES |
	2003	2049		2050
Austria	3.2	4.0	0.21	2.5
Belgium	1.2	2.0	0.19	1.7
Denmark	1.1	2.0	0.18	1.5
Finland	0.7	2.0	0.34	0.9
France	2.1	4.0	0.13	1.0
Germany	3.4	4.0	0.20	2.7
Greece	6.0	6.0	0.17	2.6
Iceland	2.1	4.0	0.14	–
Ireland	2.9	5.0	0.22	3.6
Italy	3.3	5.0	0.26	1.4
Luxembourg	6.0	6.0	0.22	3.6
Netherlands	1.9	2.0	0.29	2.1
Norway	1.7	2.0	0.56	–
Portugal	6.0	6.0	0.17	3.2
Spain	3.3	5.0	0.28	2.1
Sweden	1.3	2.0	0.43	1.8
Switzerland	1.7	2.0	0.43	–
United Kingdom	2.7	4.0	0.17	2.2
Median	2.4	4.0	0.22	2.1
Standard deviation	1.7	1.6	0.12	0.85

national estimates towards the cross-country median of the values, by taking the average of the country-specific estimate and the median. The final values are given in column κ of Table 3.4.

In the same way as for mortality, the UN has not provided alternative variants for net migration at all. The finding from the comparison between the UPE and Eurostat assumptions (ES) is that the high–low intervals have a half-width which is slightly over one-half of the one-sigma interval specified by the UPE project. In fact, the uncertainty is only slightly lower than the UPE values corresponding to the first forecast year 2003. In this case the cumulative effect of the uncertainty specification of the Eurostat forecasts may come close to that of the UPE project because of the implicit assumption of perfect autocorrelation. Note also that in the case of migration the UPE specification was based much more on judgement than those for fertility and mortality.

As we are concentrating here on national populations, we do not discuss cross-country correlations in net migration or the other demographic processes. However, cross-country correlations can be, and were, estimated (Alho, 2005).

Implications for research on ageing

In this chapter we have shown that official forecasts continue to present alternative variants to the public that can only be considered as giving a 'reasonable range' if one believes that European demographics have become considerably less volatile than they have been during the past century. Note that this is so even though we have deliberately eliminated shocks caused by wars and similar 'outliers' from this assessment, by using robust estimation procedures.

For the population as a whole the chances are about two-thirds that the future will be in the official high–low range, but for both the young and the old the chances are much less. Interestingly, the UN and Eurostat arrive at approximately the same level of uncertainty for the total population by assumptions that are in stark contrast. For the UN the uncertainty comes entirely from births, whereas Eurostat also provides variants for mortality and migration.

The fact that the uncertainty in the number of elderly is clearly underestimated by both official forecasts means that policy-makers handling ageing-related problems, who rely on official forecasts, are unlikely to appreciate the true magnitude of uncertainty. As a result they may discount the possibility of future surprises whose consequences would be borne by the European citizenship.

Dealing with uncertainty in a thoughtful manner is harder than basing policy discussions on a fixed consensus view. It is not impossible, however. Papers in Auerbach and Lee (2001) have already charted a range of issues that come up. In this book we take a step closer to actual practice by presenting a range of macro-economic models that are used in the planning and evaluation of ageing policies.

Appendix: Conventional and stochastic population forecasts – pros and cons

Population renewal can be expressed as: (population at $t+1$) = (population at t) + (births during t) − (deaths during t) + (net migration during t). In the cohort-component method the book keeping is done by age and sex. *Both conventional and stochastic forecasts use the same book keeping.* In the cohort-component method, births and deaths are generated via vital rates. In conventional forecasts the rates are specified as *numbers*, whereas in the stochastic forecasts they are taken to be *random variables*. From a logical point of view, a *conventional forecast is a special case of a*

Table 3.5. *Comparison of properties of conventional and stochastic population forecasts.*

	Conventional population forecast	Stochastic population forecast
Transparency	Involves addition, subtraction and multiplication only. The results may be checked by direct inspection, and understood with only modest education.	Forecasts are carried out by simulation. Checking is more complex. Understanding the results requires more education (including probability and statistics).
Simplicity of presentation	Middle variant may be sufficient to convey the main message. Alternative calculations may be provided, with one leading to a higher population, another leading to a lower population etc. These can be printed back-to-back in a book. Results for aggregated age-groups are produced by addition.	A full predictive distribution is approximated via computer simulation. Still, it may not be necessary to display more than the point forecast for a lay audience. Prediction intervals can be published for individual ages, but to produce intervals for aggregates a database of simulated values must (and can) be accessed.
Ease of preparation	Only a point forecast needs to be specified.	In addition, the specification of variances and correlations is required.
Interpretation and logical coherence of intervals	High and low intervals are (usually) interpreted as providing a 'plausible range'. But, there is no way to guarantee the comparability of the ranges for different ages, different sexes, different forecast years, etc. The results for different demographic functionals are necessarily incoherent.	Intervals with desired probability content for the size of any population aggregate and for the size of any demographic functional (like age ratios) at any future time can be provided.
Ability to handle uncertainty	Cannot handle uncertainty in a coherent and interpretable manner.	Uncertainty is handled in a coherent and interpretable manner.
Use of past data	Only trend estimates can be used. Judgement is necessary for questions like which models and which data periods to use. Knowledge of intermediate correlations (i.e. different from ± 1) across demographic variables cannot be used.	Can utilize information on varying trends, lack of fit, changes of volatility, etc. The uncertainty related to the choice of models and data periods can be incorporated statistically. Knowledge of intermediate correlations can be incorporated.

Table 3.5. (*cont.*)

	Conventional population forecast	Stochastic population forecast
Conditional forecasts and scenarios	Can represent scenarios that correspond to, for example, assumed effects of policy interventions or exogenous factors.	Can, in addition, incorporate information about the uncertainty concerning the effects of interventions or exogenous factors.
Sensitivity analysis	Can vary values of fertility, mortality or migration to see what the effect is.	Can, in addition, vary second moments.
Ease of computation	A large number of computer programs are available. There is extensive experience of their use. Results are obtained in seconds.	Several computer programs are available, but with differing capabilities. There is experience of their use from the past 10–15 years only. Results are obtained in minutes.

stochastic forecast, where all variance parameters are zero. From a practical point of view the main properties are as listed in Table 3.5.

NOTES

1 For a normally distributed variable the two measures are equal.
2 Here, and in the sequel, we will ignore the fact that the point forecasts can have different biases. Each forecast is assessed in turn as if it were unbiased, and only the width of the interval is considered. Note also that while we present results for year 2050 only, for the intermediate years the coverage of the official high–low intervals would typically be lower than at the end, as they assume perfect autocorrelation of errors over time.
3 Program for Error Propagation. For a description, see http://joyx.joensuu.fi/~ek/pep/pepstart.htm.
4 Note that the standard deviation in 2049 differs across countries because the estimates of initial volatility differ. For Norway an additional adjustment was made.
5 The UPE project interviewed experts in fertility, mortality and migration, in addition to carrying out statistical analyses.
6 For increased accuracy one might consider modifying this assumption for countries such as Spain, for which migration at retirement age is important.

REFERENCES

Alho, J. M. (1990). 'Stochastic Methods in Population Forecasting'. *International Journal of Forecasting*, 6: 521–30.
    (1998). *A Stochastic Forecast of the Population of Finland*. Review no. 1998/4. Helsinki: Statistics Finland.

(2005). 'Simplified Approaches to Stochastic Multi-state Population Forecasts'. Paper presented at conference on *Stochastic Demographic Forecasting*, Salamanca, August.

Alho, J. M. and Spencer, B. D. (1997). 'The Practical Specification of the Expected Error of Population Forecasts'. *Journal of Official Statistics*, 13: 203–25.

(2005). *Statistical Demography and Forecasting*. New York: Springer.

Auerbach, A. J. and Lee, R. D. (2001), eds. *Demographic Change and Fiscal Policy*. Cambridge: Cambridge University Press.

Box, G. E. P. and Jenkins, G. M. (1976). *Time Series Analysis,* revised edn. San Francisco: Holden-Day.

Cannan E. (1895). 'The Probability of Cessation of the Growth of Population in England and Wales during the Next Century'. *The Economic Journal*, 5: 505–15.

Chib, S. and Greenberg, E. (1994). 'Bayes Inference in Regression Models with ARMA(p,q) Errors'. *Journal of Econometrics*, 64: 183–206.

DeGans H. A. (1999). *Population Forecasting 1895–1945*. Dordrecht: Kluwer.

Freedman, D., Pisani, R. and Purves, R. (1978). *Statistics*. New York: Norton.

Eurostat (2005). 'EUROPOP2004, Population Projections: EU25 Population Rises Until 2025, Then Falls'. News Release 448/2005, 8 April.

Keilman, N. (1990). *Uncertainty in National Population Forecasting: Issues, Backgrounds, Analyses, Recommendations*. Amsterdam: Swets and Zeitlinger.

(1997). 'Ex-post Errors in Official Population Forecasts in Industrialized Countries'. *Journal of Official Statistics*, 13: 245–77.

Keilman, N. and Pham, D. Q. (2004). *Empirical Errors and Predicted Errors in Fertility, Mortality and Migration Forecasts in the European Economic Area*. Discussion Paper no. 386. Oslo: Statistics Norway.

Keilman, N., Pham, D. Q. and Hetland, A. (2002). *Norway's Uncertain Demographic Future*. Social and Economic Studies 105. Oslo: Statistics Norway.

Lee, R. D. (1974). 'Forecasting Births in Post-transition Populations: Stochastic Renewal with Serially Correlated Fertility'. *Journal of the American Statistical Association*, 69: 607–17.

Lee, R. D. and Carter, L. R. (1992) 'Modeling and Forecasting the Time Series of U.S. Mortality'. *Journal of the American Statistical Association*, 87: 659–71.

Lee, R. D. and Tuljapurkar, S. (1998). 'Uncertain Economic Futures and Social Security Finances'. *American Economic Review*, 88: 237–41.

Modeen, G. (1934). 'The Future Development of the Population of Finland'. *Kansantaloudellinen aikakauskirja*, 6: 351–78. (In Finnish.)

National Research Council (2000). *Beyond Six Billion: Forecasting the World's Population*. Panel on Population Projections. Washington, DC: National Academy Press.

Rao, J. N. K. (2003). *Small Area Estimation*. New York: Wiley.

Shryock, H. S., Siegel, J. S. and associates (1976). *The Methods and Materials of Demography*, condensed edn by E. G. Stockwell. New York: Academic Press.

Stoto, M. (1983). 'Accuracy of Population Projections'. *Journal of the American Statistical Association*, 78: 13–20.

United Nations (2004). *The World Population Prospects: The 2004 Revision of the Population Database*. New York: United Nations.

The UPE forecasts: strengths, innovations, developments

Shripad Tuljapurkar

Introduction

The UPE project is a remarkable effort at producing solidly grounded stochastic forecasts for the majority of European countries. In this discussion I review the features that make this work remarkable, discuss key properties that distinguish these stochastic forecasts from scenario forecasts and consider some future directions in analysis and application.

The strengths of the UPE approach include:

1. *A unified approach to many countries.* This is a challenging aspect of making forecasts and UPE provides a carefully documented and reasoned approach that will serve as a model for future work.
2. *Systematic development of assumptions.* All forecasts include historical analysis and subjective judgement. UPE does an exemplary job of setting out the two components, but is especially noteworthy in using these in a complementary way and in maintaining a necessary level of scepticism about expert judgement.
3. *Careful analysis of past official assumptions and methods.* The UPE team has made excellent use of the well-known expertise of their team members in the analysis of errors in past official forecasts. This aspect of forecast error is perhaps the only way to assess assumption bias and assumption lag in expert analysis, and UPE shows clearly how it should be implemented and used.
4. Stochastic forecasts based on a general forecasting method applied consistently across several countries. The UPE forecasts are based on dynamic models of uncertainty (about which I say more below), not just randomized scenarios. The forecasts are available online which is particularly useful.

Overall, these forecasts and the underlying developments are a benchmark for future efforts to make and use stochastic population forecasts. I hope that official European agencies will make use of these forecasts to inform and evaluate their own methods and projections.

The UPE forecasts: features and questions

I now examine specific predictions and assumptions in the UPE forecasts, using as a context forecasts and features from my experience working mainly with the United States and Japan.

Difference between UPE and official forecasts

The overall median UPE population forecast for EEA+ in 2050 is about 25 million higher than Eurostat 2004 (ES) projections. What drives the difference? Clearly the answer is in differences between projected longevity, fertility and migration. The effect of the difference in longevity projections is easy to estimate: UPE has 2050 life expectancies around 2 years (women) to 2.5 years (men) higher than ES; with a final life expectancy of about eighty-eight years the longevity difference accounts for perhaps 9 million of the difference. The remainder must come from the higher migration in UPE, offset somewhat by the slightly lower fertility. It would be useful to know how much of the difference is due to each factor. The effects of the factors can be worked out by rough computation and by simulation with alternative assumptions. Similarly, it would be informative to know how different the forecasts are with respect to dependency ratios and to the variability in total population and dependency ratios, as well as the sources of those differences.

Specification of forecast error structure

UPE employs a useful flexible equation to specify the uncertainty over *time*. The logarithm of the 'error' in a rate at age j in year t is described by

$$\varepsilon(j, t) = S(j, t)(\eta(j) + \delta(j, t))$$

where S is a scaling factor, and the terms in parentheses are components of stochastic perturbations. I think the forecasting enterprise as a whole would benefit from a more detailed presentation of how the UPE assessments of temporal correlation were made.

In particular, I find the specification of the fertility errors to be rather different from what Ron Lee and I observed for the United States (Lee and Tuljapurkar, 1994). The absence of serial correlation seems surprising. Also, the UPE assumptions about long-run total fertility rate clearly reflect some cross-country convergence of fertility behaviour, but also some persistent differences. Given that so much recent fertility change in Europe came as a clear surprise to demographers and other

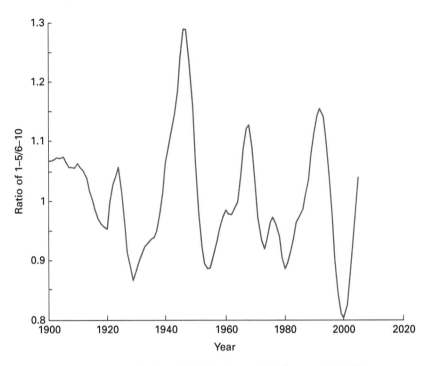

Figure IC.1. Volatility of birth cohorts: Sweden, 1900–2005.

informed observers, I am not sure that UPE includes sufficient provision for changes in volatility over the many decades of the projection.

Persistent variability: a key feature of stochastic forecasts

Forecasters often have a difficult time conveying the dynamic nature of stochastic forecasts. Long custom has cued users to expect what we would call point forecasts, perhaps with a spread. The presentation of uncertainty as a fan of single-year prediction intervals is limited in its information content. To see how much variability is contained in the UPE forecasts I looked at variability in Swedish birth cohorts. Figure IC.1 plots the ratio of the Swedish population in the age-group 0–4 to that in the age-group 5–10 – this is essentially a growth rate for the youngest cohort. The plot is for the past century and shows substantial variability, and a surprisingly (to me) high level of variability in the past two decades. The variability here is complicated in the sense that it can be driven by variability in mortality (though not much in recent times), fertility and

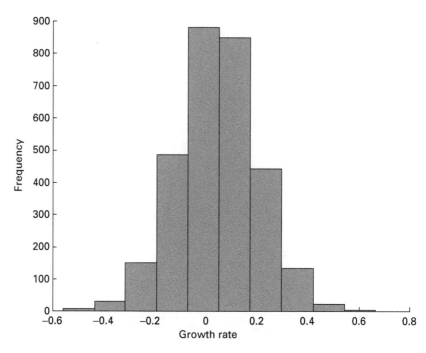

Figure IC.2. Growth of 1–5 cohort: Sweden, 2010–2020. (*Source:* UPE Project.)

age structure. Given all these factors, what happens to this variability in the UPE forecasts?

I computed the growth rate of the under-five population of Sweden using the 2010 and 2020 figures, and again using the 2040 and 2050 figures, from the UPE website. The growth rates are computed for each of the 3000 sample paths. Figure IC.2 displays a histogram of the growth rate for the earlier decade, and Figure IC.3 displays the histogram for the later decade. I find it striking, and reassuring, that the variability is similar in the two periods, which is consistent with past experience.

Mortality and the distribution of deaths

The UPE process for modelling mortality change follows past practice in focusing on age-specific mortality rates. Recently Edwards and Tuljapurkar (2005) looked at this question in a different way, analysing the change over time in the variance in age at death (as measured by period mortality rates). They showed that this variance decreased throughout

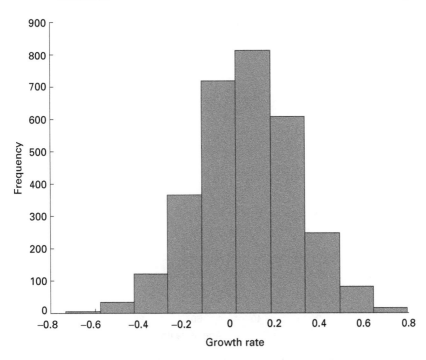

Figure IC.3. Growth of 1–5 cohort: Sweden, 2040–2050. (*Source:* UPE Project.)

most of the twentieth century but that the rate of decrease has slowed in recent years. They also found (but did not report) that the skew of the distribution has decreased over time. These observations indicate robust patterns of change; they are robust relative to analyses based on fitting mortality distributions over a wide age range. To see how UPE forecasts fare in terms of the variance and skew of the distribution of age at death, I plotted the age-at-death distributions based on period rates for Sweden using the UPE 2002 baseline data and the UPE 2048 forecast; these are shown in Figure IC.4. The changes shown there appear consistent with the findings of Edwards and Tuljapurkar (2005), which supports the validity of the modelling approach used in UPE.

Sources of variability

Users of demographic forecasts focus on a few key measures, including population growth rate and dependency ratios (elderly to workers, young

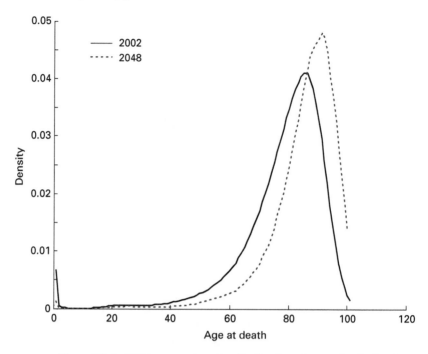

Figure IC.4. UPE assumptions for distribution of age at death: Sweden, 2002 and 2048.

to workers). A significant question that the UPE analyses do not address is how much of the forecast variance is due to the following factors:
1. changing rates;
2. changing population structure;
3. changing immigration.

Tuljapurkar and Lee (discussed by Tuljapurkar, 1990) examined population growth rate and found that the variance in annual growth rates for human population projections can be decomposed as being roughly two-thirds due to variance in rates (mortality and fertility) and one-third due to variance in age structure. Lee and Tuljapurkar (2000) discuss the significance of this and similar decompositions. An analysis of the UPE forecasts along these lines would be valuable.

Analytical approaches

Lee and Tuljapurkar (1994) made an effort to use a perturbation analysis of population dynamics based on approximate recursions for population moments, and a related approach was used by Alho and Spencer (1991).

Comment 61

I see useful applications for analyses of this type of the UPE forecasts, especially so that demographers can develop insights into the determinants of projected uncertainty. In addition, it should be possible and profitable to combine such demographic analytics with analytics for economic overlapping-generations models.

Applying stochastic forecasts

Demographers who make forecasts often stop with the forecasts: application and interpretation are regarded as the province of the user(s). I think a useful and valuable extension of the UPE effort should focus on the implications of the forecasts for the shape of the future. The specific topics that would be worth analysis and graphical exploration are:

1. visual representations of the persistent volatility and persistent change (quasi-steady states) of demographic structure;
2. fiscal adjustments to demographic variability as an ongoing, adaptive process that requires continuous updating;
3. engineering the future to take account of projected change in the age structure of populations, especially with respect to changes in mobility and perception that we know characterize older people; implications for the design and utilization of public spaces and transportation systems (airports, shopping, roadways); the adaptation of communication and entertainment;
4. changes in the human environment: what you see in the street – many elderly, more immigrants, fewer youths;
5. personal perspectives in ageing populations with respect to: employment, career change, asset management and childbearing at older ages.

REFERENCES

Alho, J. M. and Spencer, B. D. (1991). 'A Population Forecast as a Database: Implementing the Stochastic Propagation of Error'. *Journal of Official Statistics*, 7: 295–310.
Edwards, R. and Tuljapurkar, S. (2005). 'Inequality in Life Spans and a New Perspective on Mortality Convergence Across Industrialized Countries'. *Population and Development Review*, 31:645–74.
Lee, R. and Tuljapurkar, S. (1994). 'Stochastic Population Forecasts of the U.S.: Beyond High, Medium, Low'. *Journal of the American Statistical Association*, 89: 1175–89.
(2000). 'Population Forecasting for Fiscal Planning: Issues and Innovations', in *Demography and Fiscal Policy*, ed. A. J. Auerbach and R. D. Lee. Cambridge: Cambridge University Press, pp. 7–57.
Tuljapurkar, S. (1990). *Population Dynamics in Variable Environments*. New York: Springer.

Part II

Measuring sustainability in a
stochastic environment

4 Fiscal implications of demographic uncertainty: comparisons across the European Union

Martin Weale

Introduction

It is now well understood that many countries may face considerable budgetary problems as a result of demographic change and population ageing. A number of different countries have a range of economic models intended for making long-term projections and these are traditionally used to assess the budgetary impact of population change. The best summary statistic of budgetary imbalance is provided by an estimate of the immediate permanent change in taxation needed to deliver fiscal solvency. The justification for addressing the problem in this way is twofold. First of all, it corresponds to a rough notion of intergenerational equity: each generation faces the same tax burden. Second, there are now well-established arguments that fiscal policy is optimal when expected future taxes are constant (Flemming, 1987). This statistic can be calculated from a range of different types of model. It has to be remembered, however, that it is a summary statistic for the purpose of comparing different projections; in models where people's behaviour is sensitive to tax rates and which have been simulated on the assumption that taxes are varied period by period (e.g. to maintain short-term fiscal balance) the projections will be slightly different from those which would result if this constant tax increase were actually imposed.

There is, nevertheless, considerable uncertainty surrounding such projections. Two distinct sources of uncertainty can be identified. One is uncertainty in the parameters of the model used to project revenues and expenditures. This includes uncertainty about the amount of tax raised from a given tax structure or the amount of spending on health per person of a particular age. The second source is uncertainty over the population structure itself. Here we assess the implications of this second source of uncertainty for the tax adjustments which are needed to deliver fiscal solvency, summarizing results presented in country reports for Belgium, Germany (Fehr and Habermann, 2004), Finland (Lassila and

Valkonen, 2005), the Netherlands (Draper *et al.*, 2005), Spain and the United Kingdom (Sefton and Weale, 2005) in the face of prospective demographic change. Similar studies for the United States, or at least for its social security fund have been carried out by Lee, Miller and Anderson (1998) and Lee and Anderson (2005).

The methods used are reasonably straightforward, although the models to which they have been applied vary in their complexity. We generate a large number of stochastic population projections and evaluate the fiscal position in each of these population projections. We can use the outcome of these experiments to establish the frequency distribution of the tax adjustments which are needed and thus illustrate the range of uncertainty surrounding fiscal stabilization arising purely from demographic uncertainty.

In some countries the law requires that contribution rates for particular parts of government spending, such as pensions and health, be set at the rates needed to finance expenditure on a year-by-year basis. In such countries there is obviously no direct effect of demographic shocks on the budget balance through this route. There may, nevertheless, be indirect effects if the contribution rates affect labour supply and thus revenues from other forms of taxation. So as to make the simulations comparable between these countries and those where there is no automatic link between contribution rates and expenditures, we carry out our simulations for all countries with fixed rather than endogenous contribution rates. Otherwise it is difficult to make anything of the differences between different countries.

We first set out the demographic framework and summarize the resulting population projections. We then explain our measure of sustainability. This is followed by brief accounts of the models used in the different countries. We conclude with discussion of projections of the budget deficit and of the frequency distributions of the tax increases needed to restore fiscal solvency in the countries in question.

The basic demographic framework

We first set out the basic demographic arithmetic as the foundation on which to build the description of demographic uncertainty. We use the vectors $\mathbf{f}_t$ and $\mathbf{m}_t$ to represent the populations of women and men at time t. The populations at age i are denoted by f_{it} and m_{it} respectively. Our modelling framework calculates the population in period $t + 1$ as follows:

$$f_{i,t+1} = f_{i-1,t} \left\{ \frac{2 - \mu^f_{i,t+1}}{2 + \mu^f_{i,t+1}} \right\} + e^f_{i,t+1} \tag{1}$$

where $\mu_{i,t+1}^{f}$ is the mortality rate associated with females of age i in period $t+1$ and $e_{i,t+1}^{f}$ is the net inflow of female migrants aged i in period $t+1$.

It should be noted that this equation differs in form from the relationship used by the UK Government Actuary in projecting population. Their tables are consistent with the following relationship:

$$f_{i,t+1} = f_{i-1,t}\left(1 - \mu_{i-1,t}^{*f}\right) + 0.5\left(e_{i-1,t}^{*f} + e_{i,t+1}^{*f}\right) \tag{2}$$

The relationship between the two measures of mortality and net migration is given as:

$$\mu_{i,t+1}^{f} = \frac{2\mu_{i-1,t}^{*f}}{2 - \mu_{i-1,t}^{*f}} \tag{3}$$

$$e_{i,t+1}^{f} = 0.5\left(e_{i-1,t}^{*f} + e_{i,t}^{*f}\right) \text{ with } e_{0,t+1}^{f} = 0.5 e_{i-1,t}^{*f} \tag{4}$$

and thus it is simple to transform the information provided by the Government Actuary into the form needed for the programme. Similar calculations are made for men.

Births are calculated from a vector of fertility rates, ϕ_t. We denote by ψ the ratio of male to female births (assuming this to be time-invariant). The number of female births and male births in period t, b_t^f and b_t^m are given as:

$$b_t^f = \phi_t' \mathbf{f}_t / (1 + \psi); \quad b_t^m = \psi \phi_t' \mathbf{m}_t / (1 + \psi) \tag{5}$$

$\pi_{i,t}^{f}$ and $\pi_{i,t}^{m}$ denote the probabilities of surviving to age i for males and females contingent on the mortality rates in year t:

$$\pi_{i,t}^{f} = \prod_{i=0}^{i-1}\left(1 - \mu_{i,t}^{*f}\right); \quad \pi_{i,t}^{m} = \prod_{i=0}^{i-1}\left(1 - \mu_{i,t}^{*m}\right) \tag{6}$$

and it follows that the life expectancies at age i, $\lambda_{i,t}^{f}$ and $\lambda_{i,t}^{m}$ are defined as:

$$\lambda_{i,t}^{f} = \frac{1}{\pi_{i,t}^{f}} \sum_{j=i}^{i_{max}} \pi_{j,t}^{f}; \quad \lambda_{i,t}^{m} = \frac{1}{\pi_{i,t}^{m}} \sum_{j=i}^{i_{max}} \pi_{j,t}^{m} \tag{7}$$

This assumes that at the maximum age the probability of death rises to 1.

Modelling demographic uncertainty: mortality and fertility

The model of demographic uncertainty adopted is that presented by Alho and Spencer (1997); a range of other structures which might be applied to mortality is discussed by the Continuous Mortality Investigation (2004). A structure of random shocks is set up to be applied to fertility rates, death rates and migration flows. Each of the simulations is a path generated by a particular realization of the random process. Thus the fan chart which results from the repeated simulations allows one to establish the density forecast of the future population conditional on the initial position; it does not offer a means of establishing densities looking ahead from some particular point in the future although the same approach could be used in order to do this.

We consider a general error process:

$$x(i, t, \mu^f) = \sum_{k=1}^{t} \varepsilon(i, k, \mu^f) \tag{8}$$

where, in our context i refers to age. We assume that the perturbed mortality and rates are given as:

$$\log \tilde{\mu}_{i,t}^f = \log \mu_{i,t}^f + x(i, t, \mu^f) \tag{9}$$

for females, with an analogous figure for males. The disturbed fertility rates are calculated in the same way:

$$\log \tilde{\phi}_{i,t} = \log \phi_{it} + x(i, t, \phi^f) \tag{10}$$

Alho and Spencer (1997) suggest the following specification for the shocks $\varepsilon(i, t, z)$, $z = \mu^f, \mu^m, \phi^f$:

$$\varepsilon(i, t, z) = S(i, t, z)(\eta_{i,z} + \delta_{i,t,z}) \tag{11}$$

$S(i, t, z)$ are scaling factors which are assumed to be known.

We assume that $\eta_{i,z} \sim N(0, \kappa_i)$ and $\delta_{i,t,z} \sim N(0, 1 - \kappa_i^z)$ so that each shock is the combination of a random shock at each point in time and one which is common to all periods. It has the implication that $\text{Cov}(\varepsilon(i, t, z), \varepsilon(i, t+\tau, z)) = \kappa_i^z$. Given the fact that the shocks themselves are cumulatants of the $\varepsilon(i, t, z)$ shown in equation (8) the overall disturbance can be thought of as a trend which is randomly determined but fixed in each simulation and a cumulated I(1) process, with the relative size of the two effects determined by κ_i.

We do not want the shocks at the different i to be independent of each other. This would be likely to generate an anomalous situation where, for example, mortality rates would be likely to lose the property of monotonically increasing with age (at least beyond the point at which degenerative diseases become the predominant cause of death). Thus we impose the structure that

$$\text{Corr}(\eta_{i,z}, \eta_{j,z}) = \rho_{\eta,z}^{|i-j|}; \; \text{Corr}(\delta_{i,t,z}, \delta_{j,t,z}) = \rho_{\delta,z}^{|i-j|} \tag{12}$$

This obviously does not remove the risk of 'counter-intuitive' patterns of fertility emerging from the random shocks, but it is fair to say that, with high correlations, it will reduce it.

Reductions in the mortality of men and women are likely to be correlated because most medical advances benefit both sexes, as too does enhanced public health. Thus we denote

$$\text{Corr}(\eta_{i,\mu^f}, \eta_{i,\mu^m}) = \rho_{\eta,\mu^{fm}}; \; \text{Corr}(\delta_{i,\mu^f}, \delta_{i,\mu^m}) = \rho_{\delta,\mu^{fm}}$$

There is an implication that, because of the cumulative nature of the error process, the variance of $x(i, t, z)$ will tend to increase without limit and thus may eventually lead to prediction intervals which are 'too wide'. Alho and Spencer (1997) suggest that, beyond the point at which the intervals become too wide, the error should be replaced by an autoregressive process centred on the point forecast; in other words:

$$x(i, t + 1, z) = \gamma x(i, t, z) + \zeta(i, t, z) \tag{13}$$

where

$$\zeta(i, t, z) \sim N\{0, (1 - \gamma^2)\sigma^2(i, \infty, z)\} \tag{14}$$

They impose $\text{Cov}(\zeta(i, t, z), \zeta(j, t, z)) = \rho_{\eta,z}^{|i-j|}$ to maintain the same correlation pattern as the permanent shocks. If t^* is the time up to which the previous error process is allowed to run, then $x(i, t^*, z)$ provides the starting value for the autoregressive process.

This approach has been adopted by all the countries except the United Kingdom, for which the original error process has been allowed to cumulate instead. Some of the simulations for the United Kingdom did indeed have very large populations while for others the population declined to close to zero. Sixty-four of a total of a thousand simulations showed the population rising to more than 500 million people by 2152, as compared to its existing value of 60 million people. The most extreme simulation showed a population of 7,415 million people. These sixty-four simulations were suppressed.

In either case the fundamental problem with the demographic model is that it is 'open loop'. Fertility, migration and mortality rates are exogenous albeit subject to stochastic variation. One might expect, in practice, that both fertility and migration would be negatively related to the population size; with a declining population it is likely that policy measures would be taken to promote fertility. In a very densely populated country both fertility and migration rates are likely to decline; indeed, China provides an example of a country which took policy measures to stabilize its population, although in Europe fertility rates are not related to population densities. We also note that the stochastic model does not allow for the possibility of population disasters such as the Black Death or major wars. There are reasons for thinking that, because it does not allow for the effects of catastrophes, the demographic model understates the downside risk to the population.

Modelling demographic uncertainty: migration

The approach set out above cannot be applied directly to net migration, because it is the difference between immigration and emigration. A logarithmic model applied to a net migration figure of zero would imply that there was no uncertainty in it. In reality a variable calculated as the difference between forecasts of two numbers is uncertain even if small.

Alho and Spencer (1997) suggest that, given figures for either gross inflows or gross outflows, the other variable can be calculated by subtraction. They also imply that there is little reason to expect the cumulation process shown by equation (8) to be stationary although Mitchell and Pain (2003) regard it as very unclear whether there are unit root processes present or not.

Treating the inflows g_{it}^m and g_{it}^f and outflows, h_{it}^m and h_{it}^f in the same way as our earlier variables, we can denote the perturbed values as:

$$\ln \tilde{g}_{it}^m = \ln g_{it}^m + \varepsilon(i, t, g^m) \text{ etc.}$$

The $\varepsilon(i, t, g^m)$ can be defined like the other $\varepsilon(i, t, z)$ with the process again allowed to run up to t^*. However, the question arises of the correlations between the four variables $\varepsilon(i, t, g^m)$, $\varepsilon(i, t, g^f)$, $\varepsilon(i, t, h^m)$ and $\varepsilon(i, t, h^f)$, just as it arose over the shocks to the mortality rates of the two sexes. We denote the correlations between the two sexes for inflows and outflows as $\text{Corr}(\varepsilon(i, t, g^f), \varepsilon(i, t, g^m)) = \rho_{\eta g^{fm}}$, with $\rho_{\eta h^{fm}}$ the corresponding value for outflows. The correlation between the figures between inflows and outflows is denoted $\rho_{\eta gh}$.

Assessment of tax increases needed for fiscal stabilization

The government budget constraint implies that the present discounted value of government expenditure plus the value of existing net government debt must equal the present discounted value of future tax revenues. We denote government spending (excluding net interest payments) as G_t and tax revenues as generated by the models in question as T_t. GDP is assumed to take a value of Y_t. θ is the increase in taxes measured as a proportion of GDP needed to deliver budget balance, and existing debt is indicated by D_0. If the rate of interest is assumed constant, then the intertemporal budget constraint is expressed in the form

$$\sum_{s=0}^{\infty} \frac{(G_s - T_s - \theta Y_s)}{\prod_{t=0}^{s} (1 + r_t)} + D_0 = 0$$

This allows us to derive θ as

$$\theta = \frac{\sum_{s=0}^{\infty} \dfrac{(G_s - T_s)}{\prod_{t=0}^{s} (1 + r_t)} + D_0}{\sum_{s=0}^{\infty} \dfrac{Y_s}{\prod_{t=0}^{s} (1 + r_t)}} \tag{15}$$

In other words, θ, the tax increase needed, is the ratio of the present discounted sum of the government intertemporal budgetary imbalance to the present discounted sum of GDP.

Obvious issues arise over the fact that the formula requires a sum to infinity. One solution to this is to assume that, at the end of the period of simulation, T, the ratio $(G_T - T_T) / Y_T$ has stabilized, and that future rates of interest and rates of growth are constant. If T is far enough ahead, the errors arising from this sort of assumption are likely to be small. The simulations discussed here have been carried out to horizons of 150 years. This lies between the 'standard' horizon of 75 years used by Lee, Miller and Anderson (1998) and the 'infinite' horizon of 500 years considered by Lee and Anderson (2005).

In some of the models the tax rates are set endogenously to balance the budget period by period, or to balance at least a part of it, such as state pension or health fund expenditure. In this case we calculate θ as the present discounted sum of the extra tax revenues generated by the endogenous tax rates as a proportion of the present discounted sum of GDP. In the expression shown, τ_s is the endogenously generated tax revenue as a proportion of GDP and τ_0 is its value in the initial year.

$$\theta = \frac{\sum_{s=0}^{\infty} \dfrac{(\tau_s - \tau_0) Y_s}{\prod_{t=0}^{s} (1 + r_t)} + D_0}{\sum_{s=0}^{\infty} \dfrac{Y_s}{\prod_{t=0}^{s} (1 + r_t)}} \tag{16}$$

A hybrid of the two formulae ((15) and (16)) is used when some taxes or contributions are endogenous and others are exogenous.

Model descriptions

The models used to provide estimates of fiscal uncertainty fall broadly into two categories. For Belgium, Spain and the United Kingdom the models are accounting models in which economic behaviour is taken as exogenous. Such models are typically driven by income, expenditure and tax profiles, relating amounts of factor income to the population classified by age and sex in Spain and the United Kingdom, and additionally by socio-economic status in Belgium. No account is taken of possible behavioural responses; households do not adjust their labour supply as a result of changes to tax rates, and saving, which affects income from capital, does not respond to changes in life expectancy.

For the other countries, Finland, Germany and the Netherlands, the models are behavioural. In these models, typically, labour supply and consumption/saving are endogenous and the effects of this are grafted on to the purely accounting models. In the simulations presented here, the differences between behavioural and accounting models are not likely to be very large. The reason for this is as follows. As noted in the introduction, we have performed all of our simulations on the assumption that contribution and tax rates are constant; the only practical alternative is to assume that they are adjusted to clear any fiscal imbalances entirely and, for obvious reasons, one cannot, in such a situation, study the effects of demographic uncertainty on public borrowing. But, in the simulations we have performed, the main importance of behavioural responses would arise in looking at the implications of different contribution and tax rates on labour supply. With the analysis constructed around fixed tax rates this question does not arise. Nevertheless it is worth noting that, if the simulations were carried out with taxes adjusted to deliver budget balance year by year, the effects of demographic uncertainty on tax rates would be greater in models with endogenous contribution/tax rates than in those where they are exogenous. A high public expenditure burden as a result of a demographic shock would be expected to lead to higher contribution rates. This would depress labour supply; second-round and further contribution increases would be needed to balance the books.

Among the behavioural models, differing assumptions are made for different countries. For example, in Germany capital is assumed to be immobile, so that interest rates are endogenous while in the Netherlands the interest rate is set in world markets and is exogenous. Once again, it is hard to see that this difference is of great importance in the simulations presented here. We now present a brief description of the models used for the individual countries we examine.

Belgium

The study of Belgium is carried out using MALTESE (Model for Analysis of Long Term Evolution of Social Expenditure) maintained by the Federal Planning Bureau. This model is composed of modules concerning demography, socio-demographic population structure and social policy and macro-economic assumptions. Public expenditure is modelled in detail being determined scheme by scheme on the basis of the number of beneficiaries and the average benefit per beneficiary; health and long-term care expenditure are similarly modelled.

MALTESE is a sophisticated demographic/budgetary model but an accounting model nonetheless. It meets the job of translating demographic projections into budgetary developments given socio-demographic, macro-economic and social policy scenarios. Only health expenditure is endogenous, in that some elements of health expenditure are linked to GDP. There is no real macro-economic modelling, i.e. there is no structural equation for the non-accelerating inflation rate of unemployment and no feedback from tax rates to participation, and labour productivity is exogenous. Policy reaction is also absent: the public finance imbalances persist even if inherently unsustainable. The baseline simulation is provided by the effects of current legislation and policies or current observed household behaviour.

Finland

The model is an overlapping-generations model. It embodies lifetime utility-maximizing perfect-foresight households, firms and several types of public sector institutions, and generates general equilibrium price paths for labour, goods and capital. It is described in Lassila and Valkonen (2001, 2003). It reflects age-specific patterns of public spending. Contribution rates to public pension and health schemes are endogenous when the model is run. The overall tax adjustment needed for fiscal balance is, however, identified by converting changes to these to lump-sum taxes.

Germany

The situation in Germany is analysed using an overlapping-generations model. The model is one of a closed economy with the real interest rate as endogenous. People represented in the model are assumed to have perfect foresight except over their date of death; it is, however, assumed that there is no aggregate uncertainty about mortality risk and that individuals can insure against the risk they face. People derive utility from both consumption and leisure so that labour supply is endogenous. Production takes place using a CES technology and firms are assumed to maximize their net present values; productivity growth, however, is exogenous. Contribution rates for the pension and health systems are each normally endogenous in order to balance the budgets of the pension and health funds every year. The residual public budget is balanced by means of an adjustment to consumption tax.

However, to compute the sustainability gap, we fix age-dependent consumption, savings and labour supply decisions to the values in 2001 and we also fix the contribution rates and consumption taxes to their values in 2001. With this fixed behaviour and fixed taxes/contributions we compute the imbalance in all future years for the pension and health systems and the rest of government. The present value of this gap in relation to GDP is the sustainability gap.

Netherlands

The situation in the Netherlands is analysed using GAMMA, an overlapping-generations model of the Dutch economy developed by the Central Planning Bureau. The model is one of a small open economy with the real interest rate given by conditions in the rest of the world and taken as fixed. People represented in the model are assumed to have perfect foresight except over their date of death; it is, however, assumed that there is no aggregate uncertainty about mortality risk and that individuals can insure against the risk they face. People derive utility from both consumption and leisure so that labour supply is endogenous. Production takes place using a CES technology and firms are assumed to maximize their net present values; productivity growth, however, is exogenous. Private pension funds are represented as a specific form of saving and they are assumed to adjust their contribution rates so as to maintain actuarial balance. Contribution rates for all forms of public spending are exogenous. The solvency of each simulation is ensured by means of an adjustment to consumption taxes.

Spain

The model is a simple accounting model without any behavioural responses. Projections are obtained combining the population projections and the age-sex profile of revenues and expenditures which are assumed to be constant at the 2000 level. Imposed macro-economic scenarios in the projection are (i) the participation rate increases at the same rate as observed in the present until it reaches the average for the EU, and stays constant thereafter; (ii) the unemployment rate decreases linearly to reach 4.5 per cent in 2015 and stays constant thereafter; (iii) labour productivity increases linearly to reach 2.0 per cent in 2019 and is constant thereafter, and wages increase at the same rate as labour productivity.

United Kingdom

The United Kingdom simulations are performed using generational accounts (Cardarelli, Sefton and Kotlikoff, 2000). This structure does not incorporate any behavioural responses to tax rates and spending patterns, but is built round observed profiles for tax revenues and public spending patterns as a function of the age-structure of the population. In the absence of any specific information about planned changes to these profiles, it is assumed that they do not change over time. Thus, income tax revenue depends not on the overall size of the population or workforce but on an assessment of the amount of tax paid by people of different ages; this, in turn, is a consequence of age-dependent earnings differentials and the income tax base of the retired population. Productivity growth and the real interest rate are exogenously given. Contribution rates to the National Insurance Fund (which covers some health care and the state pension scheme) are exogenous, as are tax rates. The model is in effect an accounting model.

Results

Belgium

The mean tax increase needed to restore fiscal balance is zero and the standard deviation is 1.03% of GDP. Figure 4.1 shows the frequency distribution of the tax rises generated in the stochastic simulations.

Finland

The average tax rise needed to restore solvency is 0.45% of GDP with a standard deviation of 1.22%. (Figure 4.2).

Germany

The mean tax increase needed is 2.45% of GDP with a standard deviation of 1.17% (Figure 4.3).

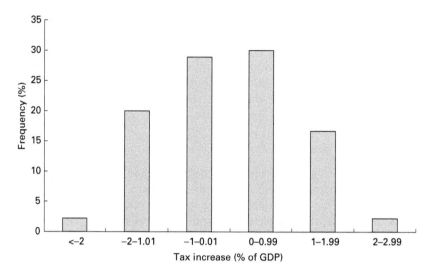

Figure 4.1. Frequency distribution of the tax increase needed to restore long-term fiscal balance: Belgium.

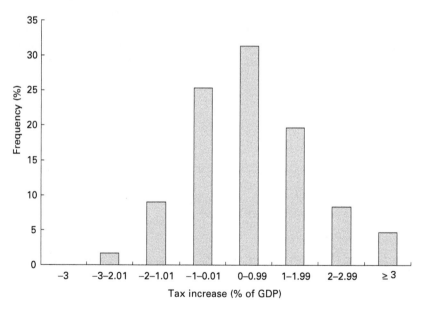

Figure 4.2. Frequency distribution of the tax increase needed to restore long-term fiscal balance: Finland.

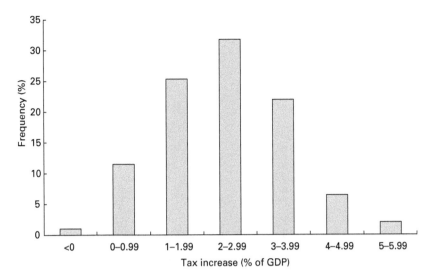

Figure 4.3. Frequency distribution of the tax increase needed to restore long-term fiscal balance: Germany.

Netherlands

The mean tax increase needed to restore fiscal solvency is 3.96% of GDP with a standard deviation of 2.59% (Figure 4.4).

Spain

The mean tax increase needed is 3.5% of GDP with a standard deviation of 0.87% of GDP (Figure 4.5).

United Kingdom

The mean tax increase needed is 2.74% of GDP with a standard deviation of 2.81% (Figure 4.6).

Summary of results and conclusions

The results presented here are in many ways very satisfactory. Stochastic demographic projections are in their infancy and it is difficult to judge whether those presented here are plausible or not. There is no single universally accepted approach to handling uncertainty in demographic forecasts. But, taking the approaches of Chapters 2 and 3 at face value,

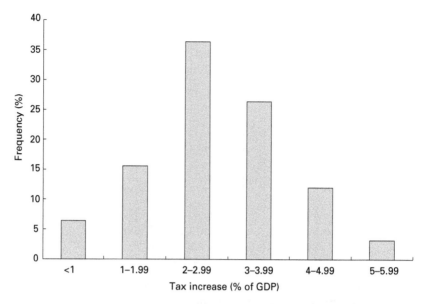

Figure 4.4. Frequency distribution of the tax increase needed to restore long-term fiscal balance: The Netherlands.

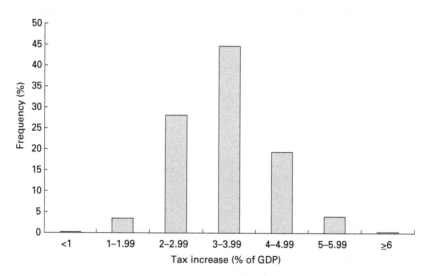

Figure 4.5. Frequency distribution of the tax increase needed to restore long-term fiscal balance: Spain.

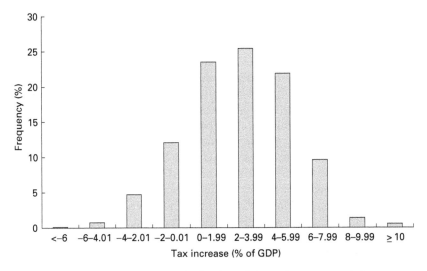

Figure 4.6. Frequency distribution of the tax increase needed to restore long-term fiscal balance: United Kingdom.

Table 4.1. *Summary statistics for tax increases needed to restore fiscal balance.*

	Mean increase (% of GDP)	Standard deviation (% of GDP)
Belgium	0	1.03
Finland	0.45	1.22
Germany	2.45	1.17
Netherlands	3.96	2.59
Spain	3.50	0.87
United Kingdom	2.74	2.81
United States	*2.99*	*1.33*

demographic uncertainty implies a substantial amount of variation in the tax adjustment needed to restore fiscal balance. Table 4.1 brings together the results on the mean and standard deviation of the tax increases needed to restore fiscal balance in the countries examined. We also include estimates calculated for the United States from the results presented by Lee and Anderson (2005)[1].

That these figures show considerable variation in the means is not surprising, since it is well known that different economies may be affected by demographic change in different ways (Alho and Vanne, 2006). However, there is also considerable variability in the standard deviations. The high standard deviation in the United Kingdom is almost certainly a consequence of the nature of the simulations. In the UK the processes set out in equations (8) to (13) were used to project fertility, migration and mortality up to 2152. In the other countries these processes were replaced in 2052 by the much less volatile processes described in equation (13). It is less clear what accounts for the high standard deviation in the Netherlands, but comparison of these results with some obtained earlier using simpler models suggests that model structure plays an important role. Since the United States figures relate only to social security we can be clear that they understate the true uncertainty; whether figures for the whole of the government budget would be as large as those for the United Kingdom is, however, impossible to know. We cannot say that the UK picture is correct and the others are incorrect or vice versa. But we can say that the implications of the different assumptions for the uncertainty surrounding fiscal sustainability are very substantial.

NOTE

1 They calculate their results only for social security and not for the whole of the government budget, finding a deficit of 5.15 per cent of employment income, with a standard deviation of 2.3 percentage points. The figures in Table 4.1 are calculated assuming that the payroll is 58 per cent of GDP at market prices, the average value for 2000–2004.

REFERENCES

Alho, J. and Spencer, B. (1997). 'The Practical Specification of the Expected Error of Population Forecasts'. *Journal of Official Statistics*, 13: 201–25.
Alho, J. and Vanne, R. (2006). 'On Predictive Distributions of Public Net Liabilities'. *International Journal of Forecasting*, 22: 725–33.
Cardarelli, R., Sefton, J. and Kotlikoff, L. (2000). 'Generational Accounting in the UK'. *Economic Journal*, 110: 547–74.
Continuous Mortality Investigation (2004). 'Projecting Future Mortality'. Continuous Mortality Investigation, Mortality Sub-committee, Institute of Actuaries. www.actuaries.org.uk/files/pdf/cmi/cmiwp3.pdf.
Draper, D., Edends, B., Nibbelink, A., Viitanen, T. and Westerhout, E. (2005). 'The Impact of Demographic Uncertainty on Public Finances in the Netherlands'. Central Planning Bureau, The Hague.
Fehr, H. and Habermann, C. (2004). 'The Budgetary Costs of Ageing in Germany'. University of Würzburg.
Flemming, J. (1987). 'Debt and Taxes in War and Peace: the Case of a Small Open Economy', in *Private Saving and Public Debt*, ed. M. Boskin, J. Flemming and S. Gorini. Oxford: Blackwell, pp. 373–91.

Lassila, J. and Valkonen, T. (2001). 'Pension Prefunding, Ageing and Demographic Uncertainty'. *International Tax and Public Finance*, 8: 573–93.

(2003). 'Ageing, Demographic Risks and Pension Reform', in *Pension Reform: Redistribution and Risk*, Occasional Paper no. 56. London: NIESR, pp. 119–66.

(2005). 'Demographic Uncertainty and Fiscal Sustainability in Finland'. ETLA, Helsinki.

Lee, R. and Anderson, M. (2005). 'Stochastic Infinite Horizon Forecasts for US Social Security Finances'. *National Institute Economic Review*, 194: 82–93.

Lee, R., Miller, T. and Anderson, M. (1998). 'Stochastic Forecasts for Social Security', in *Frontiers in Economics of Ageing*, ed. D. Wise. Chicago: University of Chicago Press, pp. 393–420.

Mitchell, J. and Pain, N. (2003). 'The Determinants of International Migration into the UK: a Panel-based Modelling Approach'. NIESR Discussion Paper no. 216, London.

Sefton, J. and Weale, M. (2005). 'Fiscal Implications of Demographic Uncertainty for the United Kingdom'. NIESR Discussion Paper no. 250, London.

5   Demographic uncertainty and pension projections

Jukka Lassila and Tarmo Valkonen

Introduction

With increasing understanding that populations are ageing and will continue to do so, long-term pension expenditure projections have become essential policy tools for all countries with pure pay-as-you-go or less than fully funded public pension systems. The most important background assumptions in these projections usually concern future demographics. It therefore seems particularly relevant to try to envision the uncertainty caused by future demographics in pension expenditure projections.

We summarize quantitative estimates of the uncertainty in long-term pension expenditure projections caused by demographic factors for Belgium, Denmark, Finland, Germany, the Netherlands, Spain and the United Kingdom. The estimates are obtained from model-based country studies. The demographic uncertainties are quantified by stochastic population simulations. The results unequivocally show a great deal of uncertainty in pension projections. There are significant differences between the uncertainty estimates in these countries. The differences partly reflect demographic factors, partly differences in pension systems and partly the properties of the models that were used.

We also relate the uncertainty estimates of the country studies to the uncertainty considerations in the recent projections by the Economic Policy Committee (EPC) of the European Commission (EPC, 2006). The EPC uses sensitivity analysis as a method to describe uncertainties. Not surprisingly, the resulting quantifications of deviations from the expected outcomes are small compared with those obtained in the country studies.

Finally, we consider the implications of the country studies for the future development of the tools for analysis. We specifically ask whether a model type that combines all the relevant features of the country-wise economic models can be identified and could be constructed. Applying such a model type to different countries would produce uncertainty estimates that are fully comparable with each other. Such a model can indeed be identified to a large extent. The implied agenda for future research

Table 5.1. *Pension expenditure as percentage of GDP in 2003 and 2050.*

	2003	2050[1]				
		d_1	Q_1	Md	Q_3	d_9
Belgium	9.2	11.1	11.8	12.6	13.4	14.1
Denmark	9.5[2]	10.8	12.2	13.6	15.2	16.6
Finland	11.0[3]	13.9	14.4	15.0	15.6	16.2
Germany	11.4[2]	11.7	12.3	13.0	13.5	14.1
Netherlands (% of wage bill)	12.0[4]	28.3	30.3	32.7	35.0	37.5
Spain	9.7	16.9	18.5	20.6	22.9	25.5
UK	6.4	6.1	6.7	7.4	8.0	8.6

Notes: [1] Column headings: Md = median; Q_1, Q_3 = first and third quartiles; d_1, d_9 = first and ninth deciles.
[2] 2001; [3] 2000–2004; [4] 2004.

includes modelling the effects of aggregate risks on behaviour and, to the extent that increases in longevity reflect factors that also increase labour productivity in old age, the links between increasing longevity and retirement behaviour.

Uncertainty in pension expenditures varies between countries

In most European countries, the ratio of pension expenditure to GDP will very likely be higher in 2050 than it is at present. This is certainly true for the countries considered here, namely Belgium, Denmark, Finland, Germany, the Netherlands, Spain and the United Kingdom, as Table 5.1 shows. In this chapter, however, our main interest is not in the increases in pension expenditures but in the demography-based uncertainty surrounding them. Table 5.1 also summarizes the uncertainty in projections concerning the year 2050.[1]

In Belgium, Denmark, Finland and Germany, where the median projected values are close to each other, the width of the 50 per cent predictive interval varies from 1.2 to 3.0 percentage points, and the 80 per cent predictive interval from 2.3 to 5.8 percentage points. Moreover, the Netherlands is also likely to be close to those numbers, if expenditures are expressed as a ratio of GDP. Adding the other two countries where the distributions are centred on different levels, we can make two observations. First, the uncertainty is non-negligible in all countries and must be deemed large in many of them. Second, there seem to be large differences between the uncertainty estimates in different countries. We

Table 5.2. *80% predictive ranges of pension expenditure and old-age ratio, as percentage of the median in 2050.*

	Pension expenditure	Old-age ratio
Belgium	24	32
Denmark	43	46
Finland	15	38
Germany	18	37
Netherlands	28	32
Spain	42	54
UK	34	43

analyse the second observation first and try to put some structure to it before returning to the first observation.

Predictability of demographics

An obvious reason for country differences in uncertainty is that some relevant demographic features are more predictable in some countries than in others. The ratio of people in old age to those in working age is clearly important here because it influences both the absolute amount of expenditure and the GDP, which is used to scale the expenditures. In Table 5.2 the width of the 80 per cent predictive intervals for both pension expenditure/GDP and the old-age dependency ratio are compared with the median. The pension numbers are calculated from Table 5.1 as differences between the ninth and first deciles, related to the median and expressed as percentages. The old-age numbers are calculated in a similar fashion from the country studies.[2] The figures show some pattern, though not very strongly. Denmark and Spain are on the high-variation end, both demographically and pension-wise. Belgium and the Netherlands show much smaller variation in both respects. Finland and Germany are outliers: in both countries the relative predictive range of pension expenditure/GDP is small, although the relative predictive range of the old-age dependency ratio is large.

Pension system rules

Some countries apply pension system rules that are aimed at limiting the effect of future demographic changes on pension expenditure. In Finland, pension benefits are adjusted for changes in longevity (see Lassila and Valkonen, this volume, chap. 8). Without this adjustment, the 80 per cent range of pension expenditure/GDP would be 22 per cent of the median in 2050. In Germany, the corresponding rule is the sustainability factor, which affects the indexation applied when the ratio of pensioners to contributors changes. Without this factor the 80 per cent range of pension expenditure/GDP would be 23 per cent of the median in 2050.

In the Finnish case there is another pension system rule which, together with the dynamics of the economic model used, limits the variation in expenditure. Earnings-related pensions are only partially indexed to wages, both in the accrual phase and after retirement. In the model used, different demographic developments lead to different wage trends and the partial indexation diminishes the variation caused by these wage differentials in pension expenditures, whereas it is fully present in GDP. This effect narrows the predictive range by 1–1.5 percentage points compared with other countries' estimates.

Modelling immigration

A third factor is the role of migration. Like partial indexation, this factor combines features of the pension system and the way it is modelled.

We assume that immigrants in Finland work like natives. But they are of different ages when they arrive, and thus generally accrue lower earnings-related pension rights than natives. They may have accrued pension rights in their country of origin, and get pensions from there, but that is not the concern of the Finnish pension system. Therefore, with positive net immigration, assuming a full-career pension for all retired people in the country overestimates the pension expenditure. With net emigration the situation is reversed: many of those emigrating have accrued pension rights, and the pensions will be paid to them even though they are no longer part of the Finnish population. Thus, assuming pensions are only paid to those retired who live in Finland underestimates the pension expenditure. So, assuming full-career pensions for all retired residents leads to a wider predictive distribution of pension expenditure, depending on the extent to which migration causes variation in the old-age population. In the Finnish model we do not assume this; migration effects on pension expenditure have been taken into account. The effect is small though; the 80 per cent predictive interval for Finland in Table 5.1 would be 0.2 percentage points, and the 50 per cent interval 0.1 percentage points wider without this correction. It appears that in some other country estimates in Table 5.1 such corrections have not been made, and their predictive ranges may thus be too large.

Including migrants in a numerical overlapping-generations model would mean that their life cycles are described and followed separately from the rest of the population. This is currently so difficult that it is usually not done. It is not done in the Finnish model either; we have simply made a correction to the aggregate pension expenditures.[3] In the Dutch model there is a different migration correction: immigrants are assumed to bring in pension wealth similar to that of natives of the same age, and the wealth is added to the pension funds. Emigrants take a corresponding wealth with them when they leave. Thus the finances of the pension system are not affected by migration, although the variation in pension expenditure estimates still is. In general, a migration correction is only needed in countries with earnings-related pensions. In Denmark, where residence-based pensions dominate, such a correction is not useful. In Spain, where, on account of the relatively young age structure and strong immigration flows, the ageing process is slow and postponed and the uncertainty in 2050 is very large, such a correction would be useful. On the other hand, it would substantially complicate the model. Finally, we may note that the migration correction should also be present in official pension projections, but in many countries this is very likely not the case.

When the three factors mentioned above are taken into account, Finland is no longer an outlier. It thus appears that the uncertainty in pension expenditure projections, due to future demographics is proportional to the size of the pension system, taking into account the differences in the predictability of future demographics, the specific features of the pension systems, and the differences in the models used in the analysis.

Models

The discussion above clearly shows the importance of the models used in the expenditure projections. The estimates in Table 5.1 have been produced by two types of model.[4] There is no economic behaviour in the accounting models employed in Belgium, Spain and the United Kingdom. The Belgian model, however, is a large and detailed accounting machine used routinely in public finance assessment, whereas the Spanish and UK models are combinations of age-specific expenditure structures and stochastic population projections.

The models describing the Danish, Dutch, Finnish and German economies are all numerical overlapping-generations models, where individuals make labour supply and savings decisions in order to maximize lifetime utility. The role of factor prices differs somewhat. The Danish and German models describe the countries as closed economies, where wages and interest rates are determined in the domestic labour and capital markets. The Dutch model describes a small open economy. In Finland there is an imperfect substitution between domestic and imported goods and the terms of trade are endogenous.

The link between labour markets and pension systems is most important. In ageing populations there are increasing numbers of pensioners and decreasing numbers of workers. If the models encompass endogenous labour supply and wages, the income and incentive effects created by the pension system become important. The exact outcome depends on the elasticity of labour demand and supply and the link between pension contributions and benefits on the individual level. Households are likely to react to lower net wages by aggravating the problem of scarce labour. Variation in productivity trends also influences the tax burden arising from pension expenditure, especially in countries where the indexation of benefits is predominantly based on consumer prices. The modelled labour markets typically adjust to population ageing without frictions.

One important, but largely unsolved, problem in the models is the retirement decision. In the numerical OLG models there are typically only one or a few representative perfect-foresight individuals in each birth cohort, which complicates the simulation of actual decision conditions near retirement. It is also difficult to separate the retirement decision from the marginal labour supply choice. Accounting models may encompass large numbers of individuals with estimated transition probabilities between labour market states, but they are vulnerable to changes in retirement rules and other pension policies.

Discussing uncertainty with sensitivity analysis

The Economic Policy Committee (EPC) of the European Commission recently made public expenditure projections for its member countries up to the year 2050 (EPC, 2006). The EPC also carried out a number of sensitivity analyses of the projections with the aim 'of providing some insight into the question of how sensitive the projections are to different assumptions and projected population and labour force developments, which inherently bring a major degree of uncertainty to long-run expenditure projections'. The sensitivity scenarios were all run in relation to the baseline scenario, changing only one factor in each sensitivity scenario from that in the baseline scenario. Sensitivity tests were made on four issues: change in labour productivity; higher life expectancy; higher employment rates; and interest rate levels.

Consider first the issue of labour productivity. The EPC used a 'production function approach' to estimate labour productivity growth. Labour productivity (output per worker) is first derived from the calculations based on the labour input projections, the assumptions concerning

Table 5.3. *Pension expenditure as percentage of GDP in 2050: the EPC's central projection and its sensitivity range.*

	Expenditure/GDP		
	2004	2050	Sensitivity range (% points)
Belgium	10.4	15.5	2.7
Denmark	9.5	12.8	1.8
Finland	10.7	13.7	1.9
Germany	11.4	13.1	0.6
Netherlands	7.7	11.2	1.5
Spain	8.6	15.7	2.5
UK	6.6	8.6	1.5

Source: EPC (2006), Tables 3–3 and 3–28.

total factor productivity (TFP) and the investment scenario. In the sensitivity analysis, an increase or decrease of 0.25 percentage points (p.p.) in the labour productivity growth rate over 2005–2015 was assumed, with the rate thereafter remaining at the 0.25 p.p. higher or lower level in comparison with the labour productivity growth rate in the baseline projection.

The higher life expectancy scenario assumes roughly that life expectancy at birth increases 1–1.5 years more than in the baseline by 2050.

The higher employment rate scenario consists of two parts. First, it assumes that the employment rate will increase by 1 p.p. over the period 2005–2015 and thereafter will remain 1 p.p. higher in the period 2015–2050 compared with the baseline projection. It is assumed that the higher employment rate is achieved by lowering the rate of structural unemployment. Second, the scenario assumes that the employment rate of older workers will increase by 5 p.p. over 2005–2015 and thereafter will remain 5 p.p. higher in the period 2015–2050, compared with the baseline projection. It is assumed that this is achieved through a reduction in the inactive population.

The higher interest rate scenarios assume interest rates of 4 per cent, compared to 3 per cent in the baseline scenario.

Table 5.3 sums up the quantitative variation in the EPC's sensitivity analysis. The 'sensitivity range' for all countries is calculated as follows. The effects of all the four issues dealt with have first been made to go in the same direction, and then they have been added together. The total deviation from the base path thus obtained varies from 0.3 to 1.4 percentage points among countries. Assuming that all the effects can also go in the other direction, the total deviations have been multiplied by two, except for labour productivity effects for which separate estimates for the other direction, available in the EPC's report, were used.

If we compare the sensitivity ranges in Table 5.3 with the predictive ranges obtained in Table 5.1, we note that for Denmark, Germany and Spain the sensitivity range is narrower than the 50 per cent predictive range, and for Belgium, Finland and the UK it is narrower than the 80 per cent predictive range. And this despite the fact that the ranges from Table 5.1 only include the effects of demographic factors, whereas the sensitivity ranges include economic factors as well. We do not have comparable predictive ranges for the Netherlands, but assuming the wage bill is of the order of 50 per cent of GDP, we can divide the predictive ranges in Table 5.1 by two and notice that the sensitivity range is much narrower than the 50 per cent predictive range. Thus we may conclude that the estimates in Table 5.1 are large in comparison with the perceptions of uncertainty obtained from an official expenditure assessment, exemplified here by the EPC's report.

Future directions

Besides its giving an impression of relatively small uncertainties, there are other reasons for a critical evaluation of the sensitivity analysis used by the EPC. The approach resembles the method of using high–low population variants in describing uncertainties in demographic projections. This method has been assessed by Alho *et al.* (2005) as follows:

Uncertainty in demographics has traditionally been accounted for by considering 'high' and 'low' scenarios in addition to a 'medium' assumption. However, it has long been known (e.g., Törnqvist, 1949) that this approach has serious shortcomings. For example, the scenarios assume a perfect (positive or negative) correlation between the vital processes of fertility, mortality and migration; the scenarios assume a perfect correlation across age and time for each vital process; combining high and low scenarios of individual age-groups produces inconsistent high and low scenarios for population aggregates; the method cannot guarantee that the high and low scenarios for different ages and different processes correspond to the same level of uncertainty; and the method is intrinsically unable to assign probabilities to its 'high–low' ranges.[5]

As an example, consider the sensitivity analysis of the labour productivity growth rate. The production function corresponds to the cohort-component framework, and TFP and the capital/labour ratio correspond to the vital rates. Without further information about the changes in the determinants of the productivity growth rate, one could assume a large number of possible combinations of the underlying factors, and each of these combinations represents a different future for the economy. The combinations which the EPC's approach chooses give a poor reflection of these possibilities, and no probabilities can be assigned to any of the ranges presented.

The shortcomings of the high–low population variants led to the development of stochastic population simulations, and their economic consequences can be studied with economic models, as this chapter has described. A similar attempt to improve the analysis of labour productivity could be made. A stochastic forecast for total factor productivity (as in Lee and Tuljapurkar, 2001, and Alho and Vanne, 2006a, b) could be included in a model with neoclassical production functions, if we believe that such functions provide a relevant description of firms' reactions to population ageing. The model thus obtained would provide an interesting interaction between TFP and the changes in the capital/labour ratio due to the variation in the size of the working-age population. On the other hand, if we believe that the size of the labour force has permanent effects on the productivity growth rate, an endogenous growth model could be used.

A similar modelling approach could be used concerning varying employment rates. The interaction of economic incentives and employment ratios is usually missing in the mechanical use of variants. This is quite surprising, considering that this interaction is one of the main reasons why population ageing is seen as so harmful to public economies and growth. In a unified model framework the assumed higher employment rates, in the form of lower unemployment, could be replaced by rational reactions to changes in the economic rewards from working, including policy changes and perhaps exogenous changes in unemployment. Also, the assumed higher employment rates, in the form of postponed retirement, could be replaced by rational reactions to changes in the economic rewards for working, changes in eligibility rules and other policy changes, and perhaps changes in disabilities.

Similarly, the assumed change in interest rates in the EPC's variant approach could be replaced by stochastic asset yield simulations (Lee and Tuljapurkar, 2001, and Alho and Vanne, 2006a, b) which, in models such as those of Fehr and Habermann (2004) and Lassila, Palm and Valkonen (1997), would interact with the possible yield effects of changes in domestic saving and investment or, as in Borgy and Alho (this volume, chap. 10), the yield effects of global saving.

Finally, the EPC assumption of higher life expectancy would be replaced by stochastic population simulations of mortality rates. This, of course, is already done in the country studies referred to above, jointly with uncertainty in fertility and migration.

Instead of making separate sensitivity calculations, all this could be done simultaneously in magnitudes that have been related to each other, taking several interdependencies between the various factors into account. The Congressional Budget Office in the United States already assesses uncertainties in this manner (CBO, 2005). A more comprehensive economic model would need to combine the relevant features of the country models referred to in this chapter. Such a model does not presently exist, but one can certainly envision its construction. We think this is the way to go. This still leaves a role for the use of variants, but the role is pedagogic and qualitative, not quantitative.

Using general equilibrium or other dynamic economic models in practical exercises to project pension expenditures provides a more comprehensive and, theoretically, more solid basis for the evaluation of uncertainty in the outcomes. In developing this approach, one aspect is to define the important exogenous factors that affect the pension system variables but are not themselves much affected by the pension system. Demographic variables are clearly important, but whether it is justifiable to treat them as exogenous, as in the country studies considered, depends on whether or not future research reveals stable effects of economic variables on the demographics.

An advantage of the model-based approach is that the framework can also be used in pension policy analysis, as Chapters 7 and 8 of this volume show. A natural line of development here would be a model in which both idiosyncratic and aggregate uncertainty influence behaviour and welfare. Those issues are discussed more closely in Chapters 10–13 of this volume.

One important question in all future evaluations of pension expenditure and the uncertainty of such evaluations is how retirement decisions should be handled. More specifically, what are the links between lower morbidity, increasing longevity and retirement behaviour? To the extent that increases in longevity reflect factors that also increase labour productivity at older ages, this must be a part of a future research agenda.

NOTES

1 The country studies are Duyck, Lambrecht and Paul (2005), Jensen and Børlum (2005), Lassila and Valkonen (2005), Fehr and Habermann (2004). Draper et al. (2005), FEDEA (2005) and Sefton and Weale (2005). We thank the authors for also providing us with some unpublished results.
2 Old-age dependency ratio: Belgium 65+/15–64, Netherlands 65+/20–64, Spain 65+/15–64 (estimated from figure), Finland 65+/15–64, UK 65+/18–64 (estimated from figure).
3 Details of the mechanism can be obtained from the authors.

4 All these models are described in Chapter 4 of this volume. The Finnish model is described in more detail in Chapter 8, the German model in Chapter 7 and the Dutch model in Chapter 9.
5 For more details, see Alho (1990), Lee and Tuljapurkar (2001) and Lee and Edwards (2002).

REFERENCES

Alho, J. M. (1990). 'Stochastic Methods in Population Forecasting'. *International Journal of Forecasting* 6: 521–30.
Alho, J. M., Jensen, S. E. H., Lassila, J. and Valkonen, T. (2005). 'Controlling the Effects of Demographic Risks: The Role of Pension Indexation Schemes'. *Journal of Pension Economics and Finance*, 4(2): 139–53.
Alho, J. M. and Vanne, R. (2006a). 'On Predictive Distributions of Public Net Liabilities'. *International Journal of Forecasting*, 22: 725–33.
    (2006b). 'On Stochastic Generational Accounting', in *Allocating Public and Private Resources across Generations*, ed. A. Gauthier, C. Chu and S. Tuljapurkar. Dordrecht: Springer, pp. 291–303.
CBO (2005). 'Quantifying Uncertainty in the Analysis of Long-Term Social Security Projections'. Background Paper, Congressional Budget Office, Washington DC.
Draper, D. A. G., Edens, B., Nibbelink, A., Viitanen, T. K. and Westerhout, E. W. M. T. (2005). 'The Impact of Demographic Uncertainty on the Dutch Pension Sector'. Central Planning Bureau, The Hague.
Duyck, J., Lambrecht, M. and Paul, J.-M. (2005). 'The Budgetary Cost of Ageing in a Stochastic Demographic Framework'. Federal Planning Bureau, Brussels.
EPC (2006). *The Impact of Ageing Populations on Public Spending: Projections for the EU25 Member States on Pensions, Health Care, Long-term Care, Education and Unemployment Transfers*. Report prepared by the Economic Policy Committee and the European Commission (DG ECFIN). European Economy, Special Report no. 1/2006, Brussels.
FEDEA (2005). 'Demographic Uncertainty and Pension System: Spanish Case', Madrid.
Fehr, H. and Habermann, C. (2004). 'Pension Expenditures in Germany'. Research Report, University of Würzburg.
Jensen, S. E. H. and Børlum, M. (2005). 'Pension Expenditures in Denmark'. Research Report, CEBR, Copenhagen.
Lassila, J., Palm, H. and Valkonen, T. (1997). 'Pension Policies and International Capital Mobility', in *Pension Policies and Public Debt in Numerical CGE Models*, ed. D. P. Broer and J. Lassila. Heidelberg: Physica-Verlag, pp. 139–66.
Lassila, J. and Valkonen, T. (2005). 'Pension Expenditures in Finland'. ETLA, Helsinki.
Lee, R. and Edwards, R. (2002). 'The Fiscal Impact of Population Aging in the US: Assessing the Uncertainties', in *Tax Policy and the Economy*, ed. J. Poterba. Cambridge, MA: MIT Press, pp. 141–81.

Lee, R., and Tuljapurkar, S. (2001). 'Population Forecasting for Fiscal Planning: Issues and Innovations', in *Demographic Change and Fiscal Policy*, ed. A. Auerbach and R. Lee. Cambridge: Cambridge University Press, pp. 7–57.

Sefton, J. and Weale, M. (2005). 'Stochastic Simulations of Pension Expenditure for the United Kingdom'. Research Report, National Institute of Economic and Social Research, London.

6 Demographic uncertainty and health care expenditure

Namkee Ahn

Introduction

One of the areas where population ageing will be particularly relevant is health care expenditure. National health expenditure already takes a substantial share of GDP in most developed countries. During the last few decades, it has increased across OECD countries. In 2003, OECD countries devoted, on average, 8.8% of their GDP to health spending, up from 7.1% in 1990 and just over 5% in 1970. However, the share of GDP allocated to health spending varies considerably across countries, ranging from less than 6% in the Slovak Republic, through 7.7% in Spain to 15% in the United States in 2003 (OECD, 2005a). Accelerating ageing of the population forecast for the first half of this century poses a serious challenge for the sustainability of the current social welfare system in Europe.

The direct link between population ageing and national health expenditure is due to the fact that per-capita health spending increases with age. The estimated ratio of per-capita health spending for a person aged 65 or over to that for a person under 65 years ranges between 2.5 and 5 in developed countries (see, for example, Anderson and Hussey, 2000), and within the elderly (aged 65 or greater) population a sharp increase in health expenditure with age is also observed in all countries (Economic Policy Committee, 2001). Increasing health spending with age accompanied by population ageing implies larger aggregate health expenditure in the future, even when age-specific per-capita expenditures stay constant.

Although ageing has similar implications for pension expenditure, it is worth noting some differences between the two. First, while pensions are paid almost exclusively to the retired population, health expenditure is relevant for the whole population.[1] The share of pensions paid to the

This chapter was originally prepared as a paper for the project DEMWEL (Demographic Uncertainty and the Sustainability of Social Welfare Systems) financed by the European Union under the Fifth Framework Programme. I am grateful for useful comments from Juha Alho and for research assistance by Juan Ramón García.

elderly (65+) population often exceeds 90 per cent of the total pension expenditure, while the share of health expenditure spent on the elderly population is usually much lower. Thus, the impact of population ageing on pension expenditure has almost one-to-one relationship while that on health expenditure is likely to be smaller. Second, per-capita pension expenditure among the elderly usually shows a flat or downward-sloping age profile, while per-capita health expenditure (especially when long-term care is included) usually shows an upward-sloping age profile. This implies that among the elderly population the health expenditure is likely to increase more rapidly than pension expenditure as longevity increases over time. Overall, as will be shown later, the impact of population ageing on health care expenditure appears to be smaller than that on pension expenditure.

Previous projections of health expenditure have been usually carried out by combining constant (over time) age-specific health expenditure with a deterministic, scenario-based population projection (see Mahal and Berman, 2001, for a survey). However, it has been shown repeatedly that the population size and structure in the future is highly uncertain and most projections have turned out wrong (see Keilman, Cruijsen and Alho and Alho, Cruijsen and Keilman, this volume, chaps. 2 and 3 respectively). Therefore, the projections based on the traditional approach are often unhelpful in evaluating future health care expenditures. In this chapter we try to improve upon the existing literature by incorporating uncertainties in future population in the projection of future health expenditure.[2] Furthermore, the age-profile of health expenditure itself may change over time on account of changes in fertility, mortality and migration rates as well as on account of changes in price, technology and preferences. We also discuss the impact of these factors in future health expenditure, and compare their impacts relative to that of pure population ageing.

We first describe age-specific health expenditures, which will be the base data for our health expenditure forecasts, and then summarize the demographic uncertainty. Health expenditure forecasts for some EU countries are presented next. In the subsequent section, we discuss uncertainties in age-profiles of health expenditure driven by uncertain demographics. Another type of uncertainty due to technology and preferences is then discussed. The main results are summarized in the final section.

Age-profile of health expenditure

In an accounting model for forecasting health expenditure, one type of basic data required is the age-profile of per-capita health expenditure. The

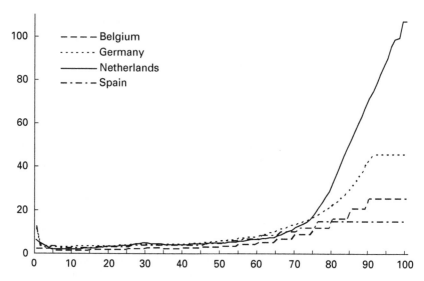

Figure 6.1. Per-capita public health expenditure (as % of GDP/capita) by age.
(*Sources:* Ahn, García and Herce (2004) for Spain; Draper *et al.* (2004) for the Netherlands; Fehr and Habermann (2004) for Germany. Data for Belgium provided by the Federal Planning Bureau.)

effect of population ageing on aggregate health expenditure will depend in part on how steep the age-profile of health expenditure is in a given country. As can be seen in Figure 6.1, a sharply increasing age-profile of health expenditure is observed in all countries.[3] However, the gradient varies somewhat among countries. The age-gradient of health expenditure seems to depend, in particular, on the extensiveness of long-term care coverage by the public health system. For example, in the Netherlands, where long-term care is most extensively covered, the gradient is highest and in Spain, where long-term care is almost non-existent, the slope is smallest.[4] Other things being equal, population ageing will have a greater impact on the aggregate expenditure in countries where the age-profile is steeper.

In most countries per-capita health expenditure is grouped by age, with a constant value within each age-group. Therefore, the age-profile differs among countries according to the degree of fineness of the age grouping for which health expenditure is estimated. The grouping is most common at higher ages. In Spain, those 76 and older are grouped together, and in Belgium and Germany those 90 and older are grouped together, while in the Netherlands single-year ages are distinguished up to age 99. This grouping may affect the magnitude of the effect of population ageing on health expenditure if real per-capita expenditure is not constant over ages within the age-interval. As is shown in the Netherlands, health care expenditure (especially when the public system covers long-term care extensively) usually increases monotonically with age up to very high ages.[5] Population ageing driven by decreasing mortality rates at higher ages means an increasing proportion of older people among the elderly. In these circumstances, the age grouping over a certain age will tend to lower projected health expenditures. The cruder the age grouping, the larger will be the magnitude of underestimation.

To illustrate the effect of age grouping on future health expenditure, we undertake a simple exercise using the data from the Netherlands. We assume that we know only the average per-capita health expenditure for those 76 or older in the Netherlands, which is computed as the average of the profile shown in Figure 6.1 weighted by the population share of each age within this age-group in the base year (2004). This gives us a per-capita health expenditure of 40.5 per cent of GDP per capita for those aged 76 or over, which would have been used in the projection of health expenditure for people in this age-group in all future years if we had not had a finer age-profile. On the other hand, if we use the true age-profile for this age-group, the average per-capita health expenditure for the age-group will increase in the future as the age-structure shifts towards the older elderly population on account of higher life expectancy. Applying the point forecast of the Dutch population in 2050, we obtain an average per-capita health expenditure for this age group of 45.1 per cent of per-capita GDP under the true age-profile. Therefore, the magnitude of underestimation of the crude age grouping is about 10 per cent for this age-group, and for the whole population it amounts to around 0.6 percentage points of GDP in 2050. This example shows the potential impact of crude age groupings in the projection of future health expenditure. Obviously, the impact will depend on the differences between the assumed and the true age-profiles and on the changes in population age-structure within age-groups.

Demographic uncertainty

Demographic uncertainty is obtained using the method developed by Alho and Spenser (1997). Keilman, Cruijsen and Alho and Alho, Cruijsen and Keilman (this volume, chaps. 2 and 3 respectively) discuss in detail the development of uncertainties in future European population, and Alho and Nikander (2004) summarize its application to eighteen European countries.

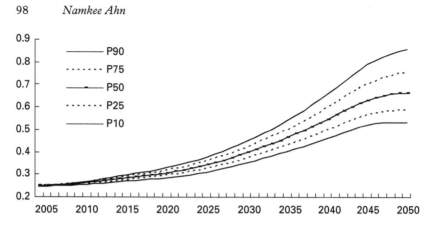

Figure 6.2. Forecast of old-age dependency ratio in Spain.

Given the steep age-profile of health expenditure, one of the most relevant demographic indicators regarding aggregate health expenditure is the old-age dependency ratio, the ratio between the numbers of those aged 65 or older and those aged 16 to 64. The higher the proportion of the elderly population relative to the working-age population, the more difficult it is to finance national health expenditure.

As an example, future demographic uncertainty in Spain is shown using 50 per cent and 80 per cent prediction intervals for the old-age dependency ratio in Figure 6.2. In Spain, the old-age dependency ratio starts at a level similar to other European countries, but then diverges from other countries, showing first a slightly lower ratio between 2010 and 2030 but later a substantially higher ratio starting from 2037. This is mainly due to the fact that the 'baby boom' in Spain occurred later (during the 1960s and 1970s instead of the 1950s and early 1960s) and that the subsequent drop in the fertility rate (the 'baby bust') has been more pronounced in Spain than in other countries.[6] By 2050, the old-age dependency ratio in Spain is predicted to lie between 0.52 and 0.85 (80 per cent prediction interval), while it will be between 0.39 and 0.55 in Belgium, Germany and the Netherlands (see Alho and Nikander, 2004). The levels and the uncertainties are substantially higher in Spain than in other countries.

Health expenditure under demographic uncertainty

Conceptually, an individual's health care expenditure at a given age depends on his/her health status at this age, the usage rate of health care services given the health status, and the unit price of health care service. Health status, in turn, depends on past health behaviour (investment),

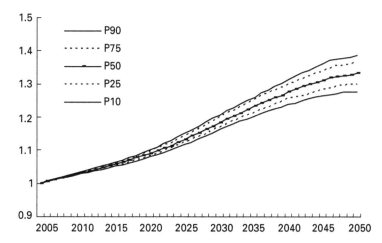

Figure 6.3. Forecasted public health expenditure (2004=1) in Spain.

genetic endowment, environment and chance. The usage rate of health services for a given health status depends, in turn, on individual characteristics and social norms (both of which form an individual's preferences) as well as their direct and indirect costs. All three elements are subject to a large random component and are interrelated in a complex manner. Therefore, the main problem with health care expenditure is that it is considerably more uncertain and difficult to model than other types of public expenditure. For example, pension legislation and work/retirement decision models provide a framework for future pension expenditure. No equivalent framework is available for the demand for, and the supply of, health care. Given this uncertainty and complexity, structural modelling which considers all the factors, as well as supply–demand interactions which determine the price, lies beyond the scope of this chapter. Therefore, we consider a simple accounting model for forecasting health expenditure. In this framework, aggregate health expenditures are computed as a product of the age-profile of per-capita health expenditures and population forecasts. Per-capita health expenditures are assumed to grow at the same rate as per-capita GDP during the period of forecast. Therefore, the aggregate health expenditure as a share of GDP is determined exclusively by the population age-structure.

Figure 6.3 shows the forecast of public health expenditure in Spain for the period 2004–2050. The increase in health expenditure (as a share of GDP) during the first half of this century will be greater than 30 per cent with a 75 per cent probability. In 2050, it will lie between 27 per cent and 38 per cent (prediction interval of 80 per cent). This relatively small

Table 6.1. *Summary statistics of uncertainty in old-age dependency ratio and health expenditure in 2050.*

| | Old-age dependency ratio in 2050 (2004 = 1) | | | |
	P90[1]	P50	P10	Relative SD[2]
Belgium	2,013	1,732	1,465	0,123
Germany	1,989	1,578	1,323	0,164
Netherlands	2,203	1,906	1,644	0,114
Spain	3,440	2,674	2,150	0,188
	Health expenditure in 2050 (2004 = 1)			
	P90	P50	P10	Relative SD
Belgium	1,671	1,489	1,345	0,085
Germany	1,362	1,248	1,175	0,058
Netherlands	1,571	1,490	1,435	0,035
Spain	1,387	1,334	1,277	0,032

Notes: [1] P90, P50 and P10 refer to the 90th, 50th and 10th percentiles, respectively.
[2] See note 7 for the definition of Relative SD.

increase and small variation in spite of the large increase and substantial uncertainty in the old-age dependency ratio is due to the fact that the health expenditure of the non-elderly population is still substantial in total health expenditure.

For the purpose of comparison, Table 6.1 summarizes the forecasted old-age dependency ratios and health expenditures in the four EU countries in 2050. First, we observe that although in all countries health expenditure increases substantially, the growth rate varies substantially among countries. For example, during the forecast period (2004–2050), according to the median (P50), it will grow by almost 50 per cent in Belgium and the Netherlands, but by less than 35 per cent in Spain and Germany. While the lower growth in Germany is mainly due to a smaller increase in the old-age dependency ratio, in Spain it is mainly due to the flatter age-profile of health spending, as shown in Figure 6.1. On the other hand, the uncertainty[7] in health spending in 2050 is largest in Belgium and Germany and smallest in the Netherlands and Spain.

Compared to the uncertainty in the old-age dependency ratio, the uncertainty in health spending is much smaller in all countries. This contrasts to the case of Medicare expenditure in the United States (Lee and Miller, 2002) or pension expenditure in European countries (Weale and Lassila & Valkonen, this volume, chaps. 4 and 5 respectively), where the correlation with the old-age dependency ratio is much higher. In conclusion, demographic uncertainties will be transferred to the uncertainties in national public health expenditures, but the magnitude of uncertainty in health expenditure will be substantially smaller.

Uncertainty in the age-profile of health expenditure

So far, we have examined the effect of demographic uncertainty on national health expenditures under the assumption of a constant (over time) age-profile of per-capita health expenditure. However, the age-profile of health expenditure may vary in the future on account of uncertainties in the vital rates of a population as well as other factors such as price, technology and preferences. We examine potential impacts of these uncertainties on the national health expenditure.

Fertility

Fertility rates affect health care expenditures in two ways. First, different fertility rates imply different numbers of newborns and therefore different health expenditure. This is easy to incorporate once we know the population by age and the age-specific health expenditure including that for those aged less than 1. Second, they imply different numbers of women who are pregnant and give birth and, therefore, different rates of medical consultation and hospital use among women of fertile age. Furthermore, maternity costs may vary with a mother's age. To incorporate this in our forecast, we need separate estimates of annual health care expenditure for women who give birth and for those who do not. For simplicity, we assume that the health care costs of a birth-giving woman are the sum of the health care costs of a non-childbearing woman and child-delivery costs.

In Spain, the unit cost of child delivery, which includes delivery costs and post-natal nursing costs, amounted to €2,456 in 1999 according to the Spanish DRG national database (Ministerio de Sanidad y Consumo, 2000). Given age-specific hospital care expenditure and the proportion of the population who used public hospitals for child delivery during the year, we can compute the hospital care expenditure separately by birth-giving status.[8]

We examined the consequences of adjusting varying maternity rates over the forecast period for Spain. According to our calculation, total expenditure after adjustment is higher than without adjusting for maternity costs since the fertility rate increases from 1.2 to 1.4 over the forecast period, but the difference is small (about 0.5 per cent of total expenditure). Even if the fertility rate doubled from 1.2 in 2004 to 2.4 in 2050, the effect of adjusting for higher maternity costs is less than 2 per cent of total health expenditure.

Mortality

Age-specific mortality rates determine the life expectancy at each given age. On the other hand, there is some evidence that health expenditure depends on the proximity to death and is concentrated during the last few years of life (Lubitz and Riley, 1993; Zweifel, Felder and Meiers, 1999; Stearns and Norton, 2002; Seshamani and Gray, 2004). Therefore, as mortality rates decline, the average length of life remaining (or time until death) increases at any given age. That is, at each given age the proportion of people who are in their last year of life diminishes as the mortality rate decreases. This will tend to decrease age-specific health expenditure at any given age. This factor should be considered seriously if the population projection is based on a relatively large improvement in mortality rates at high ages. Stearns and Norton (2002) and Seshamani and Gray (2004) show some considerable effects of changing time to death in their projections of health expenditure.

In practice, we can incorporate the effects of different mortality rates on aggregate health care expenditure by considering different health care costs by survival status. Obviously, the magnitude of the impact of changing mortality rates on future health expenditure depends on the magnitude of the improvement in mortality rates and the difference in per-capita expenditure between survivors and decedents. The greater the improvement in mortality rates and the greater the difference in expenditure by survival status, the greater will be the impact.

For the purpose of illustration, we used public-sector hospital expenditures in Spain, since for this type of health expenditure we can distinguish the expenditures for survivors and decedents using the Spanish DRG national database (Ministerio de Sanidad y Consumo, 2000).[9] As the population forecast predicts a substantial improvement in the mortality rate in the future,[10] the consideration of survival status is important in the forecast of hospital costs. Combining the age-specific per-capita hospital expenditure by survival status with the population forecast by survival status, we obtain the hospital expenditure forecast. Figure 6.4 compares the 50 per cent prediction interval (25 and 75 percentiles) of the per-capita hospital expenditure when distinguishing survival status with the same interval when not distinguishing it.

As the mortality rates decrease in the future, the hospital expenditure when we distinguish survival status is lower than when we do not distinguish it. The difference in the forecasted hospital expenditure increases over time as the mortality rate decreases continuously during the forecast period. The reduction in health expenditure when we distinguish survival status amounts to about 4 per cent by 2025 and 8 per cent by

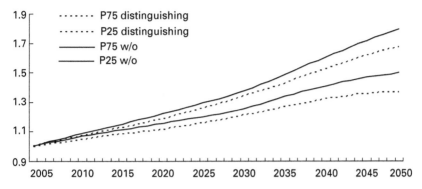

Figure 6.4. Effect of distinguishing survival status on health expenditure: 50% prediction interval of public hospital expenditure (2004=1).

2049. According to the median prediction, total hospital expenditure will increase between 2004 and 2049 by 64 per cent without distinguishing survival status; this compares to a 55 per cent increase with distinction. If we compute annual change, it amounts to 0.98 per cent without and 0.79 per cent with distinction. Uncertainty, approximated by a 50 per cent prediction interval, shows a similar magnitude in both cases. Furthermore, since the difference in levels between the two cases is not too large, there is a large area of overlap in the prediction intervals of the two cases.

At this point, a caveat is in order. Those who propose the inclusion of death-related costs claim this as an important improvement in health expenditure forecasts. For the adjustment of death-related costs to be considered as an improvement over previous forecasts, it should be the case that the age-profile of health expenditure by survival status remains stable (at least in terms of the expenditure ratio between survivors and decedents) across different mortality regimes. There is some evidence that per-capita health expenditure has increased more rapidly among survivors than among decedents during recent decades (Geppert and McClellan, 2001 for the USA; Dormont, Grignon and Huber, 2005 for France). Furthermore, a part of the decline in mortality rates among the elderly is attributable to increasing per-capita health expenditure (Lichtenberg, 2002).

To clarify the idea, we may think of two extreme cases. One is to assume that future mortality reduction is achieved through a healthier life style, such as reduced smoking and intake of other unhealthy substances and improved diet and physical exercise. In this case, reduced mortality will be translated mostly to reduced per-capita health expenditure as a result of reduced death-related costs (due to fewer decedents) and healthier survivors. The other extreme case is to assume that future mortality reduction is achieved mainly through increased and improved (usually more expensive) medical interventions in acute and chronic diseases. In this case, per-capita health expenditure will shift upwards, especially among the elderly survivors as they will be the main beneficiaries of life-prolonging medical interventions. As there is not yet convincing evidence supporting either hypothesis, it would be wise to be cautious in interpreting the effects of the inclusion of death-related costs in future health expenditure forecasts.

Migration

Migration may also affect future age-profiles of health expenditure, as immigrants are likely to have different health statuses and different utilization propensities for health care services to natives. The differences or similarities of natives and immigrants also depend on the origin country or region of the immigrants. For example, immigrants from Africa have much higher mortality and fertility rates than native Europeans, and the types of disease that they suffer are also different. If the future population is likely to be affected by a large number of immigrants, the projections of future health expenditure should consider these differences. So far, we have no data available which distinguish immigrants from natives in per-capita health expenditure.

Importance of cost pressure relative to demographic uncertainty

Many previous studies on the determinants of health expenditure have found that population ageing has small effects, while prices, preferences or technology changes[11] in the health sector have been the major factors in explaining the recent evolution in health expenditure (Cutler, 1995; Bjornerud and Oliveira Martins, 2005; Dormont, Grignon and Huber, 2005). The income elasticity of health care expenditure has been a subject of extensive research. The empirical results, however, are too varied to reach any reasonable conclusions (see OECD, 2006, for a survey). Furthermore, forecasting technology, prices or preferences in the future is an extremely difficult task, which lies beyond the scope of this chapter.

Instead, we compare the national health expenditure under two different hypotheses. One assumes that the per-capita health expenditure increases at the same rate as GDP/capita, as in previous sections. The other assumes an additional cost pressure in that the per-capita

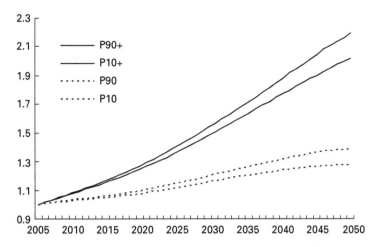

Figure 6.5. Importance of cost pressure in health expenditure (2004=1): effect of additional 1% annual increase in age-specific health expenditure (+).

health expenditure increases by one percentage point more than the GDP/capita.[12] The main purpose of this exercise is to examine the importance of uncertain future age-specific expenditure relative to uncertain demography in future health expenditure.

Figure 6.5 compares the 80 per cent prediction interval for health expenditure between the two hypotheses, with and without cost pressure. We can clearly see enormous cumulative effects over the long term in the case of cost pressure. Even a growth rate in per-capita health expenditure which is one percentage point above the GDP/capita growth rate results in a huge increase in health expenditure at the end of the projection period. Under the assumption of cost pressure, the aggregate public health expenditure in Spain is projected to increase during the projection period between 101 and 119 per cent with 80 per cent probability, while without cost pressure it will increase between 28 and 39 per cent. This is a good example which illustrates the importance of the changes in age-specific health expenditure in determining health expenditure in a nation in the long term.

Conclusions

Population ageing during the first half of this century is likely to put pressure on public health expenditure for most European countries. According to the median prediction, it will increase by two to five percentage points as a share of GDP during this period. This increase is purely due to changes in population structure under the hypothesis of constant real age-specific health expenditure. This increase may be considered to be substantial but not too alarming.

Demographic uncertainty will entail some uncertainties in future health expenditure. Compared to the uncertainty in the old-age dependency ratio, uncertainty in health spending is much smaller in all countries. In conclusion, demographic uncertainty will cause some uncertainties in future national public health expenditures, but the magnitude of uncertainty in health expenditure will be substantially smaller. This contrasts with the case of Medicare expenditure in the USA or pension expenditure in Europe where the levels and the uncertainties in their expenditures follow more closely those of the old-age dependency ratio because these types of expenditure are more concentrated on the elderly population.

Most forecasts of health expenditure have used age-profiles of per-capita health expenditure which are constant over the forecast period. However, uncertain future vital rates will inevitably result in uncertain age-specific health expenditure as the health care expenditure is different by childbearing status, between survivors and decedents and between natives and immigrants. It will be necessary to consider these factors in the projection. However, some preliminary exploration shows that their effects will be modest unless there are large changes in the vital rates. On the other hand, projections carried out under even a slightly higher growth rate of per-capita health expenditure (due to price or preference change) relative to that of per-capita GDP predict a substantial increase in the share of health expenditure in GDP in the medium and long term.

NOTES

1 We can note similar differences between Medicare expenditure in the United States and health expenditure in Europe since US Medicare covers only the population of 65 years or older and the disabled below age 65.
2 Lee and Miller (2002) and Topoleski (2004) are among the few researchers who use stochastic population forecasts, but their studies are limited to the Medicare expenditure in the USA. For Europe, to our knowledge, there is only one study, by Lassila and Valkonen (2004) who study the case of Finland.
3 Because of data availability, only public-sector health expenditure is included in all countries. The age-profile of public health expenditure may vary according to the share of private health expenditure in the total, which varied between 62 per cent in the Netherlands and 78 per cent in Germany in 2000.
4 Long-term care expenditure is extremely low in Spain, estimated at 0.2 per cent of GDP (1.3 per cent in the Netherlands) in 2000 (OECD, 2005b).

5 When long-term care expenditure is not included, the age-profile flattens or even has a downward slope for ages greater than about 85 (see, for example, Economic Policy Committee, 2001).

6 The fertility rate in Spain has been around 1.2 since the early 1990s, while the average rate for Western Europe has been 1.5.

7 Uncertainty is approximated by relative standard deviation under the assumption of a normal distribution, that is, Relative SD = (P90 – P10) / (2*1.2816*P50).

8 If we assume that child-delivery and post-partum nursing costs do not vary over mothers' age, we can assign these costs to newborns.

9 See Ahn, García and Herce (2004) for more details on how we used the DRG database to calculate age-profiles of hospital expenditure by survival status. The average cost ratio between a decedent and a survivor was 24, ranging from 96 at ages 16–20 to 5 at ages 85 or more.

10 According to the point forecasts (Alho and Nikander, 2004), the mortality rate in Spain decreases by about 65 per cent at age 65 and by about 40 per cent at age 99 during the period 2004–2049.

11 This includes changes in preferences usually interpreted as income effects. That is, as income increases, people demand more and higher-quality (usually higher-price) health care services.

12 According to the OECD (2005a), over the 1990s, the gap between health spending growth and economic growth rates was about 1 per cent on average for the OECD countries.

REFERENCES

Ahn, N., García, J. R. and Herce, J. A. (2004). 'Health Care Expenditure and Demographic Uncertainty in Spain'. FEDEA, Madrid.

Alho, J. and Nikander, T. (2004). 'Uncertain Population of Europe. Summary Results from a Stochastic Forecast'. Available at www.stat.fi/tup/euupe/del12.pdf.

Alho, J. and Spencer, B. D. (1997). 'The Practical Specification of the Expected Error of Population Forecasts'. *Journal of Official Statistics*, 13: 203–25.

Andersen, G. F. and Hussey, P. S. (2000). 'Population Ageing: a Comparison among Industrialized Countries'. *Health Affairs*, 19: 191–203.

Bjornerud, S. and Oliveira Martins, J. (2005). 'Disentangling Demographic and Non-demographic Drivers of Health Spending: a Possible Methodology and Data Requirements'. Paper presented at joint EC/OECD workshop, Brussels, 21–22 February.

Cutler, D. (1995). 'Technology, Health Costs and the NIH'. Paper presented at National Institute of Health roundtable on *The Economics of Biomedical Research*, Bethesda, MD (November).

Dormont, B., Grignon, M. and Huber, H. (2005). 'Health Expenditures and the Demographic Rhetoric: Reassessing the Threat of Ageing', THEMA, Université Paris 10, Nanterre Cedex.

Economic Policy Committee (2001). *Budgetary Challenges Posed by Ageing Populations* (EPC/ECFIN/655/01-EN final), Brussels.

Geppert, J. and McClellan, M. (2001). 'Trends in Medicare Spending near the End of Life', in *Themes in the Economics of Ageing*, ed. D. A. Wise. Chicago: University of Chicago Press, pp. 201–14.

Lassila, J. and Valkonen, T. (2004). 'Prefunding Expenditure on Health and Long-term Care under Demographic Uncertainty', *Geneva Papers on Risk and Insurance – Issues and Practice*, 29: 620–39.

Lee, R. and Miller, T. (2002). 'An Approach to Forecasting Health Expenditures, with Application to the U.S. Medicare System'. *Health Services Research*, 37: 1365–86.

Lichtenberg, F. R. (2002). *Sources of U.S. Longevity Increase, 1960–1997*, Working Paper no. 8755, Boston: NBER.

Lubitz, J. and Riley, G. (1993). 'Trends in Medicare Payments in the Last Year of Life'. *New England Journal of Medicine*, 328: 1092–6.

Mahal, A. and Berman, P. (2001). 'Health Expenditures and the Elderly: a Survey of Issues in Forecasting, Methods Used, and Relevance for Developing Country', Research Paper no. 01.23, Harvard Burden of Disease Unit, Center for Population and Development Studies. Harvard University.

Ministerio de Sanidad y Consumo (2000). *Sistema National de Salud. Año 1999*, Madrid.

OECD (2005a). *OECD Health Data 2005*. Paris: OECD.

    (2005b). *Long-term Care for Older People*. Paris: OECD.

    (2006). 'Projecting OECD Health and Long-term Care Expenditures: What are the Main Drivers?', Working Paper no. 477, Economics Department, OECD, Paris.

Seshamani, M. and Gray, A. (2004). 'Time to Death and Health Expenditure: an Improved Model for the Impact of Demographic Change on Health Care Costs'. *Age and Ageing*, 33: 556–61.

Stearns, S. C. and Norton, E. C. (2002). 'Time to Include Time to Death? The Future of Health Care Expenditure Predictions', University of Aberdeen, mimeo.

Topoleski, J. (2004). 'Uncertainty about Projections of Medicare Cost Growth', Technical Paper no. 2004-13, Congressional Budget Office, Washington, DC.

Zweifel, P., Felder, S. and Meiers, M. (1999). 'Ageing of Population and Health Care Expenditure: A Red Herring?' *Health Economics* 8: 485–96.

Assessing the uncertainty in long-term fiscal projections

Pablo Antolín

1. The main difficulty when assessing the impact of future demographic developments on long-term fiscal outcomes is the uncertainty surrounding these demographic projections. In order to assess this uncertainty this volume uses stochastic modelling,[1] but it falls short of making full use of the strength of the approach. This note therefore stresses the strengths of using a stochastic approach to assess uncertainty and, in particular, the importance of using likelihoods to gauge uncertainty, and ways to convey the uncertainty surrounding the impact of demographic forecasts.

2. The uncertainty surrounding the fiscal impact of future demographic developments is better gauged by using a stochastic approach, which allows probabilities to be assigned to different forecasts. There are several approaches to forecasting demographic outcomes. The models more commonly used to produce demographic projections are extrapolative. These models express age-specific mortality as a function of calendar time using past data and, as such, can be deterministic or stochastic. Deterministic models forecast by directly extending past trends; as a consequence, they do not come with standard errors or forecast probabilities. Stochastic models, on the other hand, forecast using probability distributions. They fit a statistical model to the historical data and use that as the basis for projections into the future. As an outcome of this process, forecast values have probabilities attached that allow assessments of the likelihood that an outcome will occur and, as a result, uncertainty and risks can be gauged adequately.

3. The strength of this volume is that it uses stochastic modelling to assess the uncertainty surrounding future demographic outcomes. Governmental agencies and international organizations tend to extrapolate in a deterministic manner, using past trends and expert opinion.[2] In this context, they have traditionally dealt with the uncertainty surrounding population forecasts by providing a range of population projection variants. For example, the UN and Eurostat population projections provide low, medium and high variants (United Nations, 2004; Eurostat, 2005). Unfortunately, this deterministic approach does not assign

probabilities to the projections and, therefore, it is impossible to assess the likelihoods of these variants. In this context, stochastic models do provide forecast probabilities, allowing one to gauge how likely different demographic forecasts are. This volume uses a stochastic approach to population forecasting.[3] For example, one of the contributions by Lassila and Valkonen to this volume (Chapter 5) illustrates the advantages of the stochastic approach when the authors compare their results with the sensitivity analysis of the impact of ageing on age-related expenditure in the latest report by the Economic Policy Committee (EPC) and the European Commission (2006). The sensitivity range for Denmark, Germany and Spain in the EPC exercise is within the 50 per cent probability range, meaning that there is more than a 50 per cent chance that the impact could be greater than the range covered by their sensitivity analysis.

4. Unfortunately, the contributions to this volume and to this part in particular, are unsuccessful in fully taking advantage of a stochastic model with forecast probabilities. At times, the contributions focus more on justifying particular choices of assumptions regarding future fertility, mortality and migration (i.e. the main determinants of population developments) over the assumptions behind the UN or Eurostat projections, rather than explaining the results in terms of forecast probabilities. The purpose of this volume should not be to produce another set of projections. Instead, it should aim at assessing the uncertainty surrounding future demographics and their impacts. In this context, policymakers and economic analysts would probably not be especially concerned whether the assumptions on fertility, mortality and migration are more or less realistic than those of the UN or Eurostat.[4] They will be more interested in knowing, for example, that there is a 65 per cent chance of seeing a 1 per cent drop in the working-age population by 2050 that will translate into an increase in age-related expenditures of two percentage points by 2050; or that there is a 15 per cent chance that the increase in age-related pension expenditure could be instead four percentage points higher. This is the value-added of the stochastic approach to demographic developments used in this volume.

5. Furthermore, the contributions to this volume fall short of exploring different ways of conveying the uncertainty surrounding demographic forecasts and their impact on future fiscal outcomes in a manner that is easy to grasp. The stochastic model used to obtain forecasts on future fertility and mortality rates provides mean and central forecasts, as well as associated standard deviations. In this context, the uncertainty surrounding any possible population outcome could be conveyed by presenting the point forecast and the standard deviation, as most contributions to this

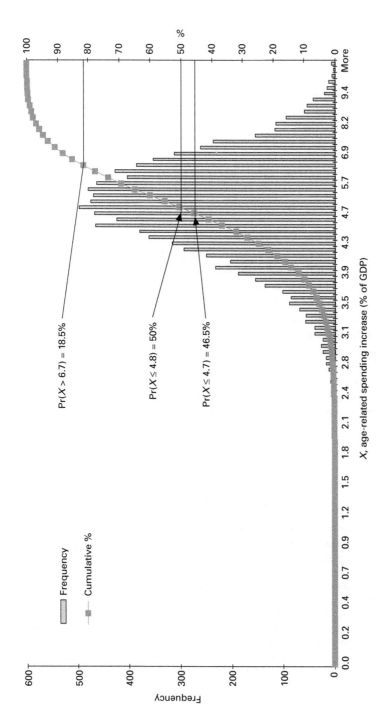

Figure IIC.1. Histogram: increase in age-related spending in 2050 (percentage points of GDP).

volume do. This uncertainty could also be presented using a fan graph, as the inflation report of the Bank of England does (King, 2004). Furthermore, it could also be conveyed by means of frequency distributions and cumulated probabilities generated from Monte Carlo simulations of the stochastic model used to forecast future population outcomes.[5] In this latter approach, the uncertainty is conveyed by presenting the most likely outcomes and their probabilities, as well as the likelihood surrounding significant deviations, as shown in Figure IIC.1.

6. An effective way to convey the uncertainty surrounding future demographic forecasts and their impact is by means of frequency distributions and accumulated probabilities. In this context, Figure IIC.1 conveys the uncertainty surrounding fiscal outcomes as a result of uncertain demographics, for a hypothetical country, by examining the cumulative probability function of an increase by 2050 in age-related spending as a share of GDP. This cumulative probability function provides the probability or likelihood associated to different forecasted values of the increase in age-related spending resulting from population ageing. Thus, Figure IIC.1 indicates that the central forecast of a 4.7 per cent increase in age-related spending lies below the median forecast. Consequently, there is a less than a 50 per cent change that the increase in age-related spending would be 4.7 per cent or lower in 2050. Furthermore, there is an 18.5 per cent chance that the increase in age-related spending as a consequence of uncertain demographics is more than two percentage points higher than the central forecasts, that is, 6.7 per cent.

NOTES

1 This approach is in line with recommendations by Antolin (2007) and by the Continuous Mortality Investigation (2004, 2005, 2006).
2 For example, Eurostat and the United States Census Bureau population projections use a deterministic approach. They use historical trends in age-specific mortality rates (ASMR), generally over the last fifteen years, and assume that they will continue in the future, weighted, however, by some expert assessment of the causes of death (Hollmann, Mulder and Kallan, 2000; Eurostat, 2005). They estimate the values of the ASMR in an intermediate year (e.g. 2018) and at the end year (e.g. 2050). This is done by applying the rate of improvement of the average mortality rate in the last three to five available years. Finally, ASMRs for each intermediate year are calculated by an interpolation method based on fitting third-degree curves. They infer the intermediate years by assuming a parametric function such as the logistic or the Gompertz function.
3 The stochastic modelling used in this volume is outlined by Alho and Spencer (2005).

4 The arguments behind the Eurostat and UN projections and those in this volume are all perfectly reasonable.
5 See Antolin (2007) for such an approach.

REFERENCES

Alho, J. M. and Spencer, B. D. (2005). *Statistical Demography and Forecasting*. New York: Springer.
Antolin, P. (2007). 'Longevity Risk and Private Pensions'. OECD Working Papers on Insurance and Private Pensions Paris.
Continuous Mortality Investigation (2004). 'Projecting Future Mortality: a Discussion Paper'. Working Paper 3, Mortality Committee, Institute of Actuaries, London.
    (2005). 'Projecting Future Mortality: Towards a Proposal for a Stochastic Methodology'. Working Paper 15, Mortality Committee, Institute of Actuaries, London.
    (2006). 'Stochastic Projection Methodologies: Further Progress and P-spline Model Features, Example Results and Implications'. Working Paper 20, Mortality Committee, Institute of Actuaries, London.
European Commission (2006). *The Impact of Ageing Populations on Public Spending: Projections for the EU25 Member States on Pensions, Health Care, Long-term Care, Education and Unemployment Transfers*. European Economy, Special Report no. 1/2006. Brussels.
Eurostat (2005). 'EUROPOP2004: Methodology for Drafting Mortality Assumptions', Brussels.
Hollmann, F. W., Mulder, T. J., and Kallan, J. E. (2000). 'Methodology and Assumptions for the Population Projections of the United States: 1999–2100'. Working Paper 38, Population Division, Bureau of the Census, Washington, DC.
King, M. (2004). 'What Fate Imposes: Facing up to Uncertainty'. *The Eighth British Academy Annual Lecture*, London.
United Nations (2004). *World Population Prospects: The 2002 Revision*. New York.

Part III

Enhancing sustainability

7 Evaluating pension reforms in the German context

Hans Fehr and Christian Habermann

Introduction

Compared to other industrialized countries, the German old-age insurance system has some special characteristics. First, the public system is very generous, offering high replacement rates at fairly low effective retirement ages. Second, since benefits are strictly linked to former contributions the system is intragenerationally fair. Finally, the system is highly centralized since the unfunded public pension system (Gesetzliche Rentenversicherung (GRV)) covers about 85 per cent of the workforce and income from funded components only amounts to about 15 per cent of current retirement income in Germany. Given these facts, it is not surprising that the German public pension system is quite expensive compared to those of other countries. Total outlays amount to about 12 per cent of GDP and the contribution rate is currently fixed at 19.5 per cent although direct government transfers already cover about a quarter of total expenditures.

In the seventies and eighties the system was almost universally accepted. However, during the last decade it came under heavy pressure in political and economic debate. One reason was the weak performance of the German economy from the mid-nineties. Rising unemployment rates and early retirement schemes decreased the contribution base and increased expenditure at the same time. The second reason was the medium-term demographic development. Due to extremely low fertility rates, Germany is ageing very fast such that the dependency ratio will almost double within thirty years. At the end of the nineties, the newly elected Red–Green government responded to these challenges with a mixture of revenue policies and future benefit cuts. Since it was afraid to increase contribution rates and labour cost, revenues from the

We would like to thank Eckart Bomsdorf for providing mortality projections, Bernd Raffelhüschen for providing age-profiles for health care, long-term care and education outlays and Susanne Schmid (Federal Statistical Office) for providing population data.

environmental tax were used to finance pension benefits after 1999. In addition, after two years of inflation indexation, the so-called Riester reform introduced a new formula for benefit adjustment in 2001 which dampened the growth of future expenditure. The main intention was to keep the contribution rate below 20 per cent until 2020 and below 22 per cent until 2030 and stabilize the pension level of a 'standard retired person' at 67 per cent of former net earnings.[1]

It soon became clear that the reform would not suffice to keep the system sustainable in the medium term. Consequently, a committee of experts (the Rürup Commission) was established in 2002 which proposed in its final report in 2003 an increase in the statutory retirement age from currently 65 to 67 from 2011 through to 2035, and the introduction of a 'sustainability factor' in the pension formula; see BMGS (2003). Due to the latter, changes in the population structure (i.e. the relation between retired people and workers) will directly affect pension benefits. After a controversial debate the government introduced the 'sustainability factor' in the latest pension reform of summer 2004. Although it was quite clear that the reform would not suffice to stabilize future contribution rates as intended, the former Red–Green government postponed the suggested increase in retirement ages. Therefore, it was no surprise that the issue appeared again on the agenda of the newly elected grand coalition in autumn 2005. At the moment, the government is preparing a new reform package in this direction.

The present study quantifies the economic and welfare consequences of two possible pension reform strategies for Germany. Similarly to Knell (2005) and Börsch-Supan and Wilke (2006), we compare an increase in the statutory retirement age with a change in the pension adjustment formula which yields the same reduction in the implicit debt level. Since our approach explicitly takes into account the uncertainty of population projections, we are able to compute probability intervals for future tax and contribution rates and assess how the reforms alter the existing inter-generational risk-sharing. Our results indicate that both reforms imply a double burden for the current older generations. They will experience not only a decrease in expected welfare, but also a higher exposure to economic risk. Consequently, we propose a reform strategy which combines a reduction in expected welfare with an improved insurance against population uncertainty for the elderly.

In the following, we first describe the simulation model of the German economy. Then we discuss the calibration and the baseline growth path. Finally we explain the modelling of alternative pension reform options and report the simulation results.

The simulation model

This section describes the simulation model which is used to compute the baseline path of the economy and evaluate the policy reforms. We start with the German pension formula, then we discuss the underlying assumptions of the stochastic population model and finally we sketch the basic structure of the behavioural model.

Calculation of pension benefits

Pension benefits in Germany are computed as the product of three elements: (1) the 'adjustment factor' (AF) for pension type and retirement age, (2) the sum of 'individual earning points' (EP), which mainly reflect the retired person's relative earning position during their working life and (3) the 'actual pension value' (APV), which defines the value of one earning point in euro. The pension of a pensioner who is age a in year t and who retired at age $\bar{a} \leq a$ in year $z \leq t$ is then

$$Pen(a, t) = AF(z) \times EP(z) \times APV(t). \tag{1}$$

Our model does not distinguish between different types of pension. Consequently, the adjustment factor only deviates from 1 if the individual retirement age deviates from the statutory retirement age, which is currently set at 65. If agents retire prior to age 65, benefits will be reduced by 3.6 per cent for each year of earlier retirement (in addition to the effect of fewer earning points). Our model assumes a constant average retirement age of $\bar{a} = 62$ during the transition. Consequently, the individual adjustment factor $AF(z)$ is 0.892 on the benchmark path. The earning points of an employee are computed from the ratio of their individual insured gross earnings to average gross earnings in each year of service. A worker who earns average gross income would receive one earnings point for each contribution year. Consequently, the sum of earning points over the working years, $EP(z)$, is also indexed by the year of retirement z. While the first two factors in equation (1) are kept constant in the years t after retirement, the actual pension value is adjusted according to

$$APV(t) = APV(t-1) \times \frac{Y(t) \times [1 - \tau^{p}(t) - \tau^{pp}(t)]}{Y(t-1) \times [1 - \tau^{p}(t-1) - \tau^{pp}(t-1)]}$$

$$\times \left\{ 1 + \kappa \left(1 - \frac{DR(t)}{DR(t-1)} \right) \right\}. \tag{2}$$

Equation (2) reflects the central elements of the adjustment formula which was introduced by the Riester reform in 2001 and the latest reform in 2004. Since then, changes in the actual pension value have been related to lagged changes of an artificial income concept which is computed from the gross income Y net of contributions to public pensions τ^p and fictitious contributions τ^{pp} to newly introduced private pension accounts.[2] Until 2008 the fictitious contribution rates to the private accounts will increase from initially 1 per cent to 4 per cent, which dampens the growth of the actual pension value. In addition, an increase in the pension contribution rate τ^p will also dampen the growth of benefits. The last component shows the 'sustainability factor', where the dependency ratio, $DR(\cdot)$, measures the ratio of pensioners to contributors (including the unemployed) of a specific year. Of course, since the dependency ratio will almost certainly increase, the new indexation rule will decrease future benefits further compared to the status quo after the Riester reform. The impact of the rising dependency ratio on benefits depends on the weight κ, which is currently set at 0.25 and will be increased in our simulation.

The sustainability factor could be interpreted as a device to insure against demographic uncertainty. If population ageing is greater than currently projected, future benefits would automatically fall more than currently projected. If population ageing is less severe, future benefits would be higher. Consequently, the benefit indexation dampens the fluctuation of the future contribution rate, while at the same time increasing the uncertainty of future benefits.

Determinants of the population model

Our stochastic population forecast is derived using the program PEP (Program for Error Propagation).[3] The starting point for our projection is the existing population structure of Germany in the year 2004 which is provided by the Federal Statistical Office. Our point forecast for age-specific fertility rates assumes that the current level of fertility will continue unchanged. This means that on average a German woman will have 1.4 children in the future. Similarly, our point forecast for immigration assumes that the current age- and sex-specific immigration rates will be stable in the long run. This implies an annual net immigration of 200,000 on average. Finally, with respect to mortality, our point forecast assumes an increase in future life expectancy. The applied sex-, age- and time-specific mortality rates are taken from Bomsdorf (2003). According to these estimates, life expectancy in Germany will increase from 80.5 to 85 years for females and from 74.5 to 78.7 for males by 2050.

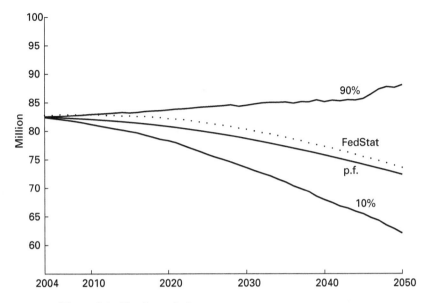

Figure 7.1. Total population.

These point estimates for fertility, immigration and mortality serve as the median of the predictive distribution of these variables. The program PEP then simulates these vital rates randomly such that future fluctuations are of similar magnitude to past fluctuations. The vital parameters are simulated randomly only between 2005 and 2050. Afterwards mortality and immigration are kept at their point forecast and a constant fertility rate is computed from the average realizations during the years 2005 and 2050. Consequently, the model arrives at a constant population structure in 2150. We simulate 300 population forecasts with different randomly selected fertility, immigration and mortality rates.[4] Consequently, for any population statistic $N(a, t)$ of the cohort which is age a at year t in the future there is an entire distribution of 300 outcomes. Given such a distribution it is possible to estimate the forecast interval.

Figure 7.1 plots our forecast of the total population in Germany, with an 80 per cent probability interval, between 2005 and 2050. As discussed above, this projection is based on our point forecast (p.f.) which is also shown in Figure 7.1. Note that our point forecast is close to the medium-variant forecast of the Federal Statistical Office of Germany (2003), which predicts a decline of the total population from 82.4 million to 74 million in 2050. According to our estimates there is an 80 per cent probability that in 2050 the total population in Germany is between 62 and 87 million people.

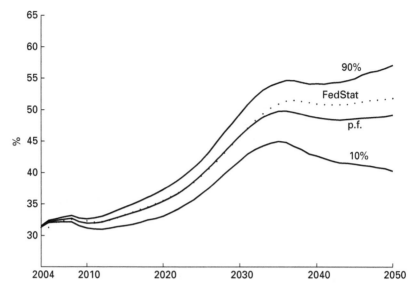

Figure 7.2. Old-age dependency ratio (population aged 65–100/ population aged 20–64), 2004–2050.

Similarly, Figure 7.2 plots the point forecast and the probability interval for the old-age dependency ratio. Until 2035 the dependency ratio in Germany will increase with certainty. However, the magnitude of the increase is quite unclear and the uncertainty will grow over the years. After 2035 there is a slight chance that the dependency ratio will fall again, while it stays almost constant in our point forecast. Note that our point forecast is more optimistic with respect to the dependency ratio than the medium prediction of the Federal Statistical Office. The main reason is that the official forecast assumes a much greater increase in life expectancy than we do.

The structure of the economic model[5]

Although the model includes immigrants from abroad, we do not distinguish between natives and immigrants on the household side. When immigrant households arrive in Germany, they are endowed with the same assets as their native counterparts of the same age.[6] The representative household is completely annuitized and, consequently, leaves no bequests at death. All agents start to make their own economic decisions at age 21.

As usual in the Auerbach and Kotlikoff (1987) tradition, our model assumes a preference structure that is represented by a time-separable, nested CES utility function. Households maximize remaining lifetime utility $U(j, t)$ which, for an agent of age j in year t, takes the form:

$$\max \ U(j, t) = \frac{1}{1 - \frac{1}{\gamma}} \sum_{a=j}^{100} \left(\frac{1}{1 + \theta}\right)^{a-j} P(a, i)$$

$$\times \left[c(a, i)^{1-\frac{1}{\rho}} + \alpha(a)\ell(a, i)^{1-\frac{1}{\rho}} \right]^{\frac{1-\frac{1}{\gamma}}{1-\frac{1}{\rho}}} \tag{3}$$

where $c(a, i)$ and $\ell(a, i)$ denote consumption and leisure, respectively and i is defined as $i = t + a - j$.

Since life span is uncertain, the utility of consumption in future periods is weighted with the survival probability $P(a, i)$ of reaching age a in year i. The parameters θ, ρ and γ represent the 'pure' rate of time preference, the intratemporal elasticity of substitution between consumption and leisure at each age a and the intertemporal elasticity of substitution between consumption and leisure in different years, respectively. The leisure preference parameter $\alpha(a)$ increases with age through the life cycle in order to generate a realistic intertemporal labour supply pattern.

Given the asset endowment $a(j, t)$ of the agent in year t, maximization of expression (3) is subject to a lifetime budget constraint defined by the sequence:

$$a(j + 1, t + 1) = a(j, t) \left[\frac{1 + r(t)}{1 - d(j, t)} \right]$$

$$+ W(j, t) - T(j, t) - c(j, t) \tag{4}$$

where $r(t)$ measures the pre-tax return on savings and $W(j, t)$ denotes the gross labour income of the age-j agent in year t, which is derived as the product of their labour supply and their wage rate. The net taxes $T(j, t)$ of an agent of age j in year t consist of consumption, capital income and wage taxes as well as social security contributions net of pensions (*Pen*). In Germany, the social security contributions for pensions (τ^P) and health care[7] are split between the employer and the employee. Pension benefits are age- and period-specific but retired persons have to pay half of their health care contributions while the other half is financed by the pension system.

The economy is populated by a large number of competitive firms, the sum of which we normalize to unity. The competitive labour market balances the labour supply of households and the demand of firms. Aggregate output $Y(t)$ is produced using a Cobb-Douglas production technology, i.e.

$$Y(t) = \phi K(t)^\epsilon L(t)^{1-\epsilon} \tag{5}$$

where $K(t)$ and $L(t)$ are aggregate capital and labour in period t, respectively. The parameter ϵ denotes capital's share in production and ϕ is a technology parameter.

Firms have to pay corporate taxes $T^k(t)$ where the corporate tax rate is applied to the output net of labour costs and depreciation. Note that the labour costs of the firm include a share of social security contributions. Capital is assumed to depreciate at rate δ and depreciation is subtracted from the tax base. Firms will employ labour up to the point where the marginal product of labour equals labour costs (which include the employer's social security contributions). Similarly they will employ capital up to the point where the net marginal product of capital is equal to the interest rate.

The consolidated government issues new debt $\Delta B(t)$ and collects net taxes and social security contributions (τ^{ss}) from households and firms in order to finance general government expenditures $G(t)$ as well as interest payments on its debt:

$$\Delta B(t) + \sum_{a=21}^{100} T(a,t)N(a,t) + \tau^{ss}(t)w(t)L(t)/2 + T^k(t)$$
$$= G(t) + r(t)B(t) \tag{6}$$

With respect to public debt, we assume that the government maintains an exogenously fixed ratio of debt to output. General government expenditures $G(t)$ consist of government purchases of goods and services, educational expenditures and health care outlays. Over the transition, government purchases of goods and services are held fixed per capita, similar to the age-specific outlays for education (which are only spent for children) and health care.

The outlays of the pension system also include half of the health care contributions of pensioners. Since the budget of the pension system must be balanced in each period, the contribution rate $\tau^p(t)$ is computed from

$$\tau^p(t)w(t)L(t) = [1 + \tau^h(t)/2] \sum_{a=\bar{a}(t)}^{100} Pen(a,t)N(a,t) \tag{7}$$

The health care contribution rate $\tau^h(t)$ is computed quite similarly to the budget of the health care system.

In general equilibrium, supply has to equal demand in all markets. Because of the closed economy assumption, assets of domestic residents $A(t)$ and immigrants $\mathcal{A}(t)$ have to balance the capital demand of companies and the government in the capital market:

$$A(t) + \mathcal{A}(t) = K(t) + B(t) \tag{8}$$

Table 7.1. *Parameter values of the model.*

	Symbol	Value
Utility function		
Time preference rate	θ	0.02
Intertemporal elasticity of substitution	γ	0.25
Intratemporal elasticity of substitution	ρ	0.8
Leisure preference parameter	$\alpha(a)$	1.0–1.8
Production function		
Technology level	ϕ	1.07
Capital share in production	ε	0.25
Economic depreciation	δ	0.05
Policy parameters		
Wage tax rate		9.5
Capital income tax rate		6.0
Corporate tax rate		20.0
Debt (as % of GDP)	B/Y	60.0
Statutory retirement age		65
Sustainability weight	κ	0.25
Replacement rate (pension/gross income)	Pen/W	0.54

Summing across budget constraints and substituting the optimality conditions, we arrive at the goods market equation, which completes the description of the model.

Calibration and simulation

In order to solve the model we have to specify the preference, technology and policy parameters. Table 7.1 reports the most important parameter values. The preference and technology parameters are mostly taken from Auerbach and Kotlikoff (1987: 52f.) or Fehr (1999: 57). Note that we allow the leisure preference parameter α to rise linearly from 1.0 (at age 21) to 1.8 (at age 100). This procedure mainly affects intertemporal labour supply, which is fairly high in early years and then is steadily reduced on approaching retirement.

On the fiscal side we specify the government per-capita purchases of goods and services as well as education and health expenditures for different age-groups. In order to finance the outlays, the wage tax rate, the capital income tax rate and the corporate tax rate are set exogenously. Since the deficit is endogenous (because of the fixed debt–output ratio), the consumption tax rate is used to balance the government budget. As already explained, we set the *statutory* retirement age at 65 whereas agents

126   *Hans Fehr and Christian Habermann*

Table 7.2. *The initial year 2004.*

	Model	Germany 2004
Expenditures (as % of GDP)		
Private consumption	49.5	59.1
Health care consumption	12.0	–
Government purchases incl. education	18.4	18.7
Aggregate education outlays	4.2	4.0
Gross investment	20.2	17.3
Exports-imports	0.0	4.9
Government indicators		
Aggregate pension benefits	11.5	12.2
Interest payment on public debt	1.6	3.0
Pension contribution rate (%)	19.5	19.5
Health care contribution rate (%)	15.9	15.9[1]
Tax revenues (as % of GDP)	19.7	20.0
Wage income tax	6.0	5.9
Interest income tax	0.8	0.8
Consumption tax	10.8	10.5
Corporation tax	2.0	1.8
Consumption tax rate (%)	21.7	–
Interest rate (%)	2.7	–
Saving rate (%)	8.3	10.8
Capital–output ratio	3.0	3.0

Note: [1] In 2004, the average health care rate was 14.2% and the long-term care rate, 1.7%.
Source: Germany, 2004: Institut der Deutschen Wirtschaft (2005).

retire *effectively* at age 62 throughout the baseline path. In addition, the weight of the sustainability factor κ is set at its current value of 0.25. Finally, the actual pension amount in the initial year is specified to yield a replacement rate for gross income of 54 per cent, which reflects the current situation for an average income-earner.

Given the parameter values described above, Table 7.2 reports the initial equilibrium in year 2004 for our point forecast.[8] The initial year is not a long-run equilibrium. Consequently, we have to specify asset endowments for the households living in the initial year. We follow Fehr (2000) and derive these asset endowments from a simulation of an artificial steady state.

While health care consumption is in reality a mixture of private and public consumption goods, it is a pure public consumption good in our model. Consequently, in our base year equilibrium private consumption expenditures are fairly low, but this difference is mainly due to health

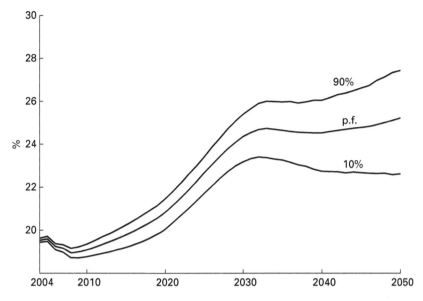

Figure 7.3. Pension contribution rates, 2004–2050.

care outlays. The remaining government consumption expenditures then include purchases for goods and services as well as education outlays. Table 7.2 shows that our benchmark calibration yields quite realistic values for these expenditures as well as for tax and contribution rates in our base year equilibrium. Note that the endogenous consumption tax rate also includes excise taxes.

Next, we consider the baseline path of our economy. Since the future is uncertain, Figure 7.3 shows the point forecast and the 80 per cent confidence interval of the endogenous pension contribution rate. Not surprisingly, the contribution rates will increase in the future quite substantially as a result of ageing.

Note that the confidence interval for the pension contribution rate in Figure 7.3 has a very similar shape to that of the confidence interval for the dependency ratio in Figure 7.2. While the contribution rate will stay almost constant up to year 2010, it will steadily increase thereafter. In our point forecast it will reach 21 per cent in 2020 and 24.3 per cent in 2030. Figure 7.3 confirms that under the current system, contribution rates could not be kept below 22 per cent up to 2030 as proposed by the government. This motivates the reforms which we analyse below.

The dynamics of health care contribution rates (Figure 7.4) are slightly different to those shown in Figure 7.3 since health care outlays increase

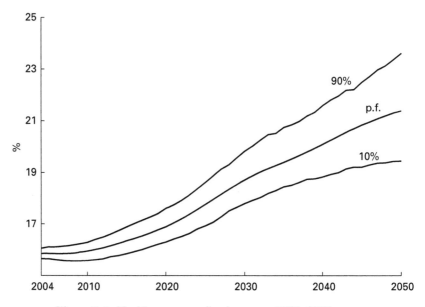

Figure 7.4. Health care contribution rates, 2004–2050.

steadily with age, and health care contributions are also paid on pension benefits. Finally, the consumption tax rates which balance the public budget in each year fall slightly until 2015 (Figure 7.5) because of the rising average productivity of the ageing population. Afterwards they most likely increase again depending on the future population structure. If the dependency ratio increases faster, contribution rates rise more rapidly and labour supply is reduced. As a consequence, income taxes decrease and consumption taxes have to increase.

Figures 7.3 to 7.5 clearly demonstrate that the current policy is not sustainable. In order to quantify the existing magnitude of the sustainability gap in Germany, we fix social security contribution rates at their current levels and compute for each population path the time-invariant consumption tax rate which would finance all current and future expenditures.[9] It turns out that on the point forecast path we would have to increase the current consumption tax rate by almost fifteen percentage points to 36.1 per cent! The revenues from higher consumption taxes would be used to build up the government assets which finance future pension and health care outlays. Of course, the sustainable consumption tax rate depends on the population projection. Table 7.3 shows that the 80 per cent predictive interval ranges from 30.6 to 44.1 per cent.

This suffices to explain the baseline path. Next we turn to the considered policy reforms.

Table 7.3. *Sustainable consumption tax rate (per cent).*

	Baseline path	Retirement age increase	Weight parameter $\kappa = 0.44$
90%	44.1	41.2	40.4
p.f.	36.1	**33.6**	**33.6**
10%	30.6	28.8	29.0

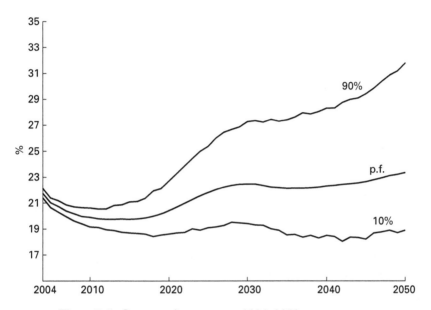

Figure 7.5. Consumption tax rates, 2004–2050.

Future benefit cuts and their impact on welfare and risk-sharing

As already explained, the objective of the current government is to reduce future benefits by increasing the statutory retirement age. In our simulations we follow the original plan of the Rürup Commission to increase the statutory retirement age of each successive annual new pensioner cohort by one month in and after 2011 (RA reform). All cohorts which retire in (and after) year 2034 would then face the new statutory retirement age of 67. Of course, since such a reform would reduce future retirement benefits, the sustainability gap would decrease as well. As Table 7.3 shows, the sustainable consumption tax rate on the point forecast path falls from 36.1 to 33.6 per cent and the 80 per cent interval reduces to 28.8–41.2 per cent as a result of the reform.

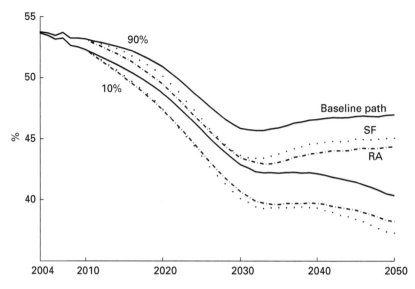

Figure 7.6. Replacement rates of reform options, 2004–2050.

Next we simulate an alternative benefit reduction where the weight κ of the sustainability factor in equation (2) is increased (SF reform). In order to compare the two reforms we calibrate an increase in κ from 0.25 to 0.44, which yields the same sustainable consumption tax rate on the point forecast path; see Table 7.3. While the point forecast is the same, the uncertainty of the sustainability gap decreases significantly, the 80 per cent interval for the sustainable consumption tax rate is now 29.0–40.4 per cent.

The latter already indicates that the two indexation reforms differ with respect to their intergenerational risk-sharing effects. In order to assess the reforms, the next sub-section compares the implied changes in contribution and replacement rates. Subsequently, the welfare and risk implications are compared.

Effects on contribution and replacement rates

Of course, both pension reforms aim to alter the path of replacement and contribution rates in the economy. Figures 7.6 and 7.7 compare the predictive distributions of the replacement and contribution rates before (solid lines) and after (dashed lines) the reforms. In our base year, the replacement rate is 54 per cent (see Table 7.1). It then falls slightly on account of the increase in the fictitious contribution rate τ^{pp} until 2008

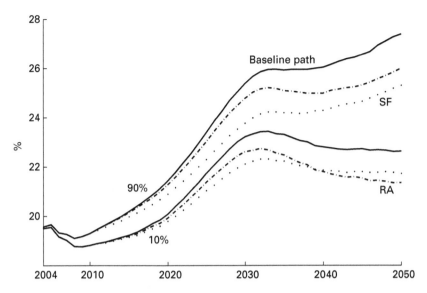

Figure 7.7. Contribution rates of reform options, 2004–2050.

and the rising contribution rate (see Figure 7.3) afterwards. The higher the future contribution rate, the lower will be the future replacement rate. If contribution rates fell again after 2030, the replacement rate would also increase slightly.

As shown in Figure 7.6, both reforms reduce replacement rates considerably compared to the baseline path. However, an increase in the statutory retirement age implies a reduced uncertainty with regard to retirement income compared to an increase in the weight parameter κ. As clearly shown in Figure 7.6, the 80 per cent predictive interval is significantly smaller for the RA reform.

While future replacement rates are more uncertain, future contribution rates become more certain with the SF reform. Figure 7.7 compares the predictive intervals for the contribution rates of the baseline scenario (solid lines, which have already been explained in Figure 7.3) and after the two reforms. Of course, lower replacement rates also reduce future contribution rates. However, as one can clearly see, the fluctuation of contribution rates is dampened under the SF reform compared to the RA reform.

Expected welfare changes and intergenerational risk-sharing

The analysis of the changes in replacement and contribution rates in the previous sub-section has already given an idea about the direction of the

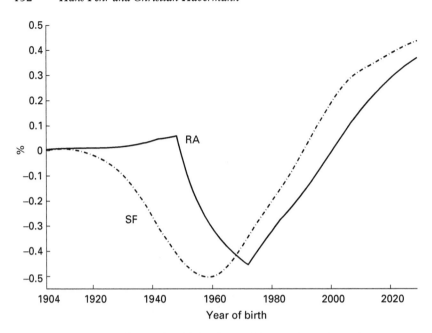

Figure 7.8. Expected welfare effects of the pension reforms (as percentage of remaining lifetime resources).

intergenerational welfare effects and risk-sharing implications of the two reform packages which are being considered. Since replacement rates as well as contribution rates fall for both reforms, the intergenerational redistribution effects of both reforms will be in favour of younger and future generations at the expense of the current elderly. However, since the probability intervals of replacement and contribution rates are quite different, we would especially expect some differences in the risk-sharing implications of the two reforms. In order to quantify the intergenerational welfare effects, we compute for each population path the generation-specific utility levels before and after the specific reform and derive the respective Hicksian equivalent variations (HEV) relative to remaining lifetime resources. Next we compute from the 300 HEV realizations the *expected* welfare change for each generation. Figure 7.8 compares the expected welfare changes of the two reform variants for generations who are born between 1904 (the oldest generation still alive in 2004) and 2025.

Consider first the solid line of the RA reform. Since those who are already retired by 2010 do not experience any benefit cuts, their welfare increases slightly due to the (slight) fall in consumption tax rates.

When the reform is implemented, in and after 2011, welfare is reduced sharply for all those cohorts who were born after 1950 (and retire after the reform). For generations born in and after 1972 (which retire in and after 2035), expected welfare increases again since they have paid much lower contributions during their working period. Finally, currently young and future generations realize significant expected welfare gains.

If the weight of the sustainability factor is increased in and after 2011, already retired generations experience some benefit cuts. Consequently, those born before 1960 are worse off with this reform than with the increase in the nominal retirement age. On the other hand, all younger and future generations are better off than before since both reforms reduce the size of the unfunded system.

Next we compare the impact of the two reforms on the generation-specific uncertainty. In order to measure the risk effects, we compute for each generation the standard deviation of the 300 utility levels (one for each path) under the baseline (σ^B) and the reform scenario (σ^R). Then we normalize the ratio of the two standard deviations to generate $\sigma^R/\sigma^B - 1$ as an index of the generation-specific risk effects. If the index is greater than zero, generation-specific risk has increased and vice versa.

Figure 7.9 shows that the RA reform only slightly reallocates risk from population uncertainty across generations. Currently medium-age households face a slightly higher risk, while future generations face a slightly lower risk. Under the SF reform, however, the risk for medium-aged households increases significantly since changes in the population structure now affect the pension level of those cohorts much more strongly. On the other hand, future generations face much lower risk than before, since the risk from population uncertainty is shifted to the older cohorts.

Conclusion

The present study aims to improve our understanding of the risk-sharing implications of alternative pension reforms. Traditional studies do not deal with such problems since they are based on models which exclude uncertainty. Our approach explicitly takes into account the uncertainty arising from future population dynamics. This allows us to quantify and compare not only the macro-economic and distributional consequences of alternative reform packages, but also their intergenerational risk-sharing implications.

The approach is applied to the recent pension debate in Germany where the government has recently linked future changes in the replacement rate to changes in the dependency ratio. We compare an increase in

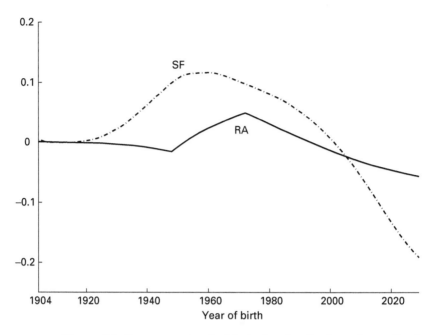

Figure 7.9. Intergenerational risk-sharing implications (normalized ratio of standard deviation).

the statutory retirement age with an increase in the weight of the sustainability factor. Although the two reforms are calibrated to yield identical reductions in the existing sustainability gap, they have quite different welfare and risk-sharing consequences for the different cohorts. The current elderly are clearly worse off under the SF reform. Not only does their expected welfare fall further, but also their exposure to risk increases considerably. Of course, the opposite happens to younger and future generations. Their expected welfare will be higher under the SF reform and their exposure to population risk will be much smaller than under an increase in the retirement age.

Consequently, taking into account the risk-sharing implications of the two reform packages, we conclude that the increase in the statutory retirement age is preferred to an adjustment of the sustainability factor since the latter would impose a double burden on currently middle-aged generations. Of course, such a policy could still be improved if it is possible to design a reform package which has exactly opposite intergenerational distribution and risk-sharing properties. A reform which redistributes welfare from the current elderly towards future generations would be better accepted if the losers were compensated by a risk reduction while the winners were to bear more risk. How to design and implement such a reform will be on the agenda for future research efforts.

NOTES

1 Börsch-Supan and Wilke (2006) provide an extensive discussion and evaluation of the recent German pension reforms.
2 Mainly for simplicity, we have lagged the variables in equation (2) by one period although in reality they are lagged by two periods.
3 A detailed description of PEP is available at www.joensuu.fi/statistics/juha. html/. The basic ideas underlying PEP are discussed in Alho and Spencer (1997) as well as in Alho *et al.* (2005) and Alho, Cruijsen and Keilmann (this volume, chap. 3).
4 This number was chosen mainly because of time constraints. However, increasing the number of simulations did not change the distribution significantly.
5 For a more detailed description, see Fehr and Habermann (2006).
6 This assumption is necessary to keep the structure of the model simple. Fehr, Jokisch and Kotlikoff (2005) apply a similar approach, whilst the model of Fehr and Halder (2006) distinguishes native and immigrant households.
7 The present model combines health and long-term care contributions and outlays, whilst Fehr and Halder (2006) separate the two systems.
8 Since households are forward-looking and tax rates are different along each population path, the initial equilibrium is affected by the population forecast. However, the effects are not very significant.
9 Similar calculations are also presented by Weale (this volume, chap. 4) as well as by Armstrong *et al.* (this volume, chap. 9).

REFERENCES

Alho, J., Jensen, S. E. H., Lassila, J. and Valkonen, T. (2005). 'Controlling the Effects of Demographic Risks: the Role of Pension Indexation Schemes'. *Journal of Pension Economics and Finance*, 4: 139–53.
Alho, J. and Spencer, B. D. (1997). 'The Practical Specification of the Expected Error of Population Forecasts'. *Journal of Official Statistics*, 13: 201–25.
Auerbach, A. J. and Kotlikoff, L. J. (1987). *Dynamic Fiscal Policy*. Cambridge: Cambridge University Press.
Bomsdorf, E. (2003). *Sterbewahrscheinlichkeiten der Periodensterbetafeln für die Jahre 2000 bis 2100*. Cologne: Eul Verlag.
Börsch-Supan, A. and Wilke, C. B. (2006). 'The German Public Pension System – How It Will Become an NDC System Look-Alike', in *Pension Reform*, ed. R. Holzmann and E. Palmer. Washington, DC: World Bank, pp. 573–610.
Bundesministerium für Gesundheit und Soziale Sicherung (BMGS) (2003). 'Nachhaltigkeit bei der Finanzierung der sozialen Sicherungssysteme', Report of the Commission, Berlin.
Federal Statistical Office of Germany (2003). 'Population of Germany Today and Tomorrow', Wiesbaden.
Fehr, H. (1999). *Welfare Effects of Dynamic Tax Reforms*. Tübingen: Mohr-Siebeck.

(2000). 'Pension Reform during the Demographic Transition'. *Scandinavian Journal of Economics*, 102: 419–43.

Fehr, H. and Habermann, C. (2006). 'Pension Reform and Demographic Uncertainty: The Case of Germany'. *Journal of Pension Economics and Finance*, 5: 69–90.

Fehr, H. and Halder, G. (2006). 'Reforming Long-term Care in Germany'. *Applied Economics Quarterly*, 52: 75–98.

Fehr, H., Jokisch, S. and Kotlikoff, L. J. (2005). 'The Developed World's Demographic Transition – the Roles of Capital Flows, Immigration, and Policy', in *Social Security Reform*, ed. R. Brooks and A. Razin. Cambridge: Cambridge University Press, pp. 11–43.

Institut der Deutschen Wirtschaft (2005). 'Deutschland in Zahlen', Cologne.

Knell, M. (2005). 'High Age – No Kids, Demographic Adjustment Factors for Sustainable PAYG Systems', Austrian National Bank, Vienna.

8   Longevity adjustment of pension benefits

Jukka Lassila and Tarmo Valkonen

Introduction

An increase in the life expectancy of elderly individuals can put a strain on the finances of a defined-benefit pension system if it means there are more retired people receiving benefits. In a pay-as-you-go (PAYG) system this increases the contribution levels. In anticipation of future increases in life expectancy, several countries have passed laws that automatically adjust pensions if life expectancy changes. The aim is to preserve the expected present value of future pensions. If benefits are received for more years, pensions per year will be lower.

The popularity of this type of adjustment among policy planners is easy to understand – it is likely to cut pension expenditure significantly if current trends in mortalities continue. In the eyes of the public it can also be defended with an intergenerational fairness argument, because changes in life expectancies would have smaller effects on the present values of future pensions of different cohorts.

In countries that have applied longevity adjustment or are considering doing so, its expected effects have been investigated in some detail. However, the fact that future mortality developments are uncertain has not received much attention. For pension contribution rates this is not a serious deficiency; the adjustment itself takes care of most of this uncertainty. But this uncertainty does exist for monthly pension benefits and replacement rates. Although the size of the adjustment will usually evolve slowly over time, it is worthwhile trying to form a picture of the effects well in advance. What has been missing thus far is an analysis that explicitly aims at both the expected implications and the risk-sharing properties of longevity adjustment when it is applied to actual populations and actual pension systems, at the same time considering the

We thank Peter Broer for fruitful comments and Juha Alho for providing us with his stochastic population simulations. We acknowledge financial support from the Ministry of Social Affairs and Health in Finland and the European Commission.

interaction between the economy, demography and the pension system rules.

We study the economic effects of longevity adjustment under demographic uncertainty, using as an example the recently reformed Finnish earnings-related pension system, where, from 2010 onwards, new old-age pensions will be affected by longevity adjustments.

First we describe the practical applications of longevity adjustment in other countries and review previous research. Then we depict the Finnish pension system and the simulation model. After that we consider the economic effects of longevity adjustment and draw conclusions.

How to adjust pensions to changes in longevity?

Details of longevity adjustment define the risk-sharing properties

Increased longevity is by itself a positive phenomenon. Besides being an indication of higher healthy life expectancy, the increased number of potential working years allows extended use of accumulated human capital. However, an increase in longevity weakens the sustainability of defined-benefit pension systems by adding to the number of pensioners and pension expenditure. The pressure to raise contribution rates may be alleviated by several policy measures. Each has different intergenerational risk-sharing properties.

Auerbach and Hassett (2001) suggest pre-funding or precautionary saving as the optimal policy against longevity risks. Due to demographic uncertainty, the precision of such up-front measures is, however, limited. In general, the desirability of waiting before policy action depends on whether the future brings a resolution of uncertainty or whether new shocks simply replace the old (Auerbach and Hassett, 2002).

In PAYG-financed pension systems the most often used reform option is to raise discretionarily the eligibility ages for pension benefits. This necessitates unpopular political decisions, which may have to be repeated since future longevity is uncertain. Political dispute can be avoided by linking the set retirement age to longevity, but this may even increase the welfare losses if the optimal retirement age varies a lot between individuals e.g. because of health, wealth or productivity differences (see Diamond, 2001).

Andersen (2005) suggests that optimal risk-sharing requires an actuarial scheme in which pensions are proportional to the expected lifetime, but the present value of pension entitlements is independent of the actual retirement age. Diamond and Orszag (2003) claim that this type of full longevity adjustment would harm the pensioners too much and propose dividing the costs of longer life times equally between benefits and contributions.

The exact details of the longevity adjustment are important for the risk-sharing properties. Adjustment of currently paid pensions with continuously updated life expectancy estimates would be problematic for retired persons; the 'demographic factor' suggested in the German Pension Act of 1999 is such a measure.

Another policy option is to let people decide when to retire (with actuarial determination of pensions), but at the same time improve the financial sustainability of the system by adjusting pensions to the expected longevity of the cohort at the time of retirement. This allows the possibility of reacting to surprises by adjusting the labour supply. There are two alternatives for the indicator of future longevity. The first is to use official cohort projections and the second is to use known *ex post* cross-sectional survival data.

Cohort projections are in use in Latvia. The process of creating projections should be transparent in order to deter political interventions (see Palmer, 2005). Lindell (2003) notes that it is not fair to adjust pensions following possibly erroneous longevity forecasts.

Use of observed data provides stronger protection from political intervention and is therefore preferred in the current Finnish and Swedish statutory earnings-related pension systems. The obvious problem is the lagging implementation of adjustments if longevity continues to increase. This slow reaction is most evident in defined-contribution or notional defined-contribution systems, where the pension capital is divided by life expectancy.

However, in the case of defined-benefit systems, this approach may still be preferable since it generates larger expected cuts to future pensions than the adjustments based on forecasted longevity. The reason is that the increase in longevity has already taken place in the base period's forecasts, but not in the observed mortality rates (see Lassila and Valkonen, 2003).

Longevity adjustment in Sweden

The Swedish pension reform of the 1990s has made longevity adjustment common knowledge in international pension circles. However, the instrument is just one part of a larger concept, the notional defined-contribution (NDC) system, which contains other automatic adjustment mechanisms as well. Although we are concentrating on longevity adjustment, its role and effects cannot fully be understood separately from the whole system.

In the Swedish pension system, the NDC part includes explicit rules that state how the mortality risk and the overall sustainability risk due to unfavourable population trends are distributed between benefits and contributions and over time.

Longevity adjustment, together with a flexible retirement age, is an essential part of the pension strategy. This adjustment is applied to the cumulative balance of the nominal account of an employee at the time of retirement. The balance is changed to an annuity, using the average life expectancy of the cohort and an imputed real rate of growth of 1.6 per cent. This imputed growth makes the annuity front-loaded: part of the expected value of the benefit stream, given the life expectancy and the 1.6 per cent growth factor, is shifted from the future to the present. The growth factor represents assumed real earned income growth. If the actual growth of real incomes is higher (lower) than 1.6 per cent, the benefit is adjusted upwards (downwards). In addition, the annuity is indexed to consumer prices, so that over the lifetime the indexation actually produces a result similar to full wage indexation. The adjustment is likely to cut pension expenditures markedly and to eliminate a major part of the variation in the contribution rate due to changes in mortality rates.

The longevity adjustment and the indexation rule leave some demographic risks to be carried by the contribution rate. Since variation in the contribution rate would be problematic in a defined-contribution system, an additional automatic balancing mechanism was created. Normally the balance in the individual account is indexed to per-capita income growth. The automatic adjustment mechanism will lower the indexation as long as the financial sustainability of the system is in danger.

The Swedish Social Insurance Agency created a large number of scenarios (72) for the future of the pension system before the automatic balancing was settled (Settergren, 2000). Uncertainty in these scenarios was related to demographics, economic growth, the labour force participation ratio and the yield of the buffer fund. Many of the studied scenarios led to the use of the balancing mechanism. The problem with this type of scenario approach is that it does not allow the attachment of any probability assessments to the results.

Other countries that are applying the adjustment include Latvia, Poland, Italy and Finland. Switzerland is planning to adopt it, and a proposal to adopt it in a defined-benefit pension scheme has been made by a pension committee in Norway.

Previous economic analysis of longevity adjustment

Previous analysis of the economic impacts of longevity adjustment has mostly been based on actuarial models, with arbitrarily chosen demographic variants. However, some exceptions are discussed below.

Lassila and Valkonen (2002) analysed the economic effects of longevity adjustment with a numerical overlapping model describing the pension system and economy of Lithuania. Future population paths were extracted from a stochastic population forecast. Thereby, the study aimed to forecast both the expected outcomes and the risk-sharing properties of the measure. It turned out that both the expected welfare losses and the changes in risks are small compared with individuals' lifetime resources. Future generations are expected to gain even though pension benefits are cut, since the lower contributions more than compensate for this. Cohorts near retirement will suffer the biggest expected welfare losses and the uncertainty of the scale of losses due to demographic uncertainty is also the largest for those generations. Lassila and Valkonen (2007) analysed the Finnish pension reform of 2005 using the same approach, but did not isolate the effects of longevity adjustment.

Fehr and Habermann (2006) used a similar method to analyse continuous adjustment of pensions for longevity ('demographic factor') by changing indexation. If ever implemented, this measure would allow the extension of incidence to currently retired generations. Still the main welfare losses and largest variation in welfare are again allocated to the middle-aged generations. The smallness of the welfare changes was also evident in these results. Other simulations based on just one population projection suggest a similar timing of expected welfare changes (Hirte, 2002; Bonin and Feist, 2003).

The issue of adjusting pensions for longevity has also been raised in the United States. Diamond and Orszag (2003) present a reform package that proposes that impacts of longevity should be divided equally between benefits and contributions. The economic outcomes of the proposal have been simulated with an actuarial model by the US Congressional Budget Office (CBO, 2004). These simulations are based on a probability distribution of possible future outcomes for the various demographic and economic assumptions used in the projections. It is impossible to isolate the impact of longevity adjustment of benefits, but it is likely to contribute markedly to the observed reduction in uncertainty.

Harris and Simpson (2005) simulated intra- and intergenerational redistribution outcomes of three pension policy measures, one of them being full longevity adjustment. These simulations utilized deterministic population forecasts. Progressive longevity indexing, which uses life expectancies by economic groups, has also been discussed in the United States.

Methodology

The Finnish earnings-related pension system

The earnings-related pension system aims to provide sufficient retirement income to cover consumption comparable to levels enjoyed during-working years and to current workers' consumption. It covers risks related to old age, disability and death of family earners. In cases where the earnings-related pension is absent or insufficient, the national pension guarantees a minimum income. Both of these first-pillar systems are mandatory. Voluntary pensions are still of minor importance in Finland but are becoming more common. Below we describe the private-sector earnings-related system. Public-sector pension systems are becoming similar, except that funding is different and there are long transition periods from old benefit rules. A more detailed presentation of the Finnish pension system can be found in Hietaniemi and Vidlund (2003).

Benefits The pensions can be thought of as consisting of both disability pensions and old-age pensions. Every year's earnings and accrual rates directly affect the future pension. The accrual rate is 1.5% per year between the ages of 18 and 52 and 1.9% between the ages of 53 and 62. Between the ages of 63 and 68 the accrual is 4.5% per year, with the aim of rewarding later retirement in a cost-neutral way.

Both pension rights and benefits are index-linked, with 80:20 weights on wages and consumer prices respectively during the working years and 20:80 weights after retirement, irrespective of retirement age. In the model, function $I(t, u, \lambda)$ states that the change in wages w from period t to period u is weighted by λ and the change in consumer prices p is weighted by $1 - \lambda$. Employee's contributions e are deducted from wages in this calculation.

$$I(t, u, \lambda) = \left(\frac{w(u)\,(1 - e(u))}{w(t)\,(1 - e(t))} \right)^{\lambda} \left(\frac{p(u)}{p(t)} \right)^{1-\lambda} \tag{1}$$

We denote the accruals with $k(x)$, where x refers to age. If retirement occurs because of disability, the pensioner is compensated for lost future accruals. The compensation depends on the age at the time of the disability event; we denote it by $f(z)$ where z refers to the age during the last working period. After receipt of the disability pension for five years there is a permanent increase in the pension. This increase is 21 per cent for a person aged 26 or less, and progressively less for older persons, so that those aged 56 or more get no increase. This feature is denoted by $a(x, z)$. Thus the pension benefit b, without longevity adjustment, for an individual i in age group x who retired at age $z + 1$ and had earned wage incomes denoted by y is:

$$b_i(t, x, z) = a(x, z) \sum_{s=1}^{z} k(s)y_i(t - s)(1 - e(t - s))I(t - s, t - x + z, 0.8)$$
$$\times\ I(t - x + z, t, 0.2) + a(x, z)f(z)y_i(t - x + z)$$
$$\times\ (1 - e(t - x + z))I(t - x + z, t, 0.2) \qquad (2)$$

where $x > z$.

Longevity adjustment The pensions are adjusted for increasing life expectancy simply by taking the increasing longevity into account in the value of the annuity. The adjustment coefficient is a ratio of two present values of a unit pension, calculated at two different periods. The present value of a unit pension, which begins in period t and is calculated forward from age 62, is:

$$A(t, 62) = \sum_{s=63}^{100} S(t - 1, 62, s)/(1.02)^{s-62} \qquad (3)$$

The present value of a unit pension is a discounted sum of terms generated during various retirement years. The terms have two parts. The first term, S, expresses the survival probability from age 62 to age s, and the first subscript of the term demonstrates that the probability is evaluated using information available in period t, when the latest observed mortalities are from period $t - 1$. The survival probabilities are actually five-year moving averages. The second term is the discount factor where the discount rate is 2 per cent per year. In the model, individuals die at the age of 100 at the latest.

The pension of a person born in period $t - 62$ is multiplied by the longevity adjustment coefficient $E(t, 62)$ after age 62. The coefficient is a ratio of two A-terms:

$$E(t, 62) = A(2009, 62)/A(t, 62) \qquad (4)$$

The median Md, the first and third quartiles, Q_1 and Q_3, and the first and ninth deciles, d_1 and d_9, for the predictive distribution of the adjustment

factors in 2030 and 2050, calculated from the 500 population paths in
this study, are:

	d_1	Q_1	Md	Q_3	d_9
2030	0.86	0.89	0.91	0.95	0.98
2050	0.79	0.82	0.87	0.91	0.97

Because of a shorter forecast horizon, the distribution is slightly narrower
than that of Alho (2003). We expect the adjustment coefficient to decline
to about 0.87 in 2050, with an 80 per cent prediction interval [0.79, 0.97].
These intervals are valid providing the volatility of the trends of mortality
during the next fifty years does not exceed the volatility of mortality during
the period 1900–1994.

Pre-funding on the individual level The Finnish earnings-related
system has collected substantial funds to smooth the contribution
increases due to population ageing in the future. Funding is collective
but based on individual pension rights. Individual pension benefits do
not depend on the existence or yield of funds. Funds only affect contributions. When a person receives a pension after the age of 65, their funds
are used to pay that part of the pension benefit that was pre-funded. The
rest comes from the PAYG part, the so-called 'pooled' component in the
contribution rate.

Equation (5) describes new funding for an individual i. A share g of
the present value of the pension right accruing in period t to workers in
the age range 18–54 is put in the funds. The present value includes all
old-age pension years, from 65 to a maximum age, assumed to be 100.
The labour income y creates a pension right for each year in old age.
Discounting includes both the so-called 'fund rate of interest' q, which
is administratively set, and survival probabilities S. For pre-funding purposes, the magnitude of the pension right is evaluated ignoring all future
changes due to wage or price developments. Thus the value of the right
is simply k times the labour income, without the employee contribution
part, for each retirement year:

$$h_i(t, x) = g \sum_{s=65}^{100} k(x) y_i(t)(1 - e(t)) S(t - 1, x, s)/(1 + q)^{s-x} \quad (5)$$

where $x = 18, \ldots, 54$.

Equation (6) states that for a retired person the amounts pre-funded
earlier (when the current pensioner was between the ages of 18 and 54)
for period t's pension, with the interest accrued to them with rate r and
leading to a total amount v, is used to pay a part of the person's pension. The interest accrued is assumed here to be constant for a simpler

exposition. In practice it follows approximately the average market yield plus a margin, and must not be lower than the fund rate in equation (5).

$$v_i(t, x) = \sum_{s=18}^{54} gk(s)y_i(t - x + s)(1 - e(t - x + s))$$

$$\times S(t - x + s - 1, x - s, x)(1 + q)^{s-x}(1 + r)^{x-s} \quad (6)$$

where $x = 65, \ldots, 100$.

Contribution and replacement rates The equations (5) and (6) are important for the aggregate dynamics of the pension system, especially for the level and time path of the contribution rates.

Let $n(t, x)$ be the number of workers and $\bar{h}(t, x)$ the average amount of new funding per worker of age x in period t. The total amount of new funding in period t is obtained by multiplying the average individual funding in age-group x by the number of workers in the age-group, and summing over all age-groups where funding takes place. Analogously, $m(t, x)$ is the number of retired persons and $\bar{v}(t, x)$ is the average amount withdrawn from the funds per retired person in each age-group, and the total amount withdrawn from the funds is obtained by multiplying the average withdrawals by the number of retired persons and summing over relevant age-groups. Three other aggregates are defined in a similar fashion: the total wage bill from which the pension contributions are collected, denoting the average wage income at age x by $\bar{y}(t, x)$; the total amount of earnings-related pension expenditure, denoting the average pension of retired persons by $\bar{b}(t, x)$; and the total amount of other transfers from the pension sector, denoting the average transfer per person by $\bar{s}(t, x)$.

The time path of the contribution rates is given by equation (7). Besides employees, employers must also pay contributions, which we denote by $c(t)$, based on the wage bill. The left-hand side of the equation is the total amount of contributions. This must be sufficient to cover that part of the pension expenditure (first term on the right-hand side) that does not come from withdrawals from the funds (second term), plus new funding (third term), plus transfers (the final term).

$$[c(t) + e(t)] \sum_{x=18}^{64} n(t, x)\bar{y}(t, x)$$

$$= \sum_{x=18}^{100} m(t, x)\bar{b}(t, x) - \sum_{x=65}^{100} m(t, x)\bar{v}(t, x)$$

$$+ \sum_{x=18}^{54} n(t, x)\bar{h}(t, x) + \sum_{x=18}^{100} [n(t, x) + m(t, x)]\bar{s}(t, x) \quad (7)$$

Employer contributions were on average 16.8 per cent, and employee contributions 4.6 per cent of wages in 2004. Future changes have been agreed to be shared 50:50 between employers and employees. Since 2005, employees aged 53 and over pay contributions that are about 1.27 times that of younger employees, reflecting their higher accrual.

From this point on, when we speak about *the* contribution rate we mean the sum of employer and employee contribution rates, where the latter is weighted from the age-dependent rates with corresponding revenue shares. By the replacement rate in age group x we mean the ratio of the average pension of retired persons $\bar{b}(t, x)$ to the average wage income $\bar{y}(t)$ of all workers.

As an intergenerational measure of the connection between benefits and contributions, we define the following. The actuarity rate is the ratio of a cohort's discounted benefits from the pension system to its discounted sum of payments to the pension system. The benefits include all pensions and transfers from the earnings-related pension system. Denoting the interest rate by r, the actuarity rate AR for the cohort born in period t is:

$$
AR(t)
= \frac{\sum\limits_{x=18}^{100} m(t+x, x)\bar{b}(t+x, x)(1+r)^{-x} + \sum\limits_{x=18}^{100} [n(t+x, x) + m(t+x, x)]\bar{s}(t+x, x)(1+r)^{-x}}{[c(t+x) + e(t+x)] \sum\limits_{x=18}^{64} n(t+x, x)\bar{y}(t+x, x)(1+r)^{-x}}
$$

(8)

The economic model

We simulate the economic impacts of introducing longevity adjustment using a perfect-foresight numerical overlapping-generations model of the type originated by Auerbach and Kotlikoff (1987). There are five sectors: households, enterprises, a government, a pension fund and a foreign sector. The labour, goods and capital markets are competitive and prices balance supply and demand period-by-period. There is no money or inflation in the model. Households and firms are forward-looking decision-makers. The unit period is five years, and the model has sixteen adult generations living in each period.

The model is adjusted to imitate the Finnish economy by a process of calibration. First, parameters for household behaviour (e.g. preference for leisure) and production technology (e.g. substitutability of capital and labour) are extracted from the economic literature and used to generate numerical versions of those model equations describing the dynamics of the economy. The current and future household cohorts are then aggregated using population statistics and forecasts. Finally, the model is scaled so that the outcomes resemble the key macro-economic, public-sector and household statistics for recent years. The earnings-related pension system is gradually brought into the model starting from the 1960s.

Household behaviour Individuals make economic decisions according to the life-cycle hypothesis. They maximize the utility from consumption and leisure in different periods and the bequests that they make. The lifetime budget constraint says that discounted lifetime net wage and pension income and discounted received bequests and transfers equal discounted consumption expenditure and bequests made. Households consider the possibility of early death by discounting future consumption and incomes by a factor that includes both the interest rate and the age-specific survival probability.

Retirement occurs at the age of 65 at the latest. At ages below 60 an exogenous share of persons, increasing with age, retire due to disability. There is also an endogenous retirement decision in the 60–64 age-group. In that group the price of leisure, besides lost wage income and discounted effects on future pensions, also includes the amount of pension one can have if retiring then. Part of the leisure so decided is interpreted as a decline in the share of people working, and the share of those retiring at the age of 65 is reduced correspondingly. The elasticity of retirement to early pensions (and resulting changes in future pensions) is calibrated to observed behaviour in Finland between 1970 and 2004, taking into account the developments in the unemployment rate at ages 60–64 and changes in the eligibility and other rules of unemployment pensions and early old-age pensions.

Decision problem for firms Firms choose the optimal amount of investment and use of labour to maximize the price of their shares. The market value of the firm is determined as a discounted sum of future dividends. The problem can be presented as maximizing at the beginning of the period the dividends distributed during the period plus the value of the firm at the end of the period, subject to the amount of initial capital stock, the cash-flow equation of the firm, the CES production function, the accumulation condition of the capital stock, the determination of the firm's debt and the investment adjustment costs.

Markets The model includes four markets, which clear in every period. In the labour market, firms demand labour according to the marginal productivity of labour rule. Households' aggregate labour supply is divided between public and private employment. The wage rate is determined by equating supply and demand in the labour market.

Firms are the sole suppliers of the domestic good in the market. The product is used by other firms as part of the composite intermediate and investment goods, by households as part of the composite consumption good and by foreign agents. The domestic agents' demand and the prices of the composite goods are determined by a cost-minimizing procedure. Domestic demand for fixed-price imported goods is also determined by minimizing the costs of the composite goods. The perfectly elastic supply adjusts to demand in this market. The fourth market is the capital market, in which saving and investment are balanced by the domestic interest rate. In the simulations, we use a model version in which the interest rate is set equal to the rate in international capital markets. In this case, total saving is the sum of domestic saving and foreign portfolio investments.

The presentation above only describes the most relevant parts of the model. The actual model includes a local and a central government, both with intertemporal budget constraints, and trade and capital flows with the rest of the world.

The role of demographics Demographic information appears in several parts of the economic model. The most important areas are cohorts and age-structures, survival probabilities and aggregation over cohorts. The model keeps track of different cohorts of population throughout their adult ages. Survival probabilities are also important. The household variables, such as consumption, labour supply and wealth, are aggregated using population weights by age to obtain aggregate consumption, labour supply and household wealth. The aggregate wage bill, pensions, various taxes and transfers are obtained by analogous aggregation.

Demographics also affect the labour markets indirectly. Part of the labour input is used to provide health and long-term care services. This share depends on the number of elderly people, weighted by per-capita need of these services in different age-groups. Similarly, part of the labour input is used for education work, whose demand depends on the sizes of young cohorts. These parts of the labour input, which vary from one population path to another, reduce the labour available for private production and affect the wages that balance the demand and supply of labour.

Real wage growth varies between population paths, even though there is a common trend growth in total factor productivity. The only partial indexation of pension accruals and benefits directly affects the replacement rates. Thus there is considerable variation in all pension outcomes, even without longevity adjustment.

Table 8.1. *Contribution and replacement rates and longevity adjustment.*

	d_1	Q_1	Md	Q_3	d_9
Contribution rate					
2030–2034					
without longevity adjustment	26.77	28.03	29.19	30.15	31.14
with longevity adjustment	26.40	27.22	28.01	28.76	29.35
2050–2054					
without longevity adjustment	26.72	28.64	30.74	32.30	34.10
with longevity adjustment	25.80	26.82	27.84	28.90	29.86
Replacement rate					
2030–2034					
without longevity adjustment	48.89	49.17	49.51	49.89	50.20
with longevity adjustment	43.75	44.85	46.22	47.67	48.88
2050–2054					
without longevity adjustment	47.17	47.80	48.44	49.04	49.53
with longevity adjustment	38.90	40.56	42.68	45.01	47.73
Effect of longevity adjustment					
On contribution rates					
2030–2034	−1.86	−1.56	−1.14	−0.72	−0.32
2050–2054	−4.52	−3.71	−2.76	−1.70	−0.69
On replacement rates					
2030–2034	−5.44	−4.60	−3.30	−2.09	−0.89
2050–2054	−8.82	−7.42	−5.77	−3.74	−1.55

Economic effects of longevity adjustment in Finland

Pension contribution and replacement rates

We describe the influence of longevity adjustment on pension contribution and replacement rates using three types of indicators. First are the medians of the predictive distributions, which can be compared with the outcomes of deterministic analysis. Second, we study the fractiles of the predictive distributions in order to find changes in the variation of the target variables. Third, we discuss how the reform changes the risk-sharing between contributions and benefits in the Finnish pension system.

Typically, longevity increases in the demographic simulations we use. Thus the likely consequence of implementing the longevity adjustment is a decline in pension benefits. Table 8.1 shows this to be the case in Finland in relation to wages as well.[1] The median of the replacement rate after the adjustment is smaller than before the adjustment in both 2030 and 2050. Smaller benefits can be financed with smaller contributions, and indeed the median predicted contribution rate has also declined.

Longevity adjustment also affects the predictability of pension outcomes. The predictive distribution of the contribution rate narrows down. The 80 per cent predictive interval in 2050, for example, declines from 7.4 percentage points to 4.1 percentage points. The reduction is larger in cases of high old-age dependency ratios, which generate high contribution rates.

Table 8.1 shows that the uncertainty in future replacement rates increases. The 80 per cent predictive interval in 2050, for example, increases from 2.4 percentage points to 8.8 percentage points. Relative to the median, the interval increases almost fourfold. One should note that there is some uncertainty in replacement rates even without longevity adjustment, although the system is defined-benefit in nature. This is caused by the reactions of wages to the capital/labour ratio in production and to the terms of trade in foreign trade, which vary from one population path to another. Because of only partial indexing of accrued pension rights and also pension benefits to wages, the ratio of pensions to wage earnings becomes lower the higher the growth in wages.

Figure 8.1 gives a visual interpretation of the results in Table 8.1. The scatterplots describe the pension situation in Finland for the years 2030 and 2050. Each of the 500 dots represents one population path. The outcome makes it evident that longevity adjustment significantly weakens the defined-benefit (DB) property of the Finnish pension system and brings in a strong defined-contribution (DC) flavour.

Diamond (2005), commenting on the three-dimensional classification of pension systems by Lindbeck and Persson (2003), notes that the distinction between DB and DC systems is really a continuum, and one can adjust both benefits and contributions to the realized financial conditions. He suggests rephrasing the DB–DC dimension as 'adjustment to stochastic realizations' (Diamond, 2005, p. 76). The observation and suggestion are certainly supported by the results presented above.

Even though the shift from horizontal allocation to vertical allocation of the observations is evident in Figure 8.1, there is still a lot of variation in contribution rates, especially in the long run. This is because longevity adjustment deals only with uncertainty in mortality. The influence of fertility risk on the contribution rate remains and its importance increases in the long term, when its full effect on the size of the labour force is realized.[2] This fact should be kept in mind when considering the proposition by Diamond and Orszag (2003) of dividing the longevity risk in half between benefits and contributions.

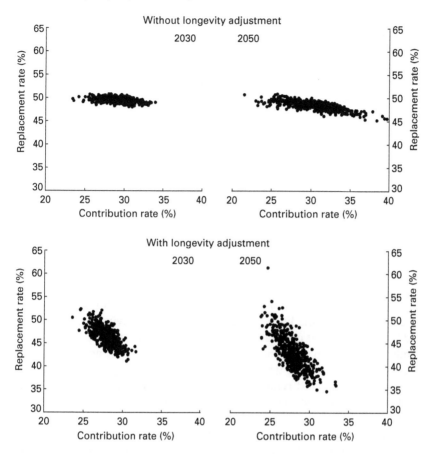

Figure 8.1. Pension contribution and replacement rates in Finland in 2030 and 2050.

The reduction in the contribution rate becomes greater the higher the rate would have been without the reform. Thus the longevity adjustment works very well as a cost-saver. Unfortunately, it does not work nearly as well as a benefit-setter: it reduces replacement rates in population paths where the rates are low to begin with, and increases the rates when they would be high anyway.

We have looked at sustainability by reporting contribution rates in some specific periods. Likewise, adequacy has been considered by showing replacement rates for some specific groups in some specific periods. Clearly, this is not sufficient for analysing the effects of policies. On the other hand, increasing the number of groups, periods and cohorts in a similar fashion to the above is probably not the answer – there is simply too much data. Thus we need summary measures.

There is a simple measure for sustainability: the 'sustainability gap'. It expresses a once-and-for-all change in the contribution rate that is needed to balance the pension system. The new contribution rate is calculated by dividing the present value of future contribution revenues by the present value of future wage bills.

For adequacy, we calculate a measure that uses the replacement rates in a base case scenario. Fixing the replacement rates from that scenario, we calculate the present value of pension expenditure in each population path and compare it with the actual present value for that path. We call the difference between the actual and hypothetical present values the 'adequacy gap', and express it as a percentage of the present value of the contribution base. Thus the gap gives the immediate and permanent change in contributions that is needed to finance replacement rates equal to those in the base case. With this definition, the adequacy gap is directly comparable to the sustainability gap.

Figure 8.2 shows how the measures correlate with life expectancy, measured by the size of the longevity adjustment factor in 2050. The lower the factor, the higher the life expectancy. Without longevity adjustment the adequacy gap is not correlated with life expectancy, whereas the sustainability gap is strongly correlated with it. With longevity adjustment, the adequacy gap increases with increasing life expectancy because monthly pensions are cut and replacement rates thus fall. This eases the effect of life expectancy on the sustainability gap considerably, but it does not remove it.

The bottom part of Figure 8.2 shows how the measures correlate with each other. Introducing longevity adjustment increases the variability of the adequacy gap and reduces the variability of the sustainability gap. In fact, comparing the ranges of the predictive distributions, we may conclude that in the Finnish system benefits take more than half and contributions less than half of adjustment to demographic realizations, when measured by contribution equivalents. Without longevity adjustment the benefits would take about 5 per cent of adjustment as a consequence of less-than-full indexing to earnings, and contributions about 95 per cent. This striking result shows that it is important to analyse quantitatively the dynamic properties of pension systems under a wide range of demographic developments.

There is one usually less discussed, but important, detail in the gap calculations. Most population forecasts extend to the year 2050. They describe a large change in population structure, ending in much higher

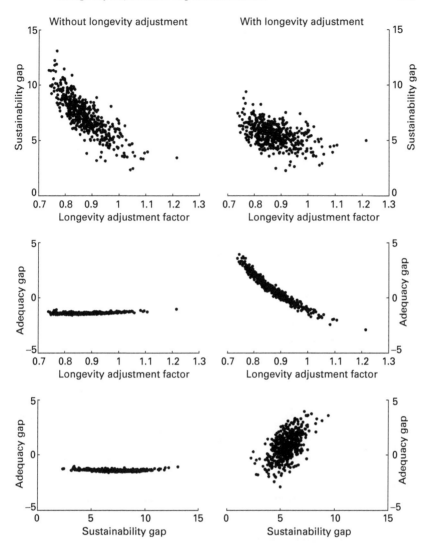

Figure 8.2. Sustainability and adequacy.

old-age ratios. Assuming the change in the age ratio is permanent, the choice of the time horizon in the gap calculations markedly influences the outcome. We have measured the gaps using a range of ninety-five years. Limiting the horizon to the year 2050 would have reduced the adequacy gap to approximately half (see Table 8.2).

Table 8.2. *Sustainability and adequacy gaps and longevity adjustment.*

	d_1	Q_1	Md	Q_3	d_9
Sustainability gap					
2005–2050					
without longevity adjustment	4.31	5.12	5.90	6.57	7.15
with longevity adjustment	4.05	4.46	4.96	5.40	5.75
2005–2100					
without longevity adjustment	5.06	6.24	7.28	8.34	9.50
with longevity adjustment	4.28	4.95	5.59	6.18	6.73
2005–2150					
without longevity adjustment	5.42	6.63	7.74	8.76	9.90
with longevity adjustment	4.57	5.15	5.73	6.30	6.78
Adequacy gap					
2005–2050					
without longevity adjustment	−0.71	−0.67	−0.63	−0.59	−0.54
with longevity adjustment	−0.30	0.03	0.40	0.77	1.07
2005–2100					
without longevity adjustment	−1.49	−1.45	−1.41	−1.36	−1.31
with longevity adjustment	−0.80	0.03	0.79	1.53	2.29
2005–2150					
without longevity adjustment	−1.73	−1.68	−1.62	−1.55	−1.49
with longevity adjustment	−0.93	0.05	0.92	1.81	2.61
Effect of longevity adjustment					
On sustainability gap					
2005–2050	−1.46	−1.19	−0.89	−0.56	−0.23
2005–2100	−2.91	−2.35	−1.76	−1.15	−0.41
2005–2150	−3.32	−2.72	−2.00	−1.30	−0.48
On adequacy gap					
2005–2050	0.28	0.65	1.03	1.39	1.71
2005–2100	0.52	1.45	2.22	2.98	3.70
2005–2150	0.60	1.66	2.56	3.48	4.26

Intergenerational fairness

The Finnish earnings-related pension system was started in 1962, and the first participants get more out than they have paid in, as is usual in (partly) PAYG arrangements. Their actuarity rates are greater than 1 under all demographic futures considered. All further cohorts are likely to have actuarity rates below 1 and thus pay more than they will get back.

Figure 8.3 presents the actuarity rates and their changes for three cohorts. The boxes in the left column plot the actuarity rates for population paths with and without longevity adjustment against each

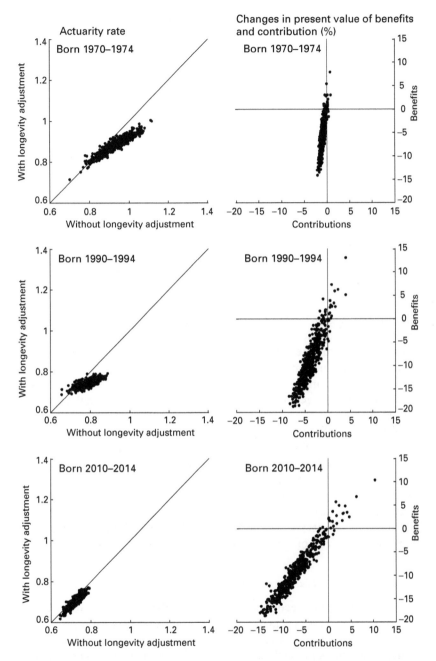

Figure 8.3. The effect of longevity adjustment on the actuary rates of three cohorts.

other. It is useful to first look at the position and scattering of the dots before considering the measure. Actuarity rate medians for successive generations decline due to the PAYG principle and population ageing. The variation also declines. There is practically no variation in the contributions paid by the oldest working-age cohorts, but the longevity risk affects the present value of their future benefits. For the younger generations, the contributions start to react to demographic scenarios. Since benefits and contributions are positively correlated, the actuarity rate risk becomes smaller.

A dot below the diagonal means that longevity adjustment lowers the actuarity rate of the cohort in that particular population path. The actuarity rates of cohorts born in the 1970s and 1990s (and in between) are likely to be reduced. For cohorts born between 2000 and 2030 the changes are minimal, and the cohorts born after 2030 are expected to win in the form of higher actuarity rates.

The right-column boxes break the changes in the actuarity rate down into corresponding changes in the present values of benefits and contributions. The cohort born in 1970 is likely to experience quite a large loss in lifetime benefits but only a small reduction in contributions. The benefit cuts are largest for the future generations, but their overall outcome will be positive because of the even bigger reductions in contributions.

Longevity adjustment limits the benefits in an actuarially fair way. As it scales down the pension system, which is unsustainable, it improves efficiency in the long term. But the incentives to work more are actually weakened for those generations that are near retirement when the measure is introduced.

As a summary measure for intergenerational equality we use a standard inequality measure, the Gini coefficient. We calculate it using cohort-wise actuarity rates as data. The results are in Table 8.3. Longevity adjustment has an extremely small effect on that measure. If we were to include more future cohorts in the calculation, it is likely that the Gini coefficients would become smaller on average. That would mean, however, using population forecasts well beyond the year 2135, which itself is already far beyond the horizon of genuine stochastic population forecasts.

Saving and labour supply

The most important economic reaction to the implementation of the reform is the increase in saving, which initially lowers consumption. The main reason for extra saving is the need for old-age consumption, but for future generations in particular the role of larger net wages generated by lower pension contributions is also evident.

Table 8.3. *Actuarity rates and generational equality.*

	d_1	Q_1	Md	Q_3	d_9
Actuarity rate					
Born 1970–1974					
without longevity adjustment	0.84	0.89	0.93	0.98	1.02
with longevity adjustment	0.83	0.86	0.89	0.92	0.94
Born 1990–1994					
without longevity adjustment	0.74	0.76	0.79	0.81	0.84
with longevity adjustment	0.72	0.73	0.75	0.76	0.77
Born 2010–2014					
without longevity adjustment	0.69	0.70	0.72	0.74	0.75
with longevity adjustment	0.67	0.69	0.71	0.72	0.74
Gini coefficient					
without longevity adjustment	0.112	0.118	0.127	0.136	0.143
with longevity adjustment	0.114	0.121	0.129	0.139	0.147

Note: Calculated from actuarity rates of five-year cohorts born between 1940 and 2034.

Changes in the aggregate labour supply are, by contrast, quite small. Implementation of the reform reduces the additional pension benefit gained by a marginal increase in the labour supply, but it also provides a higher net wage because of lower contributions. The divergent income and substitution effects just about cancel each other out.

At least in Finland, Norway and Sweden, longevity adjustment has been described in terms of the number of extra months each cohort needs to work in order to cancel the adjustment effect on pensions. From a theoretical point of view there is no reason why a rational person would like to 'cancel' one element among the many that affect the benefit level. In practice, however, marketing the issue may have a bearing on behaviour. In any case, it is important to assess what effect longevity adjustment has on the effective retirement age. In our model, retirement is endogenous in the 60–64 age group, which facilitates analysing how retirement changes.

Lassila and Valkonen (2005) analysed the Finnish pension reform of 2005, which included several elements. The marginal effect of longevity adjustment on retirement age varied, depending on the base case. If the comparison was with the old system, which broadly speaking had poor incentives for remaining at work in old age, longevity adjustment raised the effective retirement age slightly. But when the comparison was made with the new system (without longevity adjustment), adding longevity adjustment lowered the retirement age a little. The new system improved incentives to continue working, and cutting benefits by longevity adjustment reduces this reward.

The analysis in Lassila and Valkonen (2005) was made with just one demographic projection. Repeating the exercise using 500 population paths gives similar results. The retirement age declines more when the adjustment is larger. In the model, people do not compensate for the cut by postponing retirement; rather, they react by retiring earlier. But they work more when young, and the overall labour supply effects are minimal. Retirement age effects concern the timing of the work more than the amount of work over the life cycle. The changes in retirement age are usually less than 0.1 years, in practice one month or less. Note that this analysis ignores the possibility that increasing life expectancy may well be linked to factors that also increase work efficiency at older ages, thus making potential wages higher and postponing retirement.

Conclusions

We have analysed the effects of longevity adjustment using the Finnish earnings-related pension system as an example. The analysis has been carried out by simulations under uncertain future demographics.

Our results confirm the earlier results of the expected effects of longevity adjustment: it cuts future benefits and thus facilitates a decrease in future contributions. The current middle-aged generations, whose pensions are reduced more than contributions, experience the largest welfare losses. The full gains are observed far in the future.

Besides demographic realizations, the quantitative results depend on the specifics of the pension system. They also depend on the assumptions and features of the model, especially how the agents react to changes in pension policies and how the labour markets behave.

Longevity adjustment usually reduces the contribution rates, and the reduction is bigger the higher the rate would have been without the reform. Thus longevity adjustment works very nicely as a cost saver. On the other hand, contribution rates are higher in demographic worlds where labour is scarce, wages higher and replacement rates lower. Thus longevity adjustment increases the uncertainty in replacement rates. In the long run, the ratio of discounted benefits and contributions is not much affected by the measure since the induced changes in benefits and contributions are highly correlated.

Longevity adjustment significantly weakens the defined-benefit nature of the Finnish pension system and brings in a strong defined-contribution flavour. But it is important to note that demographic uncertainty in itself reduces the defined-benefit feature. Fertility risks, and other risks that may cause changes in wage trends, are important here; without them, and without longevity adjustment, the Finnish system would be very close to DB, and adopting longevity adjustment then would make the system very close to DC. But because fertility risks are significant, adopting longevity adjustment means a shift towards DC while keeping within a mixed state.

The relative timing of longevity and fertility risks is also important. For the next twenty to thirty years the effects of future fertility changes on pension outcomes are small. Longevity adjustment then narrows down the dominant uncertainty effect of demographics. After thirty years future fertility starts to affect the labour supply more, and longevity adjustment alone is inadequate in controlling the effects of demographic risks. In countries where migration risks are large, the practical significance of this timing feature is reduced.

NOTES

1 Replacement rate is measured here by the ratio of average pension income of 65- to 69-year-old people to the average wage income of 20- to 59-year-old people. The average pension income combines pensions that may have started as disability pensions for some young or middle-aged people and then changed to old-age pensions, and pensions that have started directly as old-age pensions for those at eligible ages. Thus the replacement rate here does not describe the pension of a full-career worker relative to his last or average wage income.
2 A comparable defined-benefit pension scheme rule that redistributes the fertility risk more equally between generations is indexation of pensions to the wage bill (see Alho *et al.*, 2005).

REFERENCES

Alho, J. M. (2003). 'Predictive Distribution of Adjustment for Life Expectancy Change'. Working Paper 3, *Finnish Centre for Pensions*, Helsinki.
Alho, J. M., Jensen, S. E. H., Lassila, J. and Valkonen, T. (2005). 'Controlling the Effects of Demographic Risks: the Role of Pension Indexation Schemes'. *Journal of Pension Economics and Finance*, 4(2): 139–53.
Andersen, T. (2005). 'Social Security and Longevity', CESifo Working Paper no. 1577, Ifo Institute for Economic Research, Munich.
Auerbach, A. J. and Hassett, K. (2001). 'Uncertainty and the Design of Long-Run Fiscal Policy', in *Demographic Change and Fiscal Policy*, ed. A. J. Auerbach and R. D. Lee. Cambridge: Cambridge University Press, pp. 73–92.
    (2002). 'Optimal Long-Run Fiscal Policy: Constraints, Preferences and the Resolution of Uncertainty', Working Paper no. B02–10, Robert D. Burch Center for Tax Policy and Public Finance, University of California, Berkeley.
Auerbach, A. J. and Kotlikoff, L. J. (1987). *Dynamic Fiscal Policy*. Cambridge: Cambridge University Press.
Bonin, H. and Feist, K. (2003). 'Measuring Redistribution Between Living Generations: The Case of German Pension Reform', in *Pension Reform:*

Redistribution and Risk, ed. M. Weale. Occasional Paper no. 56. London: NIESR, pp. 40–67.

CBO (2004). 'Long-term Analysis of the Diamond–Orszag Social Security Plan', Congressional Budget Office, Washington, DC.

Diamond P. A. (2001). 'Comment', in *Demographic Change and Fiscal Policy*, ed. A. J. Auerbach and R. D. Lee. Cambridge: Cambridge University Press, pp. 93–7.

(2005). 'Conceptualization of Non-Financial Defined Contribution Systems', in *Pension Reform: Issues and Prospects for Non-Financial Defined Contribution (NDC) Schemes*, ed. R. Holzmann and E. Palmer. Washington, DC: World Bank, pp. 76–80.

Diamond, P. A. and Orszag, P. R. (2003). *Saving Social Security, A Balanced Approach*. Washington, DC: Brookings Institution Press.

Fehr, H. and Habermann, C. (2006). 'Pension Reform and Demographic Uncertainty: The Case of Germany'. *Journal of Pension Economics and Finance*, 5: 69–90.

Harris, A. R. and Simpson, M. (2005). 'Winners and Losers under Various Approaches to Slowing Social Security Benefit Growth'. *National Tax Journal*, 58: 523–43.

Hietaniemi, M. and Vidlund, M. (2003), eds. *The Finnish Pension System*. Helsinki: Finnish Centre for Pensions.

Hirte, G. (2002). 'Welfare and Macroeconomic Effects of the German Pension Act of 1992 and 1999 – A Dynamic CGE Study'. *German Economic Review*, 3: 81–106.

Lassila, J. and Valkonen, T. (2002). 'Ageing Policies and Demographic Uncertainty in Lithuania: A Dynamic CGE Analysis'. Available at www.etla.fi/lithuania.

(2003). 'Ageing, Demographic Risks and Pension Reform', in *Pension Reform: Redistribution and Risk*, ed. M. Weale. Occasional Paper no. 56. London: NIESR, pp. 119–66.

(2005). 'Yksityisalojen eläkeuudistuksen taloudelliset vaikutukset' (The Economic Effects of the Private Sector Pension Reform in Finland). ETLA B 211, Helsinki.

(2007). 'The Finnish Pension Reform of 2005'. *Geneva Papers on Risk and Insurance*. (Forthcoming.)

Lindbeck, A. and Persson, M. (2003). 'The Gains from Pension Reform'. *Journal of Economic Literature*, 41: 74–112.

Lindell, K. (2003). 'Longevity is Increasing – What about the Retirement Age?' *Working Paper no. 6, Finnish Centre for Pensions*, Helsinki.

Palmer, E. (2005). 'What is NDC?', in *Pension Reform: Issues and Prospects for Non-Financial Defined Contribution (NDC) Schemes*, ed. R. Holzmann and E. Palmer. Washington, DC: World Bank, pp. 17–33.

Settergren, O. (2000). *'Automatisk balansering av lderspensionssystemet. Redovisning av regeringens beräkningsuppdrag'*. *RFV Analyserar*, no. 1, National Social Insurance Board, Stockholm.

9   Ageing, demographic uncertainty and optimal fiscal policy

Alex Armstrong, Nick Draper, André Nibbelink and Ed Westerhout

Introduction

As with many other industrialized countries, the ageing population of the Netherlands is expected to render current fiscal policies unsustainable in the coming decades (Van Ewijk *et al.*, 2006). The sizeable changes in the ratio of retired persons to workers will increase demographically sensitive public expenditures beyond the ability of current revenue arrangements to cope. Adequate remedies may take a variety of forms like tax rate or contribution increases, spending reductions or institutional reforms.

Uncertainty in the scale and direction of future demographic developments presents an added problem to policy-makers because the magnitude of the required adjustments is not fully known. Possible strategies for dealing with this uncertainty include delaying policy reforms until the uncertainty is resolved or making adjustments based on the assumption that demography will develop according to the most likely scenario. In this chapter, however, we show that a government faced with demographic uncertainty whose interest is in maximizing the expected welfare of society should pursue a precautionary fiscal policy. A precautionary policy in this case involves front-loading taxes: that is, setting tax rates such that they are expected to decrease over time.

It is a well-known result in the public finance literature that a policy that smoothes tax rates over time minimizes the excess burden from distortionary taxation (Barro, 1979). This result holds if the government has perfect foresight about future revenue requirements. In an uncertain world, a policy that minimizes expected tax distortions will not in general meet the necessary condition for a socially optimal policy: expected marginal utility smoothing over time.

The authors wish to thank Peter Broer and Casper van Ewijk for their advice and assistance in the preparation of this study as well as the participants at the DEMWEL conferences in Copenhagen, Denmark (26–27 January 2006) and Kittila, Finland (21–23 March 2006).

Consumer theory suggests that future uncertainty may be a reason for households to engage in precautionary saving (Leland, 1968; Sandmo, 1970). In the simplest form of the theory, consumption levels while young are negatively correlated with the variance of future economic outcomes. However, this type of precautionary behaviour is typically assumed to occur over the life cycle and does not account for the intergenerational implications of uncertainty. As a result there may be a role for the government to act as an agent on behalf of future generations. In doing so, the government pursues a policy of fiscal precaution (Auerbach and Hassett, 2001; Steigum, 2001). If capital markets are complete, portfolio strategies can be constructed that completely eliminate future uncertainty by, in essence, insuring the government against unexpected shocks (Lucas and Stokey, 1983). In reality, markets are far from complete and it is an empirical issue to determine what gains can be achieved from portfolio strategies (Bohn, 1990).

Using a dynamic applied general equilibrium model of the Dutch economy in combination with stochastic population forecasts, we assess the utility loss to society arising from demographic uncertainty as it pertains to the fiscal system. It is demonstrated that this loss can be mitigated by increasing tax rates on presently living generations above the level required to sustain government finances in expectation. This analysis not only confirms the current theory on optimal dynamic taxation but also quantifies the magnitude of the problem, as well as the extent to which government policy can help to solve it. Gomes, Kotlikoff and Viceira (2006) use a simulation model to assess the welfare loss resulting from government procrastination in announcing policy decisions. However, as far as we are aware, ours is the first study to use simulation techniques combined with stochastic population forecasts to address the optimal fiscal response to social risk resulting from demographic uncertainty.

The chapter is organized as follows. The next section briefly discusses the dynamic applied general equilibrium model that we use for our simulations. This is followed by a description of the projected development of the Dutch economy and fiscal position if policies were to remain as they are in 2006. This motivates the need for policy reforms that restore sustainability. The subsequent section reports the simulation results of a sustainable policy in a deterministic setting and derives the social welfare maximizing tax policy under the condition of demographic certainty. This will serve as a baseline reference to determine the implications of demographic uncertainty on optimal policy. The results of simulations based on stochastic projections of the population development in the Netherlands are then presented. These simulations produce a probability distribution of the required one-time increase in the tax rate that will enforce fiscal sustainability. The final section determines the welfare consequences of demographic uncertainty and indicates its influence on optimal policy using stochastic simulations.

The GAMMA model

This chapter uses the dynamic general equilibrium overlapping-generations model, GAMMA, to produce stylized projections of long-term economic and fiscal developments in the Netherlands.[1] The model features thorough descriptions of the public sector and the private pension system as well as of household and firm behaviour.

Each household in GAMMA is represented by an adult whose life is finite and whose economic behaviour is guided according to life-cycle theory. Households maximize their expected lifetime utility subject to a budget constraint by choosing a time path of total consumption. Lifetime expenditure is constrained by total wealth, which equals the sum of financial wealth and the discounted value of potential future labour and pension income.[2] The necessary condition for intertemporal utility maximization implies total consumption smoothing, where the slope of the time profile of total consumption depends on the difference between the interest rate and the rate of time preference.

Total consumption consists of both goods and leisure consumption so the labour supply decision results from an instantaneous household utility maximization problem. The instantaneous utility function is such that labour supply depends only on the marginal reward of labour; that is, there is no wealth effect.[3] Because households smooth total consumption, increases in labour supply must be compensated by more consumption of commodities, implying a positive correlation between goods consumption and labour supply.

Taste shift parameters that determine the demand for leisure and goods consumption for each age cohort are calibrated with estimated lifetime consumption and labour profiles of the Netherlands. A result of the calibration procedure is that, given that the wage elasticity of leisure demand is constant, the wage elasticity of labour supply is age-specific.

GAMMA considers the Dutch economy to be small relative to the outside world. In particular, goods produced at home are perfectly substitutable with those produced abroad, so commodity prices are determined by the global market. Domestic policies do not affect the interest rate, which is determined on world capital markets. Households have no market power in the labour market so wages are determined by the user cost of capital through the factor price frontier. This implies that the incidence of profit taxation is fully shifted to labour.

Table 9.1. *Parameters in the GAMMA model.*

Rate of labour-augmenting technological progress (%)	1.7
Substitution elasticity labour and capital	0.5
Rate of time preference (%)	1.3
Intertemporal substitution elasticity	0.5
Rate of inflation (%)	2.0
Nominal rate of return on bonds (%)	3.5
Risk premium on shares (%)	3.0
Real discount factor (%)	3.0
Substitution elasticity leisure and consumption	0.3

Production takes place with labour and capital according to a CES production technology. The model assumes a perfect labour market: wage accommodation takes place without any delay. The productivity of labour is assumed to depend on age. Otherwise labour supplied by households of different ages is homogeneous. Capital also adjusts without any delay. The fast adjustment of wages and capital may not be realistic from a short-term point of view, but is acceptable for the long-term analysis of this study. Table 9.1 summarizes the parameter values relevant for household and firm behaviour as well as public finance in GAMMA.

Revenues for the public sector consist of contributions to the public pension scheme and receipts from profit and income taxation as well as indirect taxation, which is levied on consumption and investment. Base-path tax rates are calculated as the ratio between tax revenues and the tax base in the base year, so there is no progressivity in the income tax system. The sale of publicly owned land and ownership of other public assets are also sources of income for the government. The government is assumed to keep the holdings of government assets constant relative to the net output of the private sector.

Public-sector expenditures are modelled according to a generational accounting framework. Expenditures on age-sensitive items such as health care, education and public pensions have their own age-profiles so aggregate expenditures on these items develop from year to year according to demographic changes. In addition, they grow over time proportionally with the wage rate. All individuals are assumed to receive the same benefit from defence and public administration spending. These expenditures rise with GDP.

The private pension sector has a large influence on the government budget, if only through its size. Pension contributions can be deducted from income before taxes are determined, while pension benefits are taxed. The difference between the tax rate on labour income and pensions implies a subsidy. This is a subsidy on labour market participation since private pensions are mandatory for workers. The large direct influence of the pension system is thus twofold: it implies a delay of the tax receipts and it gives a subsidy on pension savings. The total pension premium rate consists of two components, the contribution rate and the catching-up premium rate. The actuarially fair contribution rate finances the accrual of pension rights while the catching-up premium finances (possible) wealth deficits of a pension fund. It is assumed that old-age benefits, including government pensions, are a certain percentage of average wages earned over the working period. Furthermore, old-age benefits are indexed to prices and partly to wages, reflecting the situation for the average Dutch pension fund.

Essentially the model is deterministic. Agents have perfect foresight; that is, their expectations coincide with realizations. Lifetime uncertainty is recognized, but perfect capital markets enable households to insure against this type of risk.[4] In this study, however, the deterministic model is integrated with stochastic population projections in order to produce uncertainty at the macro-economic level. In addition, tax rate changes caused by demographic shocks are unanticipated by households. So while there is no influence of this uncertainty on individual behaviour, the expected utility of cohorts who experience demographic risk is affected. This effect will be further explained later in the chapter.

Ageing and unsustainable government finances

As a first step in the analysis, it must be determined what effect population changes will have on the government's budget balance in the coming years if fiscal arrangements stay unchanged from their state in 2006 and the population develops along a deterministic path. Since fiscal pressures will almost inevitably force the government to introduce reforms eventually, this scenario is not considered to be realistic. However, it will serve as a baseline against which the policy measures presented later in the chapter will be compared. A simulation covering the years 2006–2206 has been calculated using a point forecast of demographic developments in the Netherlands. The baseline population projection presented here deviates from the projection used in Van Ewijk et al. (2006) which was based on an estimate by Statistics Netherlands (CBS).[5]

Table 9.2 shows the projected total demographic development in the baseline scenario. It can be seen that the total population of the Netherlands is expected to increase to a significant extent over the next century. Moreover, there probably will be large changes in the composition of the population. A large increase in the projected number of elderly people

Table 9.2. *Key indicators under the baseline scenario with unchanged policies.*

	2006	2020	2040	2060	2100
Demography					
Total population (000s)	16354.55	17257.10	18317.38	18909.65	19801.06
Number of newborns (000s)	181.78	188.40	192.10	205.60	201.62
Life expectancy – females	81.15	81.95	84.78	86.32	86.32
Life expectancy – males	76.89	78.36	81.18	82.57	82.57
Number of net immigrants (000s)	−10.19	45.57	47.73	47.33	44.81
Number of children (000s)	3975.64	3836.79	4073.05	4142.80	4246.21
Number of potential workers (000s)	10071.53	10137.87	9781.02	10289.27	10718.92
Number of retired persons (000s)	2465.61	3405.07	4622.33	4653.68	5023.35
Old-age dependency ratio	0.25	0.34	0.47	0.45	0.47
Total dependency ratio	0.64	0.71	0.89	0.85	0.86
Government finance					
Primary expenditures (% GDP)	45.6	47.4	53.1	53.8	53.9
Revenue (% GDP)	45.1	47.2	49.6	49.4	49.8
Primary deficit (% GDP)	0.6	0.2	3.5	4.4	4.2
Debt (% GDP)	56.1	65.1	144.0	292.2	716.0
Economic development					
GDP (€billion)	509.8	642.5	878.0	1265.6	2610.0
Labour supply (000s of man-years)[1]	6462.1	6841.0	6606.0	6850.3	7165.2
Capital stock (€billion)	1761.1	2305.1	3145.1	4547.0	9389.3
Private consumption (% GDP)	45.8	50.9	55.7	54.6	54.5
Current account balance (% GDP)	9.7	2.8	−7.4	−6.5	−6.4

Note: [1] Full-time equivalents.

due to greater life expectancies will cause the old-age dependency ratio, the number of pensioners divided by the number of workers, to almost double by 2040. In the following decades, the ratio stabilizes at this high level. In addition, the total dependency ratio, the number of children plus pensioners divided by the number of workers, is also expected to increase, though to a lesser degree. The current net outflow of migrants is projected to be reversed, but this will be insufficient to compensate for the overall greying of the population.

These changes will have significant effects on government finances if fiscal arrangements remain as they are. The debt-to-GDP ratio is projected to explode to an unmanageable level, a development that is directly connected to the ageing population. Table 9.2 shows a gradual increase of public revenue as a percentage of GDP due to increased tax receipts from the consumption tax levied on retired cohorts and the taxation of supplementary pension incomes. However, this favourable development is not enough to offset the comparatively strong growth of demographically sensitive public expenditure, specifically public pension outlays and health care expenditure. Sustained primary budget deficits combined with the accumulated interest burden results in a debt-to-GDP ratio of more than 700 per cent by 2100 in this baseline scenario. This figure greatly exceeds the estimate presented in Van Ewijk et al. (2006) which projects a debt-to-GDP ratio of about 200 per cent in 2100 with unchanged policies. The difference is partly due to the omission in the simulations in this study of government income from taxes on asset wealth[6] as well as the differing assumptions about the population development. However, we do not expect the nature of the baseline scenario to have any effect on the qualitative results of our stochastic simulation analysis.

The ageing of the population is also reflected in macro-economic developments. Although GDP shows growth over the long run due to productivity improvements and the increase in the size of the workforce associated with a higher population, increased national consumption due to ageing results in a current account deficit of more than 7 per cent of GDP by 2040.

Optimal policy under demographic certainty

It is clear that at some point current policies will require adjustment and that the government must implement fiscal changes that decrease expenditures and/or increase revenues. In order to set a reference point, we run a tax-smoothing simulation in a deterministic setting. The tax-smoothing policy is a one-off increase in 2006 of the labour income tax rate that sustains government finances indefinitely into the future. Note that this tax-smoothing policy is not the same as a policy that balances the budget from year to year. The algorithm in the GAMMA model that adjusts tax rates to make government finances sustainable takes a long-run view of the fiscal situation. It requires only that the debt-to-GDP level should stabilize at a steady-state level which is sufficient to ensure that the present value of all future revenues will cover the present value of all future expenditures. This level may be either positive or negative but the permanent tax rate increase that enforces it is unique. As such, the tax rate increase can be interpreted as a measure of the fiscal sustainability gap.

Table 9.3 shows the fiscal and macro-economic effects of the required 13.4 percentage points increase in the labour income tax rate.[7]

Table 9.3. *Fiscal and macro-economic development under labour income tax smoothing.*

	2006	2020	2040	2060	2100
Government finance					
Primary expenditures (% GDP)	47.0	48.7	54.8	55.7	55.9
Revenue (% GDP)	50.5	53.6	55.8	55.5	56.0
Primary deficit (% GDP)	−3.4	−4.9	−1.0	0.2	−0.1
Debt (% GDP)	53.6	−18.6	−72.8	−75.4	−78.9
Economic development					
Real GDP (€billion)	490.4	619.3	842.5	1,211.5	2,498.4
Labour supply (000s of man-years)[1]	6,280.1	6,678.1	6,449.6	6,681.6	6,990.1
Capital stock (€billion)	1,711.2	2,247.4	3,068.3	4,430.5	9,151.6
Private consumption (% GDP)	42.7	46.3	49.6	48.0	47.8
Current account balance (% GDP)	21.2	6.3	−2.9	−1.7	−1.5

Note: [1] Full-time equivalents.

The tax increase has obvious beneficial effects on government finances, allowing for sustained primary surpluses and reducing the debt ratio to a stable and sustainable level. However, higher taxes have the effect of reducing net marginal wages and, as a result, labour supply is permanently lower by 2–3 per cent. The erosion of the tax base means that tax rate increases must be proportionally higher than the shortfall in revenues. In addition, the capital stock adjusts quickly to accommodate the lower labour supply and so domestic production suffers. The impact of the tax on households can be seen in the decline of private consumption relative to the baseline scenario. Not only is consumption lower relative to GDP, but since GDP is lower in the tax-smoothing scenario, the absolute level of private consumption is only about 90 per cent of its level in the baseline scenario each year.

Obviously, tax-smoothing is not the only policy that will close the sustainability gap. For instance, balancing the budget year to year would also be sufficient. However, theory suggests that such a policy would come at the cost of a higher excess burden because of the distortionary effects of variable tax rates over time. Conversely, in the context of a dynamic economy with multiple agents and a long time horizon, tax-smoothing is not necessarily optimal either, as we demonstrate below.

In order to determine the effects on social welfare of discontinuous tax policies using the GAMMA model, the simulation is split into two periods, 2006–2025 and 2026–2205. As a money measure of household

Table 9.4. *Labour income tax rate increases in the deterministic policy scenarios.*

	−8	−6	−4	−3	−2	−1	0	1	2	3	4	6	8
2006–2025	5.4	7.4	9.4	10.4	11.4	12.4	13.4	14.4	15.4	16.4	17.4	19.4	21.4
2026–2205	15.7	15.1	14.5	14.2	14.0	13.7	13.4	13.1	12.9	12.6	12.3	11.8	11.3

utility, the per-individual equivalent variations ev for a variety of tax policies are calculated using:

$$U_0(W_0 + ev) = U_1(W_1)$$

where U_0 and U_1 are ordinal utility levels as functions of lifetime wealth W_0 and W_1 in the baseline and alternative scenarios respectively. In this instance, the baseline scenario is the simulation with a tax-smoothing policy, so the equivalent variation is the lump-sum money transfer that would have the same influence on lifetime utility as a policy change away from tax-smoothing. Thus a positive equivalent variation implies a welfare improvement over tax-smoothing, and vice versa. In order to construct a social welfare function, the equivalent variations for all cohorts, present and future, are aggregated:

$$SWF = \sum_{a=20}^{99} ev_a^{2006} p_a^{2006} + \sum_{y=2007}^{\infty} ev_{20}^y p_{20}^y$$

where the subscript a indicates the age of the cohort, y indicates the year and p_a^y is a weight indicating the population size of the cohort aged a in the year y.[8]

Twelve alternative policy simulations are run relative to the tax-smoothing policy by setting the tax rate some number of percentage points[9] above or below the tax-smoothing rate in the first period and readjusting the rate in the second period to make government finances sustainable.[10]

The government's sustainability constraint implies that a tax rate below (above) the tax-smoothing rate over the first period will require a tax rate above (below) the tax-smoothing rate in the second period as is illustrated in Table 9.4. It can be seen that the deviations from the tax-smoothing rate in the second period are substantially less than the corresponding deviations in the first period. This is because the second period is much longer than the first. As a result, the required budgetary response to deficits or surpluses carried over from the first period can be drawn out over a longer time frame, so the tax rate response will be proportionally smaller.

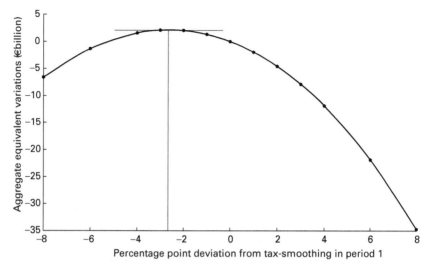

Figure 9.1. Optimal tax policy curve in the deterministic scenario.

It is clear that each simulation will involve some intergenerational redistribution relative to the baseline. Aggregating the equivalent variations over all cohorts gives a measure of the net welfare consequences of each policy. Figure 9.1 plots the aggregate equivalent variation levels for each policy against the percentage points deviation from the tax-smoothing rate (indicated by 0 on the horizontal axis) in the first period. The points are joined by a welfare curve, the peak of which indicates the optimal policy given the restrictions presented here.

It can be seen from the figure that the optimal policy under demographic certainty sets the tax rate in the neighbourhood of 2.6 percentage points below tax-smoothing in the first period (2006 to 2025). Referring to Table 9.4, one can verify that this implies that the optimal tax should be approximately 0.7 percentage points above the tax-smoothing rate in the second period (2026 to 2205).

Why is tax-smoothing not optimal in these simulations? The dynamic taxation literature typically presents the problem in the context of a representative agent with a finite time horizon. In contrast to the real world as well as to a complex simulation model such as GAMMA, this constitutes a significant simplification. Kingston (1991) derived the necessary and sufficient conditions for the optimality of equalizing wage tax rates over time in a dynamic general equilibrium framework. These conditions include constant labour supply elasticity and constant relative risk aversion. Since constant aggregate labour supply elasticity is not necessarily present in the GAMMA model, there is no reason to expect that a constant tax rate policy would maximize social welfare.

There is another reason why tax-smoothing is not optimal in the GAMMA model. Indeed, the labour income tax rate is not the only government policy variable that has an influence on the marginal reward of labour. The baseline scenario features the decline of premiums for the VUT, the Dutch PAYG-financed early retirement scheme, and decreasing catching-up premiums. Wedge smoothing then calls for increasing rather than constant tax rates. Also, there appear to be influences on optimal tax policy from productivity growth, inflation, the depreciation allowance for firms, revenues from natural gas exploitation and population growth. Only when all these factors are eliminated from the model do the simulation results show that tax-smoothing is socially optimal with this methodology.[11] This result is not important here, however. We only establish the optimal policy in the deterministic setting as a reference in order to compare it to the optimal policy when demographic uncertainty is present.

Stochastic demographics

In this section we formalize the effects that uncertainty in demographic developments can have on economic and fiscal variables by simulating projections based on population forecasts of the Netherlands produced by the PEP program.[12] The program applies stochastic processes to the forecasted development of fertility, immigration and mortality rates. By generating a large number of stochastic population paths and using them as bases for GAMMA simulations, we arrive at a distribution of possible macro-economic and fiscal outcomes that can be given a probabilistic interpretation.

The most important demographic statistic concerning fiscal policy is the total dependency ratio. Since the funding of health care, public pensions and education makes up a substantial proportion of government outlays and labour income tax constitutes a large share of government income, an increase in this ratio is bound to put pressure on fiscal balances. Figure 9.2 shows the stochastic distribution of the total dependency ratio as forecast until 2050 based on 207 PEP forecasts.[13]

The base-run line corresponds to the population point forecast that was used in the deterministic scenario in the previous section. The percentile lines are not single paths of the PEP simulations. Rather, they are trend lines connecting cumulative distributions in each forecast year. So at each point on the 10th percentile line, 90 per cent of the dependency ratio forecasts for that year lie above the line. The symmetry of the forecasts is

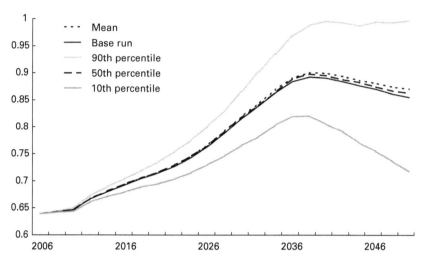

Figure 9.2. Stochastic distribution of the total dependency ratio.

evident in that the base-run, 50th percentile and mean lines all lie very close to one another in the figure.

It can be seen that the dependency ratio is almost certain to increase in the coming decades, but it is uncertain by how much. By around 2040 the ratio will level off and possibly decline thereafter. However it will remain at a relatively consistent level somewhere between 0.75 and 0.95 with a 60 per cent level of probability.

This interpretation of forecasted demographic developments naturally leads to a probabilistic interpretation of the sustainability gap as characterized by the immediate and permanent labour income tax increase that is required to sustain the budget in each stochastic demographic scenario. Figure 9.3 presents the required increases as a frequency distribution. The average necessary labour income tax increase is 14.0 percentage points from the baseline level of 29 per cent. Compare this to the necessary tax increase of 13.4 percentage points calculated in the deterministic scenario.

It is evident that the required tax rate change distribution is not symmetric.[14] This contrasts with the highly symmetric dependency ratio forecasts produced by the PEP program. The explanation for this lies in the non-linear relationship between tax revenues and tax rates. Tax distortions have the effect that a given increase in the tax rate is not matched by a proportional increase in revenues because of erosion of the tax base. Furthermore, this disparity is exacerbated at higher tax rates. As a result, while the stochastic distribution of revenue requirements may

Table 9.5. *Labour income tax rate increases in the stochastic policy scenarios.*

	−8	−6	−4	−3	−2	−1	0	1	2	3	4	6	8
2006–2025	5.4	7.4	9.4	10.4	11.4	12.4	13.4	14.4	15.4	16.4	17.4	19.4	21.4
2026–2205[1]	16.3	15.7	15.1	14.8	14.5	14.2	14.0	13.7	13.4	13.1	12.9	12.4	11.9

Note: [1] Expected tax rate increase.

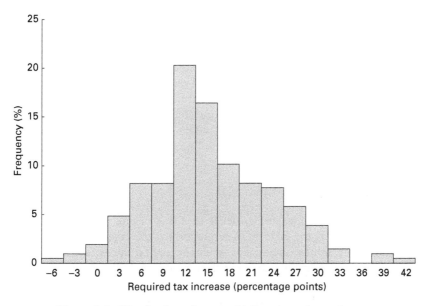

Figure 9.3. Distribution of required labour income tax increases.

be quite symmetric, the mean of the required tax rate increases is driven towards the upper end of the distribution. So because of the influence of this excess burden, it is not sufficient to impose the sustainable tax rate associated with the most likely demographic scenario. Sustaining government finances in expectation requires imposing the *expected* sustainable tax rate, which in general will be higher than the sustainable tax rate in the expected path.

As Table 9.5 illustrates, this effect from stochastic revenue requirements will have an influence on the second-period tax rates in the welfare experiments that were presented above. For each of the thirteen policy strategies, the first-period tax rate is set to the same level as in the deterministic scenarios. However, it can be seen that the expected second-period tax rate is proportionally higher in each case. This effect can be interpreted as a shift in the government's sustainability constraint due to the excess burden of distortionary taxation.[15]

Optimal policy under demographic uncertainty

In this section, the optimal fiscal policy under demographic uncertainty is determined in a similar way to that for demographic certainty in the deterministic scenario. In addition, the consequences for social welfare of this uncertainty can also be assessed. As before, a grid of first-period tax rates is chosen around the central policy of a 13.4 percentage point increase. For each of these scenarios, 207 stochastic simulations are run and for each simulation the tax rate is adjusted in the second period to sustain the budget. Because the second-period tax rate depends on the demographic development, it is determined by the stochastic process. Therefore the lifetime utility of those cohorts which are economically active in those years is also stochastic. The expected equivalent variation for each household relative to the baseline scenario (tax-smoothing as in the deterministic scenario) is calculated:

$$U_0(W_0 + ev_u) = E[U_1(W_1)]$$

Note that the lifetime utility level in the baseline scenario is non-stochastic, so only the RHS of the equation has the expectation operator. As in the deterministic scenarios, the expected equivalent variations are aggregated to construct a social welfare function:

$$SWF_u = \sum_{a=20}^{99} ev_{u_a}^{2006} E[p_a^{2006}] + \sum_{y=2007}^{\infty} ev_{u20}^{y} E[p_{20}^{y}]$$

The expected welfare consequences of each policy are plotted in Figure 9.4 and joined by the welfare curve denoted *uncertainty*. For reference, the welfare curve from the deterministic scenario is also included in the figure and denoted *certainty*. This is the same curve as that depicted in Figure 9.1. The welfare curve denoted *certainty equivalent* is constructed by running a series of deterministic policy simulations, setting the tax rates exogenously to be the same as the expected tax rates in the stochastic scenarios (as in Table 9.5). These simulations reflect the influence of the shift in the sustainability constraint on welfare while omitting the influence of net income risk for households.

It can be seen that the peak of the expected welfare curve for the stochastic scenarios is located below and to the right of the peak of the welfare curve associated with the deterministic scenarios. The shift

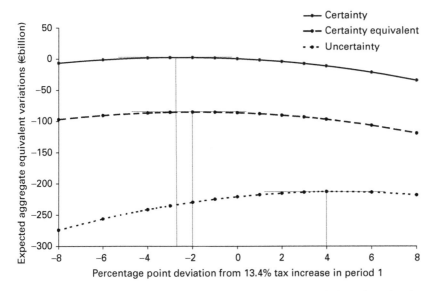

Figure 9.4. Optimal tax policy curves in the deterministic and stochastic scenarios.

downwards represents the welfare loss to society arising from the presence of risk stemming from demographic uncertainty in the second period. Since the baseline scenario is the (certain) tax-smoothing path, moving from a state of certainty to a state of uncertainty is equivalent in utility terms to reducing the aggregated lifetime wealth of all cohorts affected by the uncertainty. For example, at the tax-smoothing rate, the total cost of uncertainty to all cohorts is approximately €221 billion (1.45 per cent of the lifetime wealth for all cohorts aggregated through time) – the vertical distance between those two curves. The vertical distance between the uncertainty curve and the certainty equivalent curve represents the social welfare loss solely attributable to the implied shift in the government's expected sustainability constraint. At the tax-smoothing rate, it constitutes approximately €87 billion (0.57 per cent of lifetime wealth) of the total welfare loss from demographic uncertainty.

In order to account for the remaining loss of welfare and to illustrate the effect of demographic uncertainty on optimal policy, consider the following two-period stylized example. Suppose that the government directly taxes the wealth of a representative household in order to satisfy revenue requirements. Assume that there is no labour supply or savings behaviour so the household consumes all of its wealth in each period. A budget constraint implies that, in setting the first-period tax rate, the government is

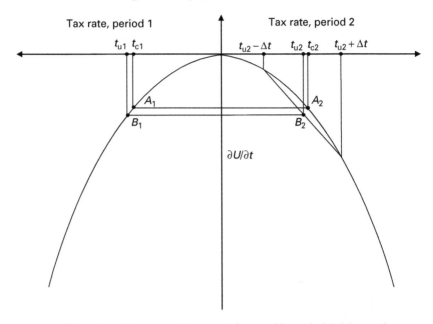

Figure 9.5. Demographic uncertainty and household risk aversion.

effectively determining household consumption levels in both periods 1 and 2. Household utility is a function of consumption with the standard properties.[16] So marginal utility is decreasing and concave in tax rates. If the household's time preference parameter is zero, optimality requires that the government should set the first-period tax rate such that the expected marginal utilities in each period are equal.

Figure 9.5 graphically illustrates the government's problem under both certainty and uncertainty. Tax rates in each period increase in opposite directions outwards along the horizontal axis. The inverted U-shape denotes household marginal utility in tax rates under certainty. Since the figure is symmetric, the optimal government policy under certainty is to set the first-period tax rate such that it is equal to the second-period rate. In the figure, the optimal tax rates t_{c1} and t_{c2} result in marginal utility levels of A_1 and A_2 respectively.

The problem under uncertainty is as follows. When the government chooses the tax rate in the first period, it faces a 50 per cent probability that the tax rate in the second period will be Δt less than the expected second-period tax rate and a 50 per cent probability that it will be Δt greater than the expected second-period tax rate. Due to the curvature of the marginal utility function, choosing the first-period tax rate such that it equals the expected second-period tax rate will not result in expected marginal utility smoothing. It can be seen in the figure that the first-period tax rate that equalizes marginal utility in the first period to expected marginal utility in the second period is t_{u1}. The expected second-period tax rate is t_{u2} and the (expected) marginal utility levels are B_1 and B_2. It can be seen that t_{u1} is greater than t_{c1}. Choosing a higher tax rate in the first period is equivalent to a policy of pre-funding in response to uncertainty in the second period. The government effectively engages in precautionary savings on behalf of the risk-averse household.[17]

However, this policy will only partially compensate the household for the utility loss arising from the consumption uncertainty in the second period. Because the household is risk-averse, it will always prefer a sure bet to an equivalent expected result from a gamble.

In Figure 9.4 the vertical distance between the expected welfare curve for the uncertainty case and the certainty equivalent curve represents the welfare loss resulting from uncertainty not attributable to the implied shift in the government's expected sustainability constraint. This loss, valued at approximately €134 billion in welfare equivalents (0.88 per cent of lifetime wealth), arises solely because of the income risk suffered by households. The rightward shift in the expected welfare curve shows the effect of uncertainty on optimal policy in the simulations. Because the consequences of demographic uncertainty are borne almost entirely by future generations, the government can reduce the net welfare loss to society by decreasing their expected tax burden and setting the tax rate in the period 2006 to 2025 at almost 4 percentage points above the tax-smoothing rate (and 1.1 percentage points below the expected tax-smoothing rate in the period 2026–2205). By doing so, the government distributes the costs of uncertainty more evenly over all generations, present and future. For example, the expected gain in welfare of future generations[18] from shifting from the optimal policy under certainty to the optimal policy under uncertainty is approximately €271 billion (2.6 per cent of lifetime wealth) in money equivalents. The expected welfare loss to current generations[19] from the same policy change is approximately €249 billion (5 per cent of lifetime wealth). On balance, this policy minimizes the aggregate consequences of uncertainty.

Figure 9.6 shows more explicitly the relationship between the optimal tax rates and the sustainability constraint. The solid diagonal line represents the combination of first- and second-period labour income tax increases (from their present rate) that will sustain the government budget if the demographic development follows the deterministic path, as in Table 9.4. The dashed line represents the combination of first- and second-period tax increases that will sustain the budget in expectation if

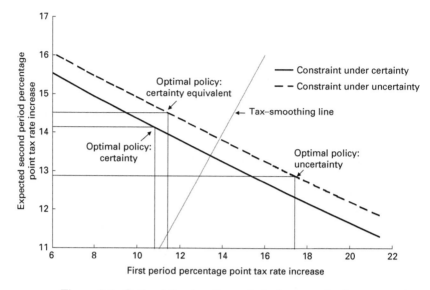

Figure 9.6. Optimal fiscal policy and the long-run budget constraint under certainty and uncertainty.

the demographic development is uncertain, as in Table 9.5. It is easy to see that the introduction of uncertainty can be interpreted as a shift in the constraint. In addition, the three optimal policy points are indicated along with a ray depicting the (expected) tax smoothing policies along each of the sustainability constraints.

Conclusions

Judging from this analysis, it is clear that the welfare implications of demographic uncertainty are quite large. It is equally clear that, given the assumptions made here, the extent to which the government can mitigate its effects is relatively small. If evaluated at the expected tax-smoothing rate, the welfare loss from demographic uncertainty is valued at €221 billion for all cohorts into the indefinite future. Increasing the tax rate by four percentage points over the next twenty years will only reduce this loss by about €8 billion.

Of course, this story relies on a few significant abstractions from reality. First, in each of the stochastic simulations there is no behavioural reaction to the consequences of demographic risk by households. As a result, the impact on social welfare of precautionary savings at the micro-economic level is neglected. For those cohorts who face the prospect of a tax increase at some point in the future, precautionary savings may preclude the need for the government to front-load taxes to some degree. As stated earlier, however, it seems unlikely that households would act in a precautionary manner for the sake of future generations who face demographic risk at some time in the distant future. Hence, there remains an argument for the government to redistribute intergenerational risk.

Second, demographic uncertainty is only one source of risk influencing optimal fiscal policy. Other sources include a variety of economic uncertainties such as variability in productivity, interest and inflation rates and labour participation rates, among others. Naturally these types of risks are bound to interact with each other, as they are bound to interact with demographic risk. Focusing on only one type of risk may underestimate the extent to which the government should exercise precaution when setting fiscal policy.[20]

Finally, the simulation experiment presented here is a stylized representation of the problem facing policy-makers. It is assumed that the government is somewhat naïve about future developments and also that it is quite restricted as to when it can implement policy reforms. The government makes an immediate reform decision in 2006 and then has to delay any policy adjustment until 2026 when the uncertainty about the true demographic structure of the population is resolved. In the mean time, it is completely ignorant about how the population is developing. Of course, governments are typically better informed than this and would be able to make gradual policy readjustments as new information became available. This flexibility should help to mitigate the adverse effects of demographic uncertainty to some extent.

These qualifications may have effects, one way or another, on the quantitative conclusions of this analysis. However, the focus here is on the qualitative question of how governments facing fiscal pressure from ageing populations should allow for uncertainty in the consideration of policy reforms. Rather than delaying reforms or assuming that the demographic development will follow the most likely path, it has been shown here that a precautionary policy maximizes the expected welfare of society.

Appendix: A stylized two-period example

Suppose that the government must choose labour income tax rates τ_1 and τ_2 for the present and future periods respectively. Government expenditure requirements g_1 and g_2 are satisfied by the revenue functions $R_1(\tau_1)$ and $R_2(\tau_2)$. Assume that the government can borrow funds at no cost, so letting the total expenditure requirements be $G = g_1 + g_2$ implies the budget constraint $G = R_1(\tau_1) + R_2(\tau_2)$. The government's goal is to set the tax rates in such a way as to maximize a utilitarian social welfare function composed of the sum of aggregated (cardinal) utility levels $V(\tau)$ of households. The problem is represented by the Lagrangian function:

$$\max_{\tau_1 \tau_2} V_1(\tau_1) + V_2(\tau_2) + \lambda(G - R_1(\tau_1) - R_2(\tau_2)) \tag{1}$$

The optimal tax rate schedule satisfies:

$$\frac{\dfrac{\partial V_1}{\partial \tau_1}}{\dfrac{\partial R_1}{\partial \tau_1}} = \frac{\dfrac{\partial V_2}{\partial \tau_2}}{\dfrac{\partial R_2}{\partial \tau_2}} \tag{2}$$

and

$$G = R_1(\tau_1) + R_2(\tau_2) \tag{3}$$

The influence of demographic uncertainty on budgetary requirements can be demonstrated by characterizing the exogenous expenditure level in the future period as a random variable $\tilde{g}_2$ whose true value is revealed in the second period. This implies that $\tilde{G} = g_1 + \tilde{g}_2$ is also a random variable. Assume the expectation of this uncertain expenditure requirement is equal to expenditure under certainty: $E_1(\tilde{G}) = G$. Then the expected second-period tax rate under uncertainty can be shown by rearranging the budget constraint, inverting the second-period revenue function and taking expectations of both sides of the equation:[21]

$$E_1[\tau_2^u] = E_1[R_2^{-1}[\tilde{G} - R_1(\tau_1)]] \tag{4}$$

Now compare (4) to the second-period tax rate under demographic certainty:

$$\tau_2^c = R_2^{-1}[E_1[\tilde{G} - R_1(\tau_1)]] \tag{5}$$

For a concave revenue function, it can be easily shown that $E_1[\tau_2^u] > \tau_2^c$.[22]

So for any given first-period tax rate, demographic uncertainty will increase the expected second-period tax rate. Viewed *ex ante*, this effect on expenditure requirements can be considered a shift in the government's (expected) sustainability constraint.

In order to isolate the effect of household risk aversion on optimal policy from the shift in the expected budget constraint, assume that the revenue functions are linear in tax rates and time-invariant. For constant preferences, tax-smoothing is the optimal policy under certainty:

$$\bar{\tau}_1^c = V_\tau^{-1}[V_\tau(\tau_2^c)] = \tau_2^c \tag{6}$$

and the optimal policy under uncertainty is:

$$\bar{\tau}_1^u = V_\tau^{-1}[E_1[V_\tau(\tau_2^u)]] \tag{7}$$

Because of the simplifying assumptions on the revenue functions $E_1[\tau_2^u] = \tau_2^c$, it can be shown that $\bar{\tau}_1^u > \bar{\tau}_1^c$ given standard assumptions on the utility function.[23]

NOTES

1 For a detailed description of the GAMMA model, see Draper and Armstrong (2007).
2 Potential labour income is defined as income with labour time equal to the total available time.
3 The wealth effect is assumed to be zero. Lumsdaine and Mitchell (1999) conclude in their survey article that the wealth effect on labour supply is small relative to the price effect.
4 Longevity risk is assumed to be diversified; each household receives an annuity from a life insurance company in return for bequeathing it its remaining assets upon death (Yaari, 1965). This type of idiosyncratic risk is fundamentally different from the aggregate risk arising from demographic uncertainty which the government faces. The government has no insurance market available to it. Alho and Määttänen (this volume, chap. 11) discuss aggregate mortality risk.
5 In the baseline forecast used here, the population reaches a level of almost 20 million by 2100 while in the CBS projection it reaches only about 17.3 million. The two population forecasts deviate mainly because of differences in the assumptions made about longevity. For example, in this projection, average life expectancy in 2050 is 86.2 years for females and 82.4 years for males, while in the CBS projection, average life expectancy in 2050 is 82.5 years for females and 79.5 years for males. As a result, the dependency ratio estimates are higher in this projection than in the CBS projection.
6 This simplification was made to facilitate consistency between the discount rates of households and the government, a requirement of the welfare analysis in this study.
7 From an average labour income tax rate of 29 per cent in 2006.
8 Although the solution period for the simulations is only 2006 to 2205, all lead variables including utility and wealth levels are solved forward from the steady-state year as infinite sums. As a result, the utility of cohorts entering the economy after 2205 is accounted for.
9 −8, −6, −4, −3, −2, −1, 1, 2, 3, 4, 6, 8.
10 The choice of 2026 as the dividing line between the two periods is completely arbitrary, since the focus here is on the scale of policy measures rather than the timing.
11 Results are available from the authors on request.
12 See Alho and Spencer (1997) and the PEP user manual at http://joyx.joensuu.fi/ẽk/pep/userpep.htm.

13 Originally 250 simulations were run. Those simulations that failed to solve or that produced total population levels above 50 million in the final simulation year (2205) were omitted from the sample. Note that, in the baseline simulation, the total population in 2205 is 20.2 million. We have found that increasing the number of stochastic simulations above 250 does not significantly increase the robustness of the demographic estimates. This number was chosen in view of the enormous demand on computing time from running numerous policy variants for each of the stochastic projections.

14 Skewness $= 0.374505$. A rule-of-thumb test for the significance of skewness is: if the ratio of the sample skewness divided by its standard error is greater than 2 or less than -2, skewness is different from zero. The standard error of skewness can be approximated by $(6/N)^{1/2}$, with N the sample size. The calculated test statistic is 2.1997, so the null hypothesis that skewness is zero is rejected.

15 See the appendix to this chapter for a simple mathematical example of the shift in the constraint.

16 $U_c > 0, U_{cc} < 0, U_{ccc} > 0$

17 See the appendix for a mathematical example.

18 Those who will turn 20 years old in 2007 and all cohorts afterwards.

19 Those aged 20 or older in 2006.

20 For a discussion of the relative impact of demographic risk versus economic risk, see Bonenkamp, Van de Ven and Westerhout (2006).

21 If f is a function with domain X then f^{-1} is its inverse, if for every $x \in X$, $f(f^{-1}(x)) = f^{-1}(f(x)) = x$.

22 If the revenue function is concave: $R_\tau > 0, R_{\tau\tau} < 0$, then the inverse of the revenue function is convex: $R_\tau^{-1} = \frac{1}{R_\tau} > 0, R_{\tau\tau}^{-1} = -\frac{1}{R_\tau^2} R_{\tau\tau} > 0$. So by Jensen's Inequality: $E[R^{-1}(\cdot)] > R^{-1}(E[\cdot])$.

23 Let net household wealth be $w(\tau)$ with $w_\tau < 0$ and $w_{\tau\tau} = 0$. Then assume:

$$V_w > 0 \Rightarrow V_\tau < 0$$
$$V_{ww} < 0 \Rightarrow V_{\tau\tau} > 0$$
$$V_{www} < 0 \Rightarrow V_{\tau\tau\tau} > 0$$

So V_τ is convex in tax rates and $E[V_\tau(\cdot)] > V_\tau(E[\cdot])$ which implies that $V_\tau[E[V_\tau(\cdot)]] < V_\tau[V_\tau(E[\cdot])]$. So:

$$\tau_1^u = V_\tau^{-1}[E[V_\tau(\cdot)]] = \frac{1}{V_\tau[E[V_\tau(\cdot)]]} > \frac{1}{V_\tau[V_\tau E[(\cdot)]]}$$
$$= V_\tau^{-1}[V_\tau E[(\cdot)]] = \tau_1^c$$

REFERENCES

Alho, J. M. and Spencer, B. D. (1997). 'The Practical Specification of the Expected Error of Population Forecasts'. *Journal of Official Statistics*, 13: 201–25.

Auerbach, A. J. and Hassett, K. (2001). 'Uncertainty and the Design of Long-run Fiscal Policy', in *Demographic Change and Fiscal Policy*, ed. A. J. Auerbach and R. D. Lee. Cambridge: Cambridge University Press, pp. 73–92.

Barro, R. J. (1979). 'On the Determination of the Public Debt'. *Journal of Political Economy*, 87: 940–71.

Bohn, H. (1990). 'Tax Smoothing With Financial Instruments'. *American Economic Review*, 80: 1217–30.

Bonenkamp, J., Van de Ven, M. and Westerhout, E. (2006). *A Small Stochastic Model of a Pension Fund with Endogenous Saving*. The Hague: CPB.

Draper, N. and Armstrong, A. (2007), eds. *GAMMA, a Simulation Model for the Netherlands*. The Hague: CPB.

Gomes, F., Kotlikoff, L. J. and Viceira, L. M. (2006). 'The Excess Burden of Government Indecision', Working Paper no. 2006-123, Retirement Research Center, University of Michigan.

Kingston, G. (1991). 'Should Marginal Tax Rates be Equalized Through Time?' *Quarterly Journal of Economics*, 106: 911–24.

Leland, H. E. (1968). 'Saving and Uncertainty: The Precautionary Demand for Saving'. *Quarterly Journal of Economics*, 82: 465–73.

Lucas, R. E. and Stokey, N. (1983). 'Optimal Fiscal and Monetary Policy in an Economy Without Capital'. *Journal of Monetary Economics*, 12: 55–93.

Lumsdaine, R. and Mitchell, O. (1999). 'New developments in the economic analysis of retirement', in *Handbook of Labor Economics*, Vol. III, ed. O. Ashenfelter and D. Card. Amsterdam: Elsevier Science.

Sandmo, A. (1970). 'The Effect of Uncertainty on Saving Decisions'. *Review of Economic Studies* 37: 353–60.

Steigum, E. (2001). 'Non-Traded Asset Risk, Precautionary Fiscal Policy, and Generational Accounting'. Paper presented at the International Institute of Public Finance Conference, Linz.

Van Ewijk, C., Draper, N., Ter Rele, H. and Westerhout, E. (2006). *Ageing and the Sustainability of Dutch Public Finances*. The Hague: CPB.

Yaari, M. E. (1965). 'Uncertain Lifetime, Life Insurance, and the Theory of the Consumer'. *Review of Economic Studies* 32: 137–50.

Computable equilibrium models in policy analysis: future directions

D. Peter Broer

Introduction

In these comments, I discuss the scope for the application of computable general equilibrium (CGE) models to ageing policy in the presence of macro-economic uncertainty, with reference to the contributions to this volume by Fehr and Habermann (chap. 7) (FH), Lassila and Valkonen (chap. 8) (LV) and Armstrong *et al.* (chap. 9) (ADNW). The application of computable general equilibrium models to ageing issues is well established, but hitherto few studies explicitly address uncertainty. I first review the application of CGE models to ageing and then discuss the options for dealing explicitly with uncertainty. Much of the potential relevance of stochastic models is determined by computational possibilities, so I also pay attention to computational issues. The last section sketches some possible future lines of research.

Deterministic CGE models of ageing

Auerbach, Kotlikoff and Skinner (1983) were the first to apply a CGE model with overlapping generations (OLG) to policy issues, in a study of the intergenerational incidence of tax reforms. Subsequently, computable OLG models also proved to be excellent tools to study the effects of ageing on growth and the intergenerational distribution. The relation between ageing and interest rates is discussed, for example, by Auerbach and Kotlikoff (1987) and Miles (1999) in a closed economy setting, and by Börsch-Supan, Ludwig and Winter (2004) in a multi-country setting. Social security reforms were taken up first by Auerbach and Kotlikoff (1987), and subsequently by, for example, Broer, Westerhout and Bovenberg (1994), Miles (1999) and Kotlikoff, Smetters and Walliser (2001). Non-linear taxes are present in Altig *et al.* (2001). Some models

I would like to thank Alex Armstrong and Nick Draper for useful discussions and comments on an earlier draft.

distinguish agents by ability as well as age, for example Kotlikoff, Smetters and Walliser (2001).

The CGE models in this volume fit into this line of research. All three chapters investigate measures to stabilize the total tax burden in response to demographic shocks. In FH and LV the measures relate to reforms in social security, and in ADNW the stabilization is achieved by means of government saving. Social security systems differ among the three countries, covering more or less the full range between defined-contribution and defined-benefit systems, which provides a useful check on the effect of the institutional characteristics on the results. The main challenge taken up by the authors is how to deal with demographic uncertainty within the confines of a deterministic model.

Demographic uncertainty

In all three chapters, the sole risk factor is the demographic development. The demographic model used contains longevity risk, fertility risk and immigration risk. The way the simulations are designed is such that households do not take any uncertainty into account in their saving and labour supply decisions. In fact, households are assumed to have perfect foresight concerning the demographic path. Given the existence of perfect annuity markets, each cohort is therefore able to insure itself fully against longevity risk. In addition, in FH and LV, households use this information to perfectly predict the actual path of taxes and contribution rates, as well as the demographic adjustment factors to be applied in the future. In these two chapters, the only agent without perfect foresight is the government, which has to choose a social security system before the uncertainty with respect to the demographic development is dispelled.

ADNW choose a somewhat different structure. Their goal is to explore the welfare effects of public precautionary saving, along the lines of Auerbach and Hassett (1999). This is only a useful exercise if the private sector does *not* possess perfect foresight. The simulation structure chosen assumes that the government chooses an initial tax rate, and revises this tax after twenty years, keeping it constant ever after (for this, it needs perfect foresight from year 20 on). The tax change at year 20 is fully unexpected for the private sector. Since the government is on an unsustainable path for the first twenty years, a tax change is unavoidable, but the private sector is in the dark about the date of the change. The simplifying assumption used is that the private sector assumes that it will never happen.

All three chapters provide useful insight into the expected range of variation of tax rates and contribution rates for different outcomes of

186 D. Peter Broer

the demographic shift as well as into how economic policy can help to stabilize these variations. Still, the incomplete treatment of uncertainty in the models raises a number of issues.

Without macro-economic uncertainty, and with all idiosyncratic risks being perfectly insured, social security does not offer any efficiency gains and serves purely as a redistribution mechanism. The redistribution leads to efficiency loss if the system is either not actuarially fair or not funded.[1] With a demographic shock, the main problem is then to keep the distortions of the system in check. However, social security was put in place as a means of *risk-sharing* between generations, and this aspect can be only crudely addressed in deterministic models.

The issue is then, first, what important effects are missing as a result of the deterministic structure chosen, and, second, can this structure be improved upon? I discuss both issues in turn.

Stochastic CGE models

To investigate the role of social security as an insurance device, it is important to consider the two types of risk that households face, the macro-economic risk of the return to their asset portfolio, including human capital, and the micro-economic risks that arise in the absence of complete insurance markets.

Idiosyncratic uncertainty

Idiosyncratic uncertainty arises in the absence of complete insurance markets. Agents are hit by individual-specific shocks that change their economic condition. As a result, *ex ante* identical agents become different *ex post*, and a distribution of agents' resources arises that evolves over time. With an infinite number of agents, individual shocks average out and at the macro level the economy evolves deterministically.

Typical idiosyncratic risk factors are longevity risk (Hubbard and Judd, 1987; İmrohoroğlu, İmrohoroğlu and Joines, 1995; Storesletten, Telmer and Yaron, 1999), and employment risk (Storesletten, Telmer and Yaron, 1999). In the absence of insurance against these risks, households attempt to smooth consumption by engaging in precautionary saving. If the government fills the missing market, this enables agents to share risk through the tax system. This may be efficient by avoiding excessive capital accumulation of individual agents at an early stage of life and a resulting imbalance between consumption in different periods of life.

The literature suggests that these efficiency gains do not materialize, however. As in the deterministic case, the general equilibrium effects of lower capital formation still dominate the outcome. Storesletten, Telmer and Yaron (1999) and İmrohoroğlu, İmrohoroğlu and Joines (1999) find that privatizing social security yields long-run efficiency gains, despite the missing insurance market. However, De Nardi, İmrohoroğlu and Sargent (1999) show that the long-run gains of privatization do not outweigh the costs on the transition path. Part of the problem is with the unfunded nature of many social security systems. Huang, İmrohoroğlu and Sargent (1997) show that a shift towards capital-funded social security may succeed in restoring private saving incentives, without sacrificing the benefits of risk-sharing.

Macro-economic uncertainty

Macro-economic shocks hit all agents at the same point in time and generate fluctuations in economic activity, in contrast to idiosyncratic risks. Hence, complete insurance is not possible. In real business cycle models, fluctuations come mostly from factor productivity risk. Over longer horizons, demographic uncertainty is also an important risk factor. Brooks (2000) and Geanakoplos, Magill and Quinzii (2004) use a stochastic OLG model with both demographic risk and productivity risk to argue that baby-boomers will face capital returns that are substantially below those of earlier generations. With capital mobility, this spills over in substantial international capital flows (Brooks, 2003).

The fundamental market incompleteness of OLG economies, that generations that do not co-exist cannot trade with each other, also applies to risk-sharing. Social security has an added value here as a means to organize intergenerational risk-sharing, in a case where the market is fundamentally unable to provide the desired insurance.

Only a few papers exist that address this issue in a CGE framework. Brooks (2000) analyses the role of a defined-contribution PAYG social security system. He concludes that this type of social security system does not provide much insurance, because PAYG benefits are positively correlated with asset market returns. Krueger and Kubler (2006) analyse the efficiency effects of a defined-contribution unfunded social security system in an economy with both productivity risk and capital return risk. Sánchez-Marcos and Sánchez-Martín (2006) analyse an economy with population growth risk (fertility risk) and a defined-benefit unfunded social security system. Both studies conclude that the gains from intergenerational risk-sharing do not compensate for the adverse crowding-out effects. Part of the adverse effects of social security occurs through the general equilibrium effects on factor prices. Miles and Cerny (2006) study the optimal PAYG component of social security for a small open economy (Japan) with exogenous labour supply. They too conclude that crowding-out dominates the long-run efficiency effects.

Computational issues

In dynamic CGE models, computational considerations often limit the scope of the model. The complexity of dynamic models arises on two accounts: first, forward-looking behaviour of agents implies that the model has to be solved for all time periods simultaneously. For the same number of agents and (undated) goods, this raises the dimension of the problem by the number of time periods. In addition, in OLG models the number of agents increases with the number of time periods, adding an order of complexity.

The second source of computational complexity of dynamic models is in the computation of the decision rules of the agents. Computational effort increases exponentially with the number of states for which decision rules have to be computed. This is Bellman's *curse of dimensionality* (Rust, 1996), which puts an upper limit on the number of state variables that can be handled. In deterministic models, the curse may be avoided if an open-loop formulation of the decision problem is feasible, for example if the decision problem is convex and has an interior solution. Papers like Altig *et al.* (2001) and Börsch-Supan, Ludwig and Winter (2004) show that it is feasible to run medium-scale OLG models of this type.

If an open-loop formulation of the decision problem is not feasible, the curse of dimensionality severely limits the scope of deterministic dynamic CGE models. For example, a proper treatment of non-convex budget constraints in a dynamic CGE model, such as may arise in the presence of a poverty trap, is out of reach.

Stochastic models

Models with purely idiosyncratic uncertainty are fully deterministic at the macro level. As such, they are comparable with heterogeneous agent models like OLG. The added complication is that the distribution of characteristics of *ex ante* identical agents is endogenous. Models of this type can be handled efficiently using a parameterized representation of the cross-sectional distribution, as in Den Haan (1997), which makes them viable as applied policy tools.

In CGE models with *macro-economic* uncertainty the curse of dimensionality can be postponed, but not avoided. For their saving decisions, agents need the distribution of future factor prices, which depend on the macro-economic state. The number of possible events increases exponentially with the number of states, so that models with more than a handful of state variables are computationally infeasible. Overlapping-generations models, in particular, have a very large state space, as a result of the heterogeneity of agents.

To postpone the curse, various dimension reduction techniques can be applied. Typically, stochastic OLG models use cohort sizes of about ten to twenty years instead of annual cohorts, which offers some relief. In addition, solution techniques try to exploit any special structure of economic models that may exist. Two main approaches may be distinguished. Sparse grid techniques, used for example by Krueger and Kubler (2006) and Sánchez-Marcos and Sánchez-Martín (2006), use only low-order polynomials in the state variables. This approach can be justified if there is not 'too much' interaction between the state variables, that is, if the cross-derivatives of the excess demand functions are bounded. Alternatively, Monte Carlo methods may be used, for example the parameterized expectations methods of Den Haan and Marcet (1990), as in Brooks (2000).

The challenge of OLG models is that the cross-sectional distribution of agents cannot be approximated well by low-order moments, in contrast to the representative agent model of Krusell and Smith (1998). Krueger and Kubler (2004) point out that the propensity of households to save varies with age, so that an approximation of the distribution in terms only of mean wealth does not work well. Given the current emphasis in economic policy on labour market participation of elderly workers, there is a need for accurate modelling of the age distribution of households that conflicts with computational possibilities.

Future directions

The discussion on computational issues shows that the curse of dimensionality prevents the inclusion of all relevant state variables in stochastic equilibrium models. While some relief may come from the application of new algorithms like sparse grid methods, for the foreseeable future shortcuts will continue to be necessary in applied policy work. That said, I think that the analyses presented in this book can be usefully generalized in a number of ways. My first few remarks build on the literature discussed in the preceding sections, and I conclude with some 'practical' suggestions.

• It is desirable to incorporate more institutional detail in deterministic CGE-OLG models of ageing. The section on deterministic CGE models reviews the current state of the art, from which it appears that models with heterogeneous agents per age cohort as well as a modest degree of tax non-linearities are within reach of current computational possibilities. This is important, as households of different ability can be affected quite differently by social security reforms. A reform that is efficiency-enhancing need not be Pareto-improving if the distributional effects are taken into account.

In addition, it would be useful to incorporate some degree of market imperfection in the models. For example, young agents are often liquidity-constrained, and they discount any mandatory contribution at a higher rate than the market rate of interest. This implies that contributions to social security are more distortionary for young agents than for old ones.

• With the current state of the art, it is possible to incorporate incomplete markets and idiosyncratic risk into models without macro-economic risk. The two main individual risk factors to be considered are labour market risk and longevity risk. This is highly relevant for policy conclusions, since the role of, especially, the first pillar of social security is in substantial measure to offer insurance against labour market risk at earlier stages in life. Politically feasible pension reforms will therefore tend to exempt the first pillar from a shift towards DC.

• It is possible to incorporate purely macro-economic risk in a CGE model with overlapping generations, provided that the number of cohorts distinguished is not 'too large'. For example, Sánchez-Marcos and Sánchez-Martín (2006) show that fertility risk can be analysed consistently in a CGE framework. Their analysis can be extended to an OLG model with annual cohorts, like those in the present volume, by applying the procedure proposed by den Haan (1997) to OLG models. This extension would allow for a more consistent analysis of crowding-out effects of social security reforms than the deterministic models reviewed above.

The points made above have the common characteristic that they strive for theoretical consistency. However, for applied policy analysis, this restriction may imply that the answer to a policy problem cannot (yet) be given. In such a case, it may be better to come up with a biased estimate of the effects of a policy measure rather than with no estimate at all. My last few suggestions should be interpreted in this light.

• The assumption used by the contributions to this volume that households know the demographic path in advance can be replaced with a forecasting rule that requires an update of the certainty-equivalent demographic path each period. This requires a recomputation of the perfect-foresight equilibrium each period, to take the realized demography into account, and is therefore computationally more demanding. This procedure provides a better approximation to the consumption uncertainty that households face under alternative social security regimes.[2]

• My second suggestion is conditional on the first one. Compute estimates of the correlations between the marginal utility of wealth and saving returns on the sample paths, in an attempt to reconstruct the applicable risk premia of the different assets. That is, let $u'(c_{a,i}(t))$ denote the marginal utility at time t of consumption of a household of age a in Monte Carlo run number i. Then we can construct a (biased) estimate of the risk premium at time t of an asset from the sample statistics of $E[u'(c_{a+1,i}(t+1))(1 + r_i(t+1))|t]$ and $E[u'(c_{a+1,i}(t+1))]$. The point is that households' consumption decisions for period $t+1$ are based on the *current* demographic forecast and are therefore properly conditioned on the available information. The computed risk premia can then be used to correct welfare estimates for variations in risk.

This suggestion resembles the parameterized expectations approach of den Haan and Marcet (1990). It is less general in that households continue to use certainty-equivalent decision rules.

• My third suggestion is to also include productivity risk in the analysis. This is especially important for the evaluation of defined-benefit pension systems. For a small open economy, one might also want to add foreign interest rates as an important risk factor, in particular to study reforms with funded pension funds.

NOTES

1 A funded actuarially fair system is equivalent to private saving.
2 The results of Alho and Määttänen (this volume, chap. 11) suggest that this procedure would take care of a large part of the effects of demographic uncertainty on the behaviour of households. However, their partial equilibrium approach cannot take into account the effects of demographic uncertainty on variations in interest rates and taxes.

REFERENCES

Altig, D., Auerbach, A. J., Kotlikoff, L. J., Smetters, K. A. and Walliser, J. (2001). 'Simulating U.S. Tax Reform'. *American Economic Review*, 91: 574–95.
Auerbach, A. J. and Hassett, K. A. (1999). *Uncertainty and the Design of Long-run Fiscal Policy*. Working Paper no. 7036. Boston: NBER.
Auerbach, A. J. and Kotlikoff, L. J. (1987). *Dynamic fiscal policy*. Cambridge: Cambridge University Press.
Auerbach, A. J., Kotlikoff, L. J. and Skinner, J. (1983). 'The Efficiency Gains from Dynamic Tax Reform'. *International Economic Review*, 24: 81–100.
Börsch-Supan, A., Ludwig, A. and Winter, J. (2004). *Ageing, Pension Reform, and Capital Flows: A Multi-country Simulation Study*. Discussion Paper no. 064-04. MEA.
Broer, D. P., Westerhout, E. W. M. T. and Bovenberg, A. L. (1994). 'Taxation, Pensions and Saving in a Small Open Economy'. *Scandinavian Journal of Economics*, 96: 403–24.

Brooks, R. (2000). *What Will Happen to Financial Markets When the Baby Boomers Retire?* Working Paper no. 00/18, International Monetary Fund. Washington, DC: IMF.

——— (2003). 'Population Aging and Global Capital Flows in a Parallel Universe'. *IMF Staff Papers*, 50: 200–21.

De Nardi, M., İmrohoroğlu, S. and Sargent, T. J. (1999). 'Projected U.S. Demographics and Social Security'. *Review of Economic Dynamics*, 2: 575–615.

Den Haan, W. J. (1997). 'Solving Dynamic Models with Aggregate Shocks and Heterogeneous Agents'. *Macroeconomic Dynamics*, 1: 355–86.

Den Haan, W. J. and Marcet, A. (1990). 'Solving the Stochastic Growth Model by Parameterizing Expectations'. *Journal of Business and Economic Statistics*, 8: 31–4.

Geanakoplos, J., Magill, M. J. P. and Quinzii, M. (2004). 'Demography and the Long Run Predictability of the Stock Market'. *Brookings Papers on Economic Activity*, 1: 241–325.

Huang, H., İmrohoroğlu, S. and Sargent, T. J. (1997). 'Two Computations to Fund Social Security'. *Macroeconomic Dynamics*, 1: 7–44.

Hubbard, R. G. and Judd, K. L. (1987). 'Social Security and Individual Welfare: Precautionary Saving, Borrowing Constraints, and the Payroll Tax'. *American Economic Review*, 77: 630–46.

İmrohoroğlu, A., İmrohoroğlu, S. and Joines, D. H. (1995). 'A Life Cycle Analysis of Social Security'. *Economic Theory*, 6: 83–114.

——— (1999). 'Social Security in an Overlapping Generations Economy with Land'. *Review of Economic Dynamics*, 2: 638–65.

Kotlikoff, L. J., Smetters, K. and Walliser, J. (2001). *Finding a Way Out of America's Demographic Dilemma*. Working Paper no. 8258. Boston: NBER.

Krueger, D. and Kubler, F. (2004). 'Computing Equilibrium in OLG Models with Stochastic Production'. *Journal of Economic Dynamics and Control*, 28: 1411–36.

——— (2006). 'Pareto Improving Social Security Reform When Financial Markets are Incomplete'. *American Economic Review*, 96: 737–55.

Krusell, P. and Smith, A. A. (1998). 'Income and Wealth Heterogeneity in the Macroeconomy'. *Journal of Political Economy*, 106: 867–96.

Miles, D. (1999). 'Modelling the Impact of Demographic Change upon the Economy'. *Economic Journal*, 109: 1–36.

Miles, D. and Cerny, A. (2006). 'Risk, Return and Portfolio Allocation under Alternative Pension Systems with Incomplete and Imperfect Financial Markets'. *Economic Journal*, 116: 529–57.

Rust, J. (1996). 'Numerical Dynamic Programming in Economics' , in *Handbook of Computational Economics*, vol. I, ed. H. M. Amman and D. A. Kendrick, Amsterdam: Elsevier, pp. 620–729.

Sánchez-Marcos, V. and Sánchez-Martín, A. R. (2006). 'Can Social Security be Welfare Improving When There is Demographic Uncertainty?' *Journal of Economic Dynamics and Control*, 30: 1615–49.

Storesletten, K., Telmer, C. I. and Yaron, A. (1999). 'The Risk Sharing Implications of Alternative Social Security Arrangements'. *Carnegie-Rochester Conference Series on Public Policy*, 50: 213–59.

Part IV

Extensions

10 Macro-economic consequences of demographic uncertainty in world regions

Vladimir Borgy and Juha M. Alho

Introduction

Demographic projections suggest that the OECD countries (notably the European countries and Japan) are expected to have large increases in their old-age dependency ratios. The other regions of the world are expected to have relatively low ratios, and their working-age populations are expected to increase. This differential timing of ageing may induce international flows of 'excess' saving from the ageing industrialized regions to the younger developing regions during the next decades. We expect such macro-economic dynamics – more precisely the saving-investment equilibrium – to be reflected in the world financial markets, in particular in the evolution of world interest rates.

While demographics have long been identified as a key variable in long-term macro-economic analysis, most previous analyses have relied on deterministic population forecasts. But, as contributions in this volume testify (e.g. Keilman, Cruijsen and Alho, chap. 2; Alho, Cruijsen and Keilman, chap. 3), demographic developments are uncertain, and attempts at describing this via scenario-based variants have serious shortcomings. As far as we know, the macro-economic consequences of demographic uncertainty have not been explored in the multi-regional setting of the world economy, but they can be of considerable interest. The asynchronous nature of the ageing process is expected to influence macro-economic trends, but it is also of interest that the uncertainty of population forecasts differs across world regions (National Research Council, 2000).

In this chapter, we investigate the impact of demographic uncertainty in a multi-regional general equilibrium, overlapping-generations model. Specifically, we will consider the level of uncertainty in ten major regions of the world, and its correlation across regions. In order to address these

We are grateful to Amina Lahrèche-Revil, Gilles Le Garrec and Valérie Mignon for their help. We would like to thank Pablo Antolin, Jean Chateau, Xavier Chojnicki and Jukka Lassila for useful comments and suggestions.

issues, we produce stochastic simulations of the population in the ten regions until 2050. Then, we will analyse the economic consequences on a path-by-path basis over the period 2000–2050.

These simulations allow us to assess the uncertainty induced in key macro-economic variables, the GDP growth rate and the world interest rate in particular, by uncertain future demographics. We will show that the assumptions regarding interregional correlations of forecast errors are important in our model: they have a large impact on the uncertainty of the macro-economic variables, and it appears that the macro-economic adjustments can differ substantially according to whether we consider independence or high correlation across the regions. In particular, the macro-economic behaviour of the agents in the current account/saving problem differs significantly across regions according to the degree of interregional correlation.

We start out by describing the main features of the point forecast for the world population, and then focus on both methodological and empirical aspects of the stochastic forecast of the world population. A non-technical overview of the economic model INGENUE 2[1] follows. Then we discuss our results on the world interest rate and the role played by the degree of interregional correlation.

Stochastic population forecasts at the world level

In order to produce point forecasts of population by region, we rely on the demographic block of INGENUE 2. The world is divided into ten regions, mainly according to geographic or cultural proximity: *North America* (including Australia and New Zealand), *Western Europe* (approximately the EU-15), *Japan*, *Eastern Europe* (including most of the newcomers to the EU), *Russian region* (including Ukraine and Belorussia), *Chinese region* (China and other East Asian countries excluding Japan*)*, *Indian region* (India, Indonesia, Pakistan, Bangladesh, Sri Lanka), *Latin region* (South and Central America and the Caribbean), *Mediterranean region* (non-European Mediterranean countries, Near and Middle Eastern countries) and *Africa* (Sub-Saharan Africa).

Main features of the point forecast

The regional point forecasts of population have been specified to match the UN forecasts from 2000 to 2050,[2] by age and sex. Using 1995 as the jump-off year, we project mortality by age and sex, and fertility by age, for each region, in the period 1995–2050. We assume that there is no migration across regions. Although this assumption is violated by a number of pairs of regions, relative to the sizes of the regions the migration flows are small. Changes in fertility and mortality rates are specified to match assumptions concerning the total fertility rate and life expectancy at birth.

According to the point forecast, the world population reaches 9.3 billion in 2050 (United Nations, 2001). The population of the Indian region grows to 2.9 billion in 2050 (31% of the world population, against 28% in 2000). The population of the Chinese region increases slowly until a peak in 2050. Its share of the world population decreases from 27% in 2000, to 22% in 2050. Or, over the next fifty years, the Indian region is expected to grow by 70%, whereas the Chinese region will grow by 25%. The African region is expected to grow the fastest due to its high fertility. In contrast, the population of Western Europe is expected to stay at the current level, so its share will decline from the current level of 6.4% to 3.5% in 2050.

Japan is expected to be the first region to undergo severe ageing. An increase in life expectancy coincides with a collapse of fertility (to 1.4 children per woman in 1995, against 2.0 in the United States and 1.7 in Europe). This leads to a decline of the working-age population, from 2005. Western Europe is also expected to undergo ageing as its dependency ratio (defined in this chapter as the ratio of retired persons to the population of working age) will rise substantially in the next decades (see Figure 10.1). In contrast, in North America fertility is expected to remain above 1.9 children, so the population is close to reproducing itself. There, the working-age population begins a slow decline in 2020.

Figure 10.1 shows that the Chinese region, Eastern Europe and the Russian region are also characterized by rapid ageing, which is expected to be even more pronounced in some countries than in Western Europe.

We concentrate first on the share of the 45–69-year-olds by region, because high savers are concentrated in these ages. Figure 10.2 shows that the proportion of high savers propagates from one region to the next over time. The proportion reaches a peak in Japan in 1995 and remains high until 2030. Then, North America has a maximum in 2025, Western Europe in 2030, and Eastern Europe, the Russian region and the Chinese region follow. All are regions with a declining labour force, which hampers future growth. In contrast, the potentially fast-growing regions are expected to see an increase in the proportion of high savers, which does not reach a peak before 2050. It follows that saving is expected to change from early high savers to late high savers in the coming decades. This is because according to the life-cycle hypothesis net savings should even out when cohorts reach the highest ages (Modigliani, 1986). This assumption is central to the saving behaviour of households in INGENUE 2.

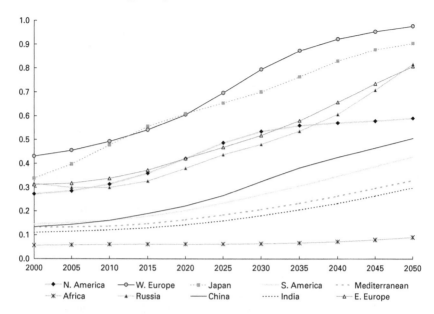

Figure 10.1. Point forecast of the dependency ratio (retired persons divided by total working-age population), 2000–2050.

Stochastic forecasts of the world population: methodological issues

For each region, the point forecast is used as input to PEP.[3] Since we assume no migration, the uncertainty of forecasting derives from fertility and mortality alone. As discussed by Alho, Cruijsen and Keilman (this volume, chap. 3) a direct empirical assessment of forecast uncertainty is a practical possibility in many countries, notably in the EU. However, for the broad regions of the world, only partial estimates are available (e.g. Alho, 1997). Thus, a different strategy had to be adopted.

To specify the uncertainty parameters we used two sources of information. First, as regards relative level of uncertainty across age and sex, we used the empirical estimates for the eighteen European countries discussed by Alho, Cruijsen and Keilman (this volume, chap. 3). Second, and more important, these estimates were proportionally calibrated to match the empirical findings concerning the overall level of uncertainty in population size, as given in chapter 7 of *Beyond Six Billion* (National Research Council, 2000).[4] These estimates were obtained for the total population of all countries included in the world forecasts of the UN, and for broad regions of the world, during the latter part of the twentieth century. In practice, we multiplied all age- and sex-specific uncertainty

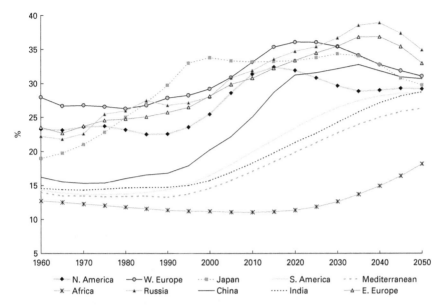

Figure 10.2. Point forecast of the high saver population (age-group 45–69 years) as percentage of the total population, 1960–2050.

parameters by one region-specific constant such that the resulting coefficient of variation[5] of the total population of each region, for year 2050, agreed with the empirical estimate. The coefficients of variation that we used for the calibration of the uncertainty parameters are presented in Table 10.1. The interpretation is that the probability of, say, Japan being within ±13 per cent of the point forecast in 2050 is about two-thirds. As discussed in Alho and Spencer (2005), these estimates depend on the volatility of population development during the past half-century. For some regions (such as Western Europe and North America) this period has been relatively calm so the level of uncertainty as specified in Table 10.1 is lower than estimates that are based on longer time periods. For others (such as the Russian region) the period may have been unusually turbulent.

In a multi-regional setting, the question of the correlation between the stochastic population forecasts is of major interest. Referring to the stochastic forecast for the world population presented in *Beyond Six Billion*, Alho and Spencer (2005) note that there were insufficient data reliably to estimate correlations across the ten regions empirically. Yet, the world forecast is sensitive to the level of interregional correlation.

Table 10.1. *Coefficients of variation used for the calibration of the uncertainty scale parameters.*

North America	Western Europe	Japan		South America	Mediterranean
0.06	0.05	0.13		0.12	0.24
Africa	Russian region	Chinese region	Indian region		Eastern Europe
0.17	0.26	0.11	0.11		0.06

Given that reliable empirical estimates of correlation were not available, we ran stochastic simulations with PEP in such a way that we could perform sensitivity analyses[6] concerning the level of correlation of interregional forecast errors. Technically, we relied on the use of seeds that has been implemented in PEP (see Alho and Spencer, 2005, chap. 9). For instance, if we want a positive correlation of 0.2 between regions, we first run the program PEP $4n/5$ times with a different seed for each region and then $n/5$ times with the same seed for all the regions. As a consequence, looking at the first $4n/5$ rounds of simulations allows us to analyse the case with the assumption of independence between the regions. By contrast, looking at the last $n/5$ rounds allows us to study the case of (essentially) perfect correlation. Results from the whole set of simulations (n times) allows us to study the case with a positive correlation of 0.2.

Stochastic forecasts of the world population: main results

Figure 10.3 depicts a stochastic forecast for the world population on the basis of 400 simulations performed with 50 per cent and 95 per cent prediction intervals that assume (unrealistically) complete independence between regions. The median of the predictive distribution for the world population in 2050 is 9.51 billion.[7] According to these estimates, there is a 50 per cent probability that the world population in 2050 is between 9.18 and 9.87 billion.

Table 10.2 presents the uncertainty of the world forecasts in the case of independence between regions compared with the cases where the interregional correlation is 0.1 and 0.2 respectively. Introducing an interregional correlation of 0.1 across the ten regions has the effect of multiplying the standard error estimates for the world by 1.19 compared to the standard errors assuming independence.[8] With an interregional correlation of 0.2, the standard error estimates for the world are multiplied by 1.30 compared to standard errors assuming independence. With the assumption of independence between the regions, the 95 per cent prediction interval is [8.71, 10.66] billion. With the assumption

Table 10.2. *Quantiles of the predictive distribution of world population in 2050 (billions).*

	0.025	0.25	0.5	0.75	0.975
Independence	8.71	9.18	9.51	9.87	10.66
Correlation of 0.1	8.45	9.15	9.50	9.87	10.77
Correlation of 0.2	8.23	9.12	9.50	9.89	10.89

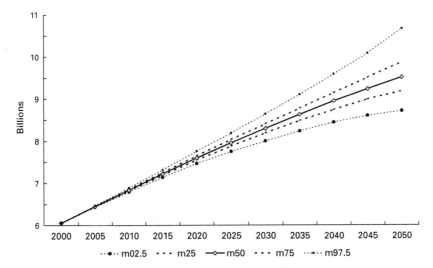

Figure 10.3. Stochastic forecasts of the world population, 2000–2050: independence of interregional forecast errors.

of an interregional correlation of 0.1, this interval is larger and ranges between 8.45 and 10.77 billion. It is even larger when we assume an interregional correlation of 0.2 as it reaches [8.23, 10.89] billion.

Table 10.3 shows that Western Europe will age rapidly in the coming decades: the median of the dependency ratio is expected to increase from 0.50 in 2010 to 0.99 in 2050, with a 90 per cent prediction interval of [0.88, 1.13]. A comparison with Table 10.4 indicates that the Russian region will age by as much, from 0.31 to 0.82 in 2050, but starting from a lower level. However, a major difference is that in the latter the 90 per cent prediction interval ranges from 0.46 to 1.30 in 2050. Furthermore, notice that the dispersion is already high in 2030.

Table 10.3. *Quantiles of the predictive distribution of the dependency ratio in the Western Europe in 2010, 2030 and 2050.*

	0.05	0.25	0.5	0.75	0.95
2010	0.49	0.50	0.50	0.50	0.50
2030	0.77	0.79	0.81	0.83	0.85
2050	0.88	0.95	0.99	1.04	1.13

Table 10.4. *Quantiles of the predictive distribution of the dependency ratio in the Russian region in 2010, 2030 and 2050.*

	0.05	0.25	0.5	0.75	0.95
2010	0.28	0.30	0.31	0.32	0.33
2030	0.33	0.43	0.50	0.56	0.63
2050	0.46	0.66	0.82	1.00	1.30

INGENUE 2: a long-term model for the world economy

Our economic simulations were made with a new version of the computable, general equilibrium, multi-regional overlapping-generations model INGENUE.[9] The model was initially constructed to assess wealth accumulation and the development of pension funds and other forms of retirement saving, in a global macro-economic setting,[10] for ten major regions of the world until 2050.

INGENUE 2 is an overlapping-generations model of Auerbach and Kotlikoff (1987) type. The model has 21 generations. The time unit is 5 years and the maximum life span is 105 years. The model includes 17 cohorts of adults (ages 20+) and 4 cohorts of young people (ages <20). Cost per child is proportional to the consumption of their parents. Labour supply is exogenous and adjusted for an age-specific participation ratio to the labour market in each region. The model does not distinguish between sexes, the young do not optimize their behaviour, and household behaviour is reduced to behaviour of individuals who progress from working age to retirement age according to region-specific patterns.

Household behaviour Individuals make economic decisions according to the life-cycle hypothesis. A voluntary bequest is left to children at age 80 (in the baseline version of INGENUE 2) subject to survival until this age. In the budget constraint, the expenditures consist of consumption (including costs of children) and saving in each age and each period. On the income side, there is, first, the return on accumulated saving corrected by one-year survival probabilities. This adjustment is equivalent to a perfect annuity market that pools the risk of death. Second, there is non-financial income that depends on age. This includes labour income (net after social security taxes) that is adjusted by region-specific age-profiles of labour force participation, a mix of labour income and pension for the partially retired population, and full pension for the retired. The lifetime utility is maximized under the intertemporal budget constraint, taking prices, social contributions and benefits as given (Modigliani, 1986).

The public sector is confined to a public pay-as-you-go (PAYG) defined-benefit pension scheme in all regions. It pays a proportion of the current net wage to retired persons. It is financed by a payroll tax on labour income. The exogenous parameters are the retirement age and the replacement ratio. They are region-specific and the contribution rate is determined so as to balance the budget, period by period.

Production system   Goods are heterogeneous. In each region there is an intermediate goods sector. It uses labour and capital to produce a region-specific intermediate good with a constant-return-to-scale Cobb-Douglas production function. The final goods sector is the product of a constant elasticity of substitution (CES) combination of a domestic intermediate good and a foreign intermediate good imported by the region from a world market (Backus, Kehoe and Kydland, 1995). This homogeneous world good is 'produced' by a fictive world producer as the output of a CES combination of all intermediate goods exported by the regions. All production functions are augmented by total factor productivity (TFP) coefficients.

Firm behaviour   In each sector (intermediate/final goods), markets are competitive. Firms maximize their profit under their production constraint, taking prices as given. In the domestic intermediate good sector the constraint is intertemporal, since the production function depends on the stock of capital that is depreciated and accumulated. Intermediate goods producers maximize net present value of future cash flows, i.e. production value minus wage cost and capital cost. The latter depends on the depreciation rate, which is itself influenced by international capital market imperfections. The depreciation rate is higher in debtor regions: the higher the ratio of net foreign debt to the stock of capital, the higher the depreciation rate. Therefore, the debt constraint increases the required gross rate of return on capital in debtor regions, which in turn lowers the demand for capital. Other types of producer face a simpler problem. In each region, a domestic goods producer maximizes current profit subject to a CES production function that includes the regional intermediate good and the world intermediate good. The world producer maximizes current profit subject to its CES production function that includes all the region-specific intermediate goods.

General equilibrium   The capital stock in each region, the age distribution of saving in each region and the initial prices of domestic commodities are the initial conditions. Exogenous variables and parameters are the demographic profiles in each region that are outputs of the demographic upstream model; the coefficients of the TFP determination in the intermediary and final sectors of each region; and the social security policy parameters in each region. The competitive world equilibrium stems from five sets of equations: intertemporal utility maximization of households; intertemporal profit maximization of firms in intermediate goods sectors; period profit maximization of firms in final goods sectors; period profit maximization of the world producer; and market clearing conditions. The markets for intermediate goods, final goods and labour in each region, and the market for the world intermediate good, are cleared in each period. These equations determine all relative equilibrium prices expressed in a common *numeraire*, which is the price of the intermediate good in North America. This convention allows us to express values in constant dollars. Finally, Walras's law implies that the world financial market equilibrium is the redundant equation.

Technological catching up   The level of TFP is exogenous and grows at a constant rate, in each region. For 1950 until 2000, the growth rate of TFP is given by historical data. After this date the rate of growth of the TFP is the result of a given, exogenous growth of 1.1 per cent per annum in the North American region, supposed to be the technological leader, and a region-specific exogenous, catching-up factor, reflecting international diffusion of technological progress. In the baseline scenario of the model, three regions have a sustained catching-up process: the take-off in the Chinese and Indian regions which had already started in the 1990s is assumed to gain momentum. Eastern Europe is also assumed to be a fast-growing region due to its accession to the European Union. The model has been calibrated on the basis of the international macro-economic database constructed by Heston, Summers and Aten (2002).

Table 10.5. *Quantiles of the predictive distribution of GDP growth in Western Europe in 2010, 2030 and 2050.*

	0.05	0.25	0.5	0.75	0.95
2010	1.85	1.88	1.90	1.92	1.94
2030	0.57	0.61	0.64	0.68	0.72
2050	0.31	0.52	0.67	0.80	1.04

Table 10.6. *Quantiles of the predictive distribution of GDP growth in the Russian region in 2010, 2030 and 2050.*

	0.05	0.25	0.5	0.75	0.95
2010	1.20	1.45	1.60	1.73	1.85
2030	0.15	0.65	0.84	0.99	1.14
2050	−1.11	−0.44	0.08	0.58	1.17

Macro-economic consequences of demographic uncertainty in a multi-regional model

In this section, we analyse the economic consequences on a path-by-path basis. The macro-economic consequences of demographic uncertainty are different from one region to another (Table 10.1). For instance, the uncertainty surrounding the GDP growth rate is higher for the Russian region than for the Western European region of the model as a result of the higher uncertainty concerning the population forecasts in the former region (Tables 10.5 and 10.6). The median of the predictive distribution of GDP growth decreases in Western Europe from 1.90% in 2010 to 0.67% in 2050 with a 90% prediction interval of [0.31%, 1.04%]. In the Russian region the median decreases sharply from 1.60% in 2010 to 0.08% in 2050. The uncertainty is substantially higher than in Western Europe with a 90% prediction interval of [−1.11%, 1.17%].

In the INGENUE 2 model, the world interest rate balances at each period the capital supply and the capital demand at a world level. The equilibrium of the world financial market is then given by the equation:

$$\sum_z p_f^z(t) K^z(t) = \sum_z p_f^z(t) S^z(t)$$

Or, at time t the world interest rate will balance the sum over all regions z, of firms' capital stocks $K^z(t)$ and assets (held by the households) $S^z(t)$, where $p_f^z(t)$ denotes the price of the final good produced in region z at t.

Table 10.7. *Quantiles of the predictive distribution of the world interest rate, 2010–2050.*

	0.025	0.25	0.5	0.75	0.975
2010	6.582	6.635	6.661	6.683	6.731
2020	5.267	5.346	5.384	5.421	5.505
2030	4.531	4.648	4.702	4.759	4.887
2040	4.193	4.333	4.397	4.479	4.646
2050	3.889	4.059	4.136	4.241	4.415

As a theoretical 'balancing variable', the interest rate does not exactly correspond to observable interest rates. In fact, our interest rate is much more stable than such rates are, in practice. There seem to be two reasons for this. First, the only source of volatility in the interest rate in our framework is unpredictable demographics. Factors such as structural shocks, changes in monetary policy etc. that can have a major impact on actual interest rates are not considered. Second, as our model assumes perfect foresight, even demographic shocks far in the future are known to the decision-makers, so that they are able to adjust to them from the outset. Together, these factors imply that the interest rate we consider behaves, roughly speaking, like a very long moving average taken over an actual interest rate, such as the real US bond yield rate of AAA companies.

In the deterministic baseline scenario, the world interest rate is expected to decline in the next fifty years as a result of the demographic evolution and the macro-economic dynamics: the working-age population is expected to decline absolutely while the age-group of high savers is expected to grow in one region after another (Figure 10.2). In the first decades, there is a substantial amount of saving by the ageing populations of Western Europe and Japan. In the long run, saving will diminish here but increase in the developing regions, where investment will become more efficient due to technological catching up. As a result, the world saving–investment equilibrium is tilted towards a lower equilibrium rate.

Introducing stochastic demographics into the economic model does not substantially change the picture: the general declining pattern of the world interest rate remains the same. The uncertainty related to this economic variable increases over time but remains quite low (see Table 10.7).

Introducing an interregional correlation of 0.2 across the regions increases the standard deviation of the world interest rate, but the effect becomes smaller with the forecast horizon (Table 10.8). In 2010 the standard deviation is multiplied by 1.375 but in 2040 by only 1.143.

Table 10.8. *Dependence of standard deviation of world interest rate on interregional correlation of population uncertainty.*

	2010	2020	2030	2040	2050
Ratio[1]	1.375	1.288	1.163	1.143	1.079

Note: [1] Defined as standard deviation when interregional correlation is 0.2 divided by standard deviation when regions are independent.

These results contrast with those obtained with the GDP growth, above. In particular, we conjecture that the narrowness of the prediction intervals for the world interest rate is primarily due to the (unrealistic) assumption of perfect foresight of the agents.

In order to analyse the effects of demographic uncertainty on the world interest rate, we compute three 'global' dependency ratios. The G3 dependency ratio includes the three most industrialized regions of the model, namely Western Europe, North America and Japan. The G5 dependency ratio includes Western Europe, North America, Japan, Eastern Europe and the Russian region, which expected to experience the most significant ageing over the next five decades. The world dependency ratio includes all ten regions.

Figure 10.4 depicts the G3 dependency ratio and the world interest rate in 2030 for the case where interregional forecast errors are independent (based on 200 simulations). There is a clear negative correlation between the dependency ratio and the interest rate ($R^2 = 0.31$). To understand this economically, note first that a higher than expected dependency ratio reflects either a high number of elderly people, a low number of working-age people, or both. Consider first the case of an unexpectedly low number of workers.[11] In our economic framework, investment is taken to be an increasing function of the working-age population, so we expect a decline in demand for investment capital. This tends to lower the interest rates. Consider now the case in which we have a higher than expected number of the elderly.[12] Under the assumption of perfect foresight, workers will save more, all through their careers, than under the most likely circumstances. Thus, there will be an increase in the supply of capital to the markets, and interest rates will again go down. With a longer perspective, the macro-economic effects of a higher than expected number of the elderly will be different. As they retire, individuals will sell their assets to finance consumption: the lower amount of assets will induce an increase of the interest rate. As the share of the elderly population increases over time, saving at the macro level will decrease and the interest rate will then rise.

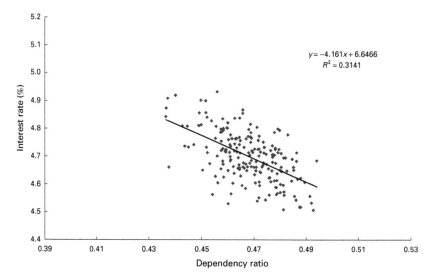

Figure 10.4. World interest rate as a function of the G3 dependency ratio in 2030 under the assumption that interregional forecast errors are independent.

The link between the world interest rate and the G3 dependency ratio is reinforced when we assume a positive correlation for the interregional forecast errors. Figure 10.5 depicts the G3 dependency ratio and the world interest rate in 2030 for the case where interregional forecast errors have a positive correlation of 0.2.[13] By comparing this result with the previous one, we note that the dispersion of the dependency ratio is higher. This results from the fact that we now take into account simulations with interregional forecast errors that have a positive correlation (i.e. stochastic simulations of populations with low fertility rate and/or higher life expectancy for one region are associated with stochastic simulations with the same characteristics for the nine remaining regions). Furthermore, the scatter of the world interest rate is also higher than in the case where interregional forecast errors are independent.[14] Or, the positive correlation between regions leads to economic situations where the tensions on the world capital market are substantial.

The G3 dependency ratio is perhaps the most accurate 'global old age' variable of the three that we have considered for the purpose of explaining the level of the world interest rate in 2030 as it has $R^2 = 0.52$ (Figure 10.5). Indeed, when interregional forecast errors have a positive

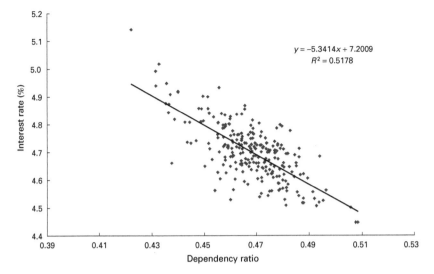

Figure 10.5. World interest rate as a function of the G3 dependency ratio in 2030 under the assumption that interregional forecast errors have a correlation of 0.2.

correlation of 0.2, the R^2 of the regressions of the world interest rate on the G5 and world dependency ratios are equal to 0.37 and 0.38, respectively.

In order to have a deeper understanding of the effect of cross-regional correlation of demographics on the world interest rate, we look at the simulation leading to the lowest level for world interest rate in 2030. This occurred under a perfect correlation simulation. In it, fertility is globally lower than in the point forecast, leading to a lower growth rate of the working population of the regions from 2030 (Figure 10.6). Also, life expectancy is higher than in the point forecast, so the dependency ratio, the contribution rate to the retirement system, and the proportion of high savers are substantially higher than under the point forecast, in the developing regions of the model. Over the period 2000–2030, the increase of saving is the highest in the regions facing the most significant rises in the dependency ratio. Thus, the supply of capital from households is high for all regions during 2000–2030 (see Figure 10.7).[15] The lower labour input leads to lower investment and a lower GDP growth after 2035. This lowers the demand for capital from firms. Over the whole period, the interest rate resulting from this saving–investment equilibrium is lower than under the most likely population development, because the global capital supply exceeds the capital demand in all regions.

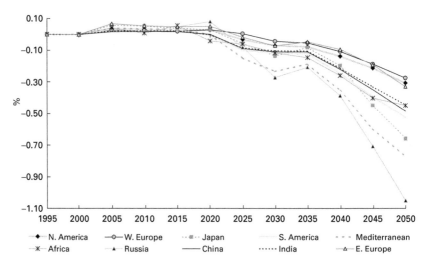

Figure 10.6. Working-age population annual growth rate, 1995–2050: difference from baseline scenario.

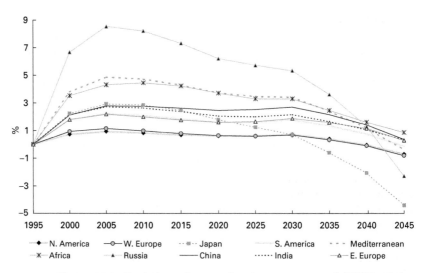

Figure 10.7. Evolution of net saving (as percentage of GDP), 1995–2045: difference from baseline scenario.

Macro-economic dynamics with perfect interregional correlation vs. independence

We have seen that the macro-economic behaviour of the agents in the regions is related to the degree of interregional correlation. In order to illustrate this point we focus on the current account/saving problem for Western Europe, North America and Japan on the one hand, and the Chinese and Indian regions on the other.

By 2025,[16] industrialized regions have begun to experience ageing: the dependency ratio of Western Europe is expected to increase to 0.7 from 0.45 in 2005, and in Japan it is expected to rise to 0.65 from 0.40 in 2005 (Figure 10.1). Although the ageing process is less pronounced in the other two Asian regions, the dependency ratio is still expected to increase by almost 0.10, reaching 0.26 in 2025 in the Chinese region. In the Indian region, the increase is expected to be much less pronounced as the ratio increases only by 0.04 during 2005–2025 to reach 0.16. According to the point forecast, the proportion of high savers would reach its peak in 2020–2025 in Western Europe (Figure 10.2). At this time, the proportion of high savers will be high in Japan,[17] but also in the Chinese region and North America. In 2025, the proportion of high savers is expected to have increased in the Indian region but to remain below 25 per cent of the total population. From the economic point of view, in 2025 the three industrialized regions are creditors *vis-à-vis* the rest of the world, because they all have current account surpluses. In contrast, the two Asian regions are net borrowers (Figure 10.8).

Indeed, our analysis shows that Western Europe could get a current account surplus: the saving of European households could flow towards the developing regions of the world that have a more sustained path of growth, due to the increase of their working-age populations. Nevertheless, these regions will also face fiscal sustainability problems in relation to ageing in the more distant future (Figure 10.1).

Our simulations highlight the potential effect of cross-regional correlation on macro-economics. For instance, there is a clear positive association ($R^2 = 0.72$) between the current account position and the level of saving in Western Europe in 2025 (see Figure 10.9) when regional demographics are independent. The level of saving depends on population structure that differs from one population simulation to another. A high level of national saving will allow the Western European region to have a more pronounced creditor position *vis-à-vis* the rest of the world. In the case in which cross-regional correlation is 0.2, the association is less important ($R^2 = 0.60$).

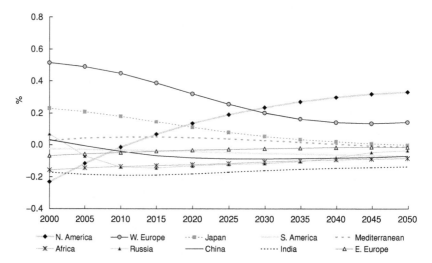

Figure 10.8. Evolution of current account balance in the INGENUE 2 model (percentage of world GDP), 2000–2050.

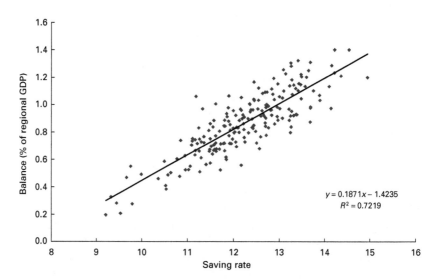

Figure 10.9. Current account as a function of saving in Western Europe in 2025 under the assumption that interregional forecast errors are independent.

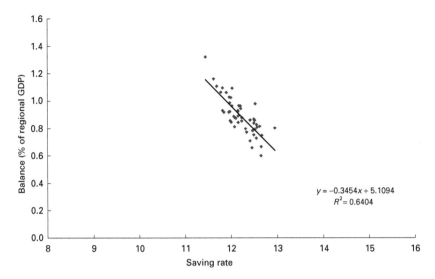

Figure 10.10. Current account as a function of saving in Western Europe in 2025 under the assumption that interregional forecast errors are perfectly correlated.

In order to understand this result, we plot in Figure 10.10 the current account and the level of saving in the case of perfect correlation of the interregional forecast errors.[18] The correlation between the economic variables is now negative. This is caused by behavioural adjustments of the economic agents.[19] Indeed, the correlation between savings for two regions is high in the case of perfect correlation. For instance, the regression of saving in North America on saving in Western Europe in 2030 shows a high positive correlation ($R^2 = 0.841$) and the regression coefficient is equal to 1.11. (In the case of independence of interregional forecast errors, $R^2 = 0.127$ only.) This statistical result concerning saving in the case of perfect correlation is observed for all the regions. For instance, for the regression of saving in Western Europe on saving in the Indian region in 2030 we have $R^2 = 0.67$, reflecting a high positive correlation in the case of perfect interregional correlation, while it is equal to zero in the case of independence between the regions.

The phenomenon we observe is caused by the fact that, for each simulation, deviations from the point forecast go in the same direction for all regions (Figure 10.6 illustrates this for the working-age population). As a consequence, once the decision-makers discover the non-anticipated new population path in 2000, households in each region will change their consumption/saving behaviour in the same way. For instance, while the

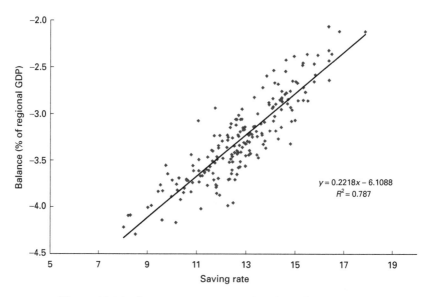

Figure 10.11. Current account as a function of saving in the Indian region in 2025 under the assumption that interregional forecast errors are independent.

households of a region will increase their saving during their working period if life expectancy is higher than in the point forecast, the same will happen in other regions as well. Therefore, the amount of capital exported by these regions (inducing a current account surplus) is not a function of the level of their national saving as in the case of independence between regions. To illustrate this further, we focus on the Indian region. In the case of independence between the regions, we observe the same statistical relation as for the Western Europe case (Figure 10.11). The current account deficit of the Indian region is all the more important when the level of saving is low in the region. In the case of perfect correlation across the regions, this positive correlation does not hold anymore (Figure 10.12): the coefficient associated with the regression (which was 0.22 in the previous case) is now –0.03. Furthermore, the range of the current account deficit is much narrower than in the case with independence.[20]

It appears that the external position of the Asian regions (Chinese and Indian regions) is less sensitive to the level of their saving in the case with perfect interregional correlation. The link between the macro-economic variables in this multi-regional setting is then distorted in the cases in which all the regions face the same type of innovations concerning their population paths.

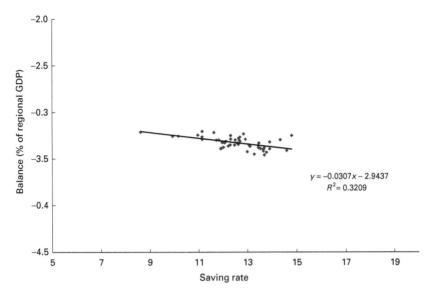

Figure 10.12. Current account as a function of saving in the Indian region in 2025 under the assumption that interregional forecast errors are perfectly correlated.

Conclusion

In this study, we have investigated, apparently for the first time, the impact of demographic uncertainty within a multi-regional general equilibrium, overlapping-generations model. A major challenge was to generate a joint predictive distribution of the population of the ten world regions by age and sex. A simplified approach was adopted that borrows age- and sex-specific information from models discussed in Chapter 3, and information about the uncertainty of the total populations from other statistical sources. It seems that such approximations will continue to be necessary far into the future, because of problems in the quality of demographic data outside the industrialized countries. We offer three main conclusions: two empirical ones relating to economics, the third a methodological one.

First, introducing stochastic population paths into the multi-regional world model indicates that the effect of the uncertainty of demography has a major impact on GDP growth. In particular, the larger the uncertainty in the size of the working-age population of a region, the larger the uncertainty in GDP growth. This effect and its timing is quantified in a setting of world regions.

Second, as one would expect, introducing stochastic demographics does not change the decreasing trend of the world interest rate during

2000–2050 that we get in the baseline scenario. However, an important finding was the narrow range of uncertainty in the interest rate, even up to 2050. This might seem surprising, since comparable interest rates, such as the bond yield rates of major companies, display much more volatility. The major reason for the difference appears to be that this aspect of our model is particularly vulnerable to the perfect-foresight hypothesis. Extensions in which this assumption can be relaxed in a realistic manner are a topic of future research.

Third, interregional correlations of population evolution appear to be important in the multi-regional model, as they have a large impact on the uncertainty surrounding the macro-economic variables. Although existing estimates of cross-regional correlation point to relatively low values, by considering the extreme assumption of perfect correlation we discovered a qualitatively different economic evolution, as compared to the case of independence. Thus, the consideration of stochastic paths revealed a structural feature of the multi-regional INGENUE 2 (specifically, the link between the current account position and the level of saving in different regions) that would have been difficult to detect using the conventional approach of considering a limited number of alternative scenarios.

NOTES

1 The INGENUE 2 model was developed at CEPII, Paris, in collaboration with CEPREMAP and OFCE, by Michel Aglietta (CEPII), Vladimir Borgy (CEPII), Jean Chateau (OECD), Michel Juillard (CEPREMAP), Jacques Le Cacheux (OFCE), Gilles Le Garrec (OFCE) and Vincent Touzé (OFCE). See Ingenue (2007) for a description of the model and detailed definitions of world regions.
2 As discussed by Keilman, Cruijsen and Alho (this volume, chap. 2), this probably understates the speed of ageing somewhat.
3 Program for Error Propagation. A detailed description of the program is available at www.joensuu.fi/statistics/juha.html.
4 Some regrouping of the countries had to be done to arrive at the final estimates for the work at hand.
5 I.e. standard deviation divided by the mean.
6 We compare the case of independence of interregional forecast errors with the one where the correlation between regions is positive and could reach 0.2.
7 In general, the median of the predictive distribution does not exactly agree with the point forecast. In addition, the calibration of the data for use in PEP was based on a number of simplifying assumptions. Finally, simulation error may contribute to the difference between 9.51 billion and the UN point forecast of 9.3 billion.
8 Based on extensive simulations Alho and Spencer (2005) find a multiplier of 1.28 for the standard-error estimate for the corresponding analysis. The

difference may be due to the limited number of simulations we have at our disposal.

9 For technical features of the new INGENUE 2 model, as well as the baseline scenario and a sensitivity analysis of the main structural parameters, see Ingenue (2007).

10 For a synthetic view of the global demographic changes issue, see IMF (2004) and Ingenue (2002). This issue is also explored in a multi-country model by Börsch-Supan, Ludwig and Winter (2006).

11 As discussed in Alho, Cruijsen and Keilman (this volume, chap. 3), this occurs typically if our forecast of net migration is too high.

12 This would typically be caused by mortality being lower than we expect.

13 Technically, the 50 simulations of stochastic populations that have been performed with PEP by taking the same seed for the different regions of the model are added to the 200 independent simulations.

14 This result has already been highlighted in Table 10.8.

15 Overall, the deviations from the baseline scenario are the largest for the regions where the uncertainty scale parameters have the highest calibrated values (see Table 10.1).

16 The results are similar for the decade 2020–2030, but they would differ for more distant periods as the relative demographic and economic features of the regions change.

17 The proportion of high savers also reaches high values in Eastern Europe and the Russian region, two regions that will also experience ageing and fiscal sustainability problems at this time horizon.

18 This corresponds to the stochastic simulations performed with the same seed for all the regions of the model.

19 We note that the same regression based on the current account and saving in the North American region in 2025 leads to the same results. In the case of Japan, there is a clear positive correlation in the case with independence of interregional forecast errors but there is no correlation in the case of perfect correlation between the regions of the model.

20 Similar adjustments occur in the case of the Chinese region. Nevertheless, the regression in the case of perfect correlation leads to a small positive value for the coefficient (0.047) associated with the regression.

REFERENCES

Alho, J. M. (1997). 'Scenarios, Uncertainty and Conditional Forecasts of the World Population'. *Journal of the Royal Statistical Society. Series A* 160: 71–85.

(1998). 'A Stochastic Forecast of the Population of Finland'. Review no. 1998/4. Helsinki: Statistics Finland.

Alho, J. M. and Spencer, B. D. (2005). *Statistical Demography and Forecasting.* New York: Springer.

Auerbach, A. and Kotlikoff, L. (1987). *Dynamic Fiscal Policy*, Cambridge: Cambridge University Press.

Backus, D., Kehoe, P. and Kydland, F. (1995). 'International Business Cycles: Theory and Evidence', in *Frontiers of Business Cycle Research*, ed. T. F. Cooley. Princeton: Princeton University Press, pp. 331–56.

Börsch-Supan, A., Ludwig, A. and Winter, J. (2006). 'Ageing, Pension Reform and Capital Flows: a Multi-country Simulation Model'. *Economica* 73: 625–58.

Heston, A., Summers, R. and Aten, B. (2002). 'Penn World Table 6.1', Center for International Comparisons at the University of Pennsylvania (CICUP).

IMF (2004). 'How Will Demographic Change Affect the Global Economy?' *World Economic Outlook* (www.imf.org/external/pubs/ft/weo/2004/02/)

Ingenue (2002). 'A Long Term Model for the World Economy', in *Market Imperfections and Macroeconomic Dynamics*, ed. J. O. Hairault and H. Kempf. Boston: Kluwer, pp. 51–73.

  (2007). 'INGENUE 2: A Long Term Intertemporal World Model for the 21st Century'. Working paper, CEPII, Paris.

Modigliani F. (1986). 'Life Cycle, Individual Thrift, and the Wealth of Nations', (Nobel Lecture), *American Economic Review*, 76: 297–313.

National Research Council (2000). *Beyond Six Billion: Forecasting the World's Population*. Panel on Population Projections. Washington, DC: National Academy Press.

United Nations (2001). *World Population Prospects. The 2000 Revision*, vol. I: *Comprehensive Tables*. New York: United Nations.

11 Informational assumptions, aggregate mortality risk and life-cycle saving

Juha M. Alho and Niku Määttänen

Introduction

The primary motivation of models discussed in this volume is the need to quantify the effects of policy measures on, for example, the pension system. Stylized models are preferred for qualitative insight (Diamond, 2001), but cannot provide precise estimates for policy formulation. The price one has to pay for the realism is the relative complexity of the models. The models are not analytically tractable and even a description of their computational solution is involved. We discuss here a related model that deals with decision-making in the presence of uncertainty about future mortality rates. While our model does not allow for analytical solutions either, it is transparent in terms of what is being optimized and permits an analysis of more general informational assumptions than the complex models used to analyse pension problems. In discussing the model we have the following three issues in mind.

First, studies of the use of population forecasts in decision-making[1] suggest that while the uncertainty of forecasts is readily acknowledged by both the users and producers of forecasts (Alho, Cruijsen and Keilman, this volume, chap. 3), there is considerable inertia in the adoption of new methods. Cohort-component forecasts of population have been produced in many European countries since the 1920s and 1930s (Alho and Spencer, 2005). Since that time, alternative forecast variants have typically been offered, but the users have almost invariably considered the middle variant only. As discussed by Alho, Cruijsen and Keilman (this volume, chap. 3), providing alternative variants is a deficient method for handling uncertainty. Nevertheless, a reason for considering only one variant may be the cost of added complexity in a decision process involving several decision-makers. Alho and Spencer (2005) note that frequent updates may similarly be costly and lead to a lack of predictability in other parts of the economic system. Thus, it is of interest to discuss low information alternatives to rational expectations. In the lowest information one, we assume that the decision-maker ('consumer', in our example) only learns the initial point forecast, makes a life-course plan and never reconsiders. In an intermediate information case we assume that the decision-maker is periodically provided with an updated point forecast that reflects the demographic development up to that time. She then produces a new plan for the rest of her life. This method of updating is continued until death. At any update, she does not take into account that she will be offered a chance to reconsider later on. Obviously, the low information alternatives should produce lower utilities than the rational-expectations solution, on average. The question is how much the decision-maker loses compared to a rational-expectations solution.

Second, the OLG models developed for Denmark, Finland, Germany, Netherlands and the UK that are discussed in this volume (Lassila and Valkonen, chap. 5; Fehr and Haberman, chap. 7; Armstrong *et al.*, chap. 9; Weale, chap. 4) have been developed in a deterministic context. In other words, only one future population path is considered, and decision-makers are assumed to know it exactly. The authors are fully aware that the assumption of perfect foresight is not natural in the context of stochastic population development, but numerical complications (caused by lack of Markovianity and the high dimensionality of the resulting optimization problem) currently preclude a formulation with rational decision-makers who take precautions in the face of uncertainty. In contrast, our setting is simple enough so that the computational problems of determining the optimal decisions can be overcome. Thus, we are able to evaluate how much a decision-maker gains if given access to the 'crystal ball' of perfect foresight as compared to the rational-expectations solution.

Third, results in this volume and other work all suggest that uncertainty of population development directly influences the sustainability of pension systems (Weale, this volume, chap. 4) and public finances as a whole (Alho and Vanne, 2006). On the other hand, although it has been established that past forecasts of mortality have had major errors (National Research Council, 2000), it has also been shown that for the sustainability of the health care systems other factors dominate (Ahn, this volume, chap. 6). In our example, we consider *aggregate mortality risk*, i.e. the uncertainty caused by the fact that the forecast of the average mortality of a cohort is uncertain. While it is well known that aggregate mortality risk is a major concern for public pension systems and insurance companies selling annuities (Blake and Burrows, 2001; Friedberg and Webb, 2005), less is known about its direct importance to consumers trying to make optimal savings decisions. We will quantify this effect relative to *idiosyncratic mortality risk*, by which we mean the uncertainty of an individual's lifetime conditional on average cohort mortality. This, of course, is a topic of classical life insurance mathematics.

The life-cycle savings problem we consider involves a consumer who has to decide how much to save for retirement. She understands the nature of idiosyncratic risk, but her understanding of the uncertainty of forecasting ranges from the low information alternatives, via knowledge of the exact predictive distribution of future mortality, to perfect foresight. Formally, the predictive distribution we use is essentially equivalent to the mortality model of Lee and Carter (1992). Instead of trying to replicate the mortality of any given country, we will numerically evaluate the model so that it is representative of mortality in Europe, as assessed in the UPE project (Keilman, Cruijsen and Alho, this volume, chap. 2). A discrete Markovian approximation will be provided that represents the uncertainty of forecasting fifty years into the future. This allows us to carry out the dynamic optimization (Filar and Vrieze, 1997) needed for the rational-expectations solution. Mathematically, the other informational settings are easier.

We will start by developing the mortality model. Then, we describe the consumer's decision problem in terms of her utility function, and the welfare measure that is used to translate utilities to equivalent consumption. Results for the various informational assumptions and different degrees of risk aversion follow. We conclude by considering the implications of our findings for future work.

Demographics

In this section, we present the stochastic process for aggregate mortality. The challenge is to specify a process which is sufficiently simple that we can solve the life-cycle savings problem of a fully rational consumer, but which can also be calibrated to be empirically relevant.

We assume that time is discrete and index the periods as $t = 1, 2, \ldots, T$ and ages as $j = 1, 2, \ldots, T$. Death occurs only at the end of a period.

Let $m_t(j) \geq 0$ be the age-specific mortality rate among consumers of age j during period $t = 1, 2, \ldots$ True future mortality rates are taken to be random. Following loosely the bilinear model of Lee and Carter (1992), we specify the probability law of future mortality as follows. Let $m(j)$ be the current mortality rate of age j and assume that it is known. Its expected rate of decline is $b(j)$, and the median mortality t years ahead is $\hat{m}_t(j) = m(j) \exp(-tb(j))$. For a simple representation of the uncertainty of the forecast, we define a Bernoulli process X_t such that $P(X_t = 1) = P(X_t = 0) = 1/2$ and then a discrete random walk $Y_t = Y_{t-1} + X_t$, where $Y_0 = 0$. This is a first-order Markov process with mean (or drift) $t/2$. Let us further define a function $Z_t(y) = (y - t/2)\phi$, where $\phi > 0$ is a volatility parameter to be specified later. Then, the true age-specific mortality is assumed to be of the form

$$m_t(j) = m(j) \exp(-(t + Z_t(Y_t))b(j)) \tag{1}$$

Denote the probability that a consumer who is alive and of age j at time t will be alive at the beginning of the next period by $s_t(j)$. For calibration purposes we assume that each period corresponds to five calendar years. Assuming that mortality is constant within a period, we have

$$s_t(j) = \exp(-5m_t(j)) \tag{2}$$

In the analysis below, we will consider only the problem of consumers who are of age 1 in period 1. That is, we specialize to the case $t = j$. We will take the first period to correspond to ages 20–24 and the last period to ages 105–109. After that everyone is assumed to die. Therefore, the latest time period we will have to consider is $T = 18$. On the other hand, it will be important to keep in mind that the probabilities in equation (2) are random, since they are functions of Y_t via equation (1). To make this transparent, when $t = j$ we will write $s_t(j) = S_t(Y_t)$ for equation (2). We assume that period t mortality rates are observed at the end of period t. Due to the Markovianity of process Y_t, both the expectation and median forecast, at time v, for the survival probability at time $t \geq v$ depend on Y_{v-1}. We denote the median by $\widehat{S}_t^v$. A technical issue that arises here is that, under our model, randomness is incorporated in a non-linear manner into survival probabilities (equation (2)), so setting aggregate variance to zero does not exactly yield unconditional expected values. Instead, the relevant quantities must be determined numerically.

The mortality process is parameterized by the values $m(j)$, $b(j)$ and ϕ. In calibrating these we aim to provide realistic values in a European context, rather than to replicate the values of any given country at any given time. Thus, we use combined male and female mortality data from Finland in 2002 for the $m(j)$,[2] and average rates of decline in mortality from eleven European countries during 1970–2000 (Alho and Spencer 2005, p. 235). These empirical data were available up to age 99. The estimates were extended to age-group 100–104 by assuming mortality to increase at the same rate as it increased from ages 90–94 to ages 95–99. The rate of decline over time was assumed to be the same as in age-group 95–99. For simplicity, we further assumed $m(j) = 0$, for $j < 10$. To specify the volatility of the process, we used data from nine European countries with long mortality series of good quality. The data suggest that a random walk can provide an approximate representation for the

Table 11.1. *Parameter values for the mortality process and the median survival probabilities.*

Age	Model age	m	b	Median survival probability
20–64	1–9	0	0	1
65–69	10	0.026	0.100	0.955
70–74	11	0.044	0.100	0.931
75–79	12	0.072	0.100	0.886
80–84	13	0.119	0.078	0.806
85–89	14	0.190	0.061	0.671
90–94	15	0.283	0.044	0.481
95–99	16	0.404	0.029	0.280
100–104	17	0.577	0.029	0.172
105–109	18	∞	0	0

forecast error of the log of the age-specific mortality, when the standard deviation of the process increment is taken to be 0.06 (Alho and Spencer, 2005, p. 256). By taking into account that an average value for the $b(j)$s is about 0.08, we arrive at a value $\phi = 3.3541$. Table 11.1 displays $m(j)$ and $b(j)$. In addition, it shows median probabilities of surviving from one period to the next.

To see how the calculations were made, note first that the rate of decline corresponds to five-year model periods, so the annual rate of decline is about $0.08/5 = 0.016$, or about 1.6 per cent. Also, note that we are displaying cohort survival probabilities here. Thus, for example, the median mortality of those in age-group 85–89 has been reduced from the value 0.190 at $t = 0$, during fourteen model periods to $0.190^* \exp(-14^*0.062) = 0.07976$. Thus, the median survival is $\exp(-5^*0.07976) = 0.671$, the value given in the last column of Table 11.1 for this age-group.

As an illustration of the degree of uncertainty attached to future mortality, we present in Figure 11.1 the distribution of average life times over 10,000 realizations of the mortality process. The standard deviation is approximately 3.3 years. Since this represents *cohort* survival fifty years into the future, it agrees well with the somewhat larger UPE values of Table 3.3 that relate to *period* survival in 2049.

A related aspect of the mortality model is the relationship between aggregate uncertainty and idiosyncratic uncertainty. Consider median mortality. An individual's life span has a standard deviation of about 6.1 years around the point forecast. (This value is somewhat too low, because we have completely eliminated the 'outliers' that occur, in reality, before

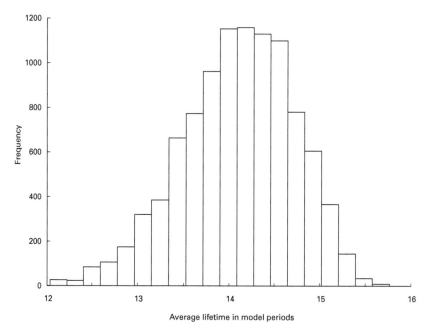

Figure 11.1. Histogram of average lifetimes in 10,000 simulations.

age 65.) This means that the total standard deviation that includes the aggregate uncertainty is approximately $(6.1^2 + 3.3^2)^{1/2} = 6.94$. We see that from an individual's point of view adding the aggregate uncertainty only adds about 14 per cent to the standard deviation, so it does not dramatically alter the prospects of longevity.

The consumer's problem

We consider a simple life-cycle savings problem. The consumer receives wage income during the earlier periods and is retired for the later periods of her life. Let w_t denote her wage income in period t. During retirement, the consumer needs to finance her consumption with her own savings. The model is a partial equilibrium one in that all prices are exogenously given. Prices are also independent of demographics. The periodic utility function is denoted by $u(c)$, where $c > 0$ stands for consumption.

We assume that the only asset available to the consumer is a financial asset, k, that pays a constant interest rate, r. We also impose a borrowing constraint: $k \geq 0$. Together with lifetime uncertainty, the absence of both annuities and a bequest motive implies that the consumer will leave accidental bequests whose value is not reflected in her lifetime utility.

In the case of rational expectations about future mortality, it is easiest to write the consumer's problem recursively. Given the simple structure of the mortality process, at the beginning of period t, a single integer, namely $Y_{t-1} \in \{0, 1, \ldots, t-1\}$, is sufficient to determine the best possible forecast about mortality in period t and beyond. Hence, Y_{t-1} is the only state variable needed to capture all relevant information about aggregate mortality in period t.[3] Denoting the value function in period t by V_t, and the discount factor by $\beta > 0$, the problem can be written recursively:

$$V_t(k_t, Y_{t-1}) = \max\{u(c_t) + \beta E_{Y_t|Y_{t-1}}[S_t(Y_t) V_{t+1}(k_{t+1}, Y_t)]\}$$

such that   (3)

$$k_{t+1} = w_t + (1+r)k_t - c_t$$

The solution to this problem includes a savings function $k_{t+1} = k_{t+1}(k_t, Y_{t-1})$ and a consumption function $c_t = c_t(k_t, Y_{t-1})$ that determine next period's savings and current consumption given age, current savings and demographic development up to period $t-1$.

We will compare the above rational-expectations problem to two alternative problems where the consumer has less information about the mortality process, and to the problem with perfect foresight. For the ease of comparison, we write these problems using backward recursion, even though, in practice, they are more easily solved directly, in a single global optimization routine. With perfect foresight, the consumer's problem can be written:

$$V_t\left(k_t, \{Y_s\}_{s=t}^{T}\right) = \max\left\{u(c_t) + \beta S_t(Y_t) V_{t+1}\left(k_{t+1}, \{Y_{s+1}\}_{s=t}^{T}\right)\right\}$$

such that   (4)

$$k_{t+1} = w_t + (1+r)k_t - c_t$$

We have included the path of future Ys as an argument of the value function to highlight the fact that the optimal decision in period t depends on all future survival probabilities which are assumed to be known with uncertainty.[4] Clearly, the consumption–savings decisions depend on demographic developments in the future.

Consider then the other extreme case where the consumer learns only the initial point forecast in period $t = 0$, makes a life-cycle savings plan believing that future mortality rates will be exactly as predicted by the point forecast, and never reconsiders the savings plan. Following again the recursive formulation, we can write the consumer's problem in this case as follows:

$$V_t(k_t) = \max\left\{u(c_t) + \beta\widehat{S}_t^1 V_{t+1}(k_{t+1})\right\}$$

such that   (5)

$$k_{t+1} = w_t + (1+r)k_t - c_t$$

Recall that $\widehat{S}_t^1$ is the period 1 point forecast for surviving period t. The solution to this problem is a sequence of consumption–savings decisions which are independent of the demographic path.

In the other low information case, the consumer updates her savings plan periodically based on the most recent point forecast. However, she still does not take uncertainty into account. For instance, in period 1 she makes a life-cycle savings plan under the assumption that her future survival probabilities will be exactly those predicted by the period 1 point forecast. Then, in period 2 she is given a new point forecast (determined by Y_2). She makes her period 2 savings decision taking her current savings as given and under the assumption that future survival probabilities will be exactly those predicted by the new point forecast, and so on. For a given aggregate mortality path, the problem the consumer faces at time t can be written down formally as a sequence of dynamic optimization problems where future mortalities are assumed to be given by point forecasts that are conditional on demographic development up to time $t - 1$. Thus, we have formally that

$$V_t\left(k_t, Y_{t-1}, \{E[Y_s|Y_{t-1}]\}_{s=t}^T\right)$$

$$= \max\left\{u(c_t) + \beta S_t(E[Y_t|Y_{t-1}]) V_t\left(k_t, Y_{t-1}, \{E[Y_s|Y_{t-1}]\}_{s=t+1}^T\right)\right\}$$
                                                                          (6)

if survival is evaluated at the conditional expectation (rather than the conditional median). In other words, the consumer decides as if she had a 'crystal ball' like in equation 4, but she actually only has conditional expectations given Y_{t-1} with which to work.

Calibration

The retirement age is set at 10, which corresponds to real age 65. Until retirement, the consumer earns a wage income of 1 every period, i.e. $w_t = 1$ for $t < 10$ and $w_t = 0$ for $t \geq 10$. Preferences are time-separable and the periodic utility function is of the constant-relative-risk-aversion form. For $\sigma \geq 0, \sigma \neq 1$ we have

$$u(c) = \frac{c^{1-\sigma}}{1-\sigma}$$ (7)

where σ measures the constant relative risk aversion. For $\sigma = 1$, we have $u(c) = \log(c)$.

Wages are paid and consumption occurs at the beginning of the period. For simplicity, we assume that both the interest rate and the subjective discount factor are zero. That is $\beta = 1$ and $r = 0$.

The welfare measure

Our welfare measure is the consumption equivalent variation. It gives the percentage increase in consumption in all periods that is needed in a benchmark case to make the expected lifetime welfare as high as in a comparison case. For instance, in order to compute the welfare cost of not taking aggregate mortality risk into account, we first solve the consumer problem with rational expectations. Then, we solve the consumer's problem assuming that she makes her decisions based on either mean (or median) mortality rates only. Next, we generate a large number N of randomly drawn aggregate mortality paths. Finally, we compute the increase in consumptions needed to make average lifetime utilities equal in the two cases.

More formally, consider simulation $i = 1, \ldots, N$ with a mortality path $\{Y_t^i\}_{t=1}^T$. Let c_t^i denote the optimal consumption level in simulation i, at age t, given rational expectations. Similarly, let $\tilde{c}_t^i$ denote the optimal consumption at age t when the consumer makes her decisions based on point forecasts alone.[5] The consumption equivalent variation measuring the welfare cost of using the median mortality rates instead of having rational expectations about future mortality is a scalar x such that

$$\sum_{i=1}^{N} \sum_{t=1}^{T} \prod_{s=1}^{t-1} S_s\left(Y_s^i\right)\beta^s u\left(c_t^i\right) = \sum_{i=1}^{N} \sum_{t=1}^{T} \prod_{s=1}^{t-1} S_s\left(Y_s^i\right)\beta^s u\left((1+x)\tilde{c}_t^i\right) \quad (8)$$

Results

The welfare cost of not taking aggregate mortality risk into account

How important is it for the consumer to take aggregate mortality risk into account? In Table 11.2 we display the welfare cost of making savings decisions based on point forecasts alone rather than having rational expectations about future mortality. The first row ('constant') corresponds to the case where the consumer receives only the period 1 point forecast. The second row ('adjust') corresponds to the case where the consumer updates her savings plan every period based on the most recent point

Table 11.2. *The welfare cost of not taking aggregate mortality risk into account under low information alternatives.*

	Risk aversion, σ		
	1	3	5
Constant	0.52%	0.62%	0.51%
Adjust	0.04%	0.06%	0.05%

forecast. The results are shown for different values of the risk aversion parameter.

The welfare cost of using just the period 1 point forecast rather than having rational expectations varies between 0.51% and 0.62% in terms of a consumption equivalent variation, depending on the degree of risk aversion. The interpretation is that in order to make the expected lifetime utility of a consumer with only the period 1 point forecast equal to that of a consumer who takes the uncertainty fully into account, we need to increase the consumption in the low information case by 0.51%–0.62% in every period. As we explained above, the point forecasts are based on median mortality. We could also consider expected mortality. In experiments not reported here, we found that that would result in slightly smaller welfare costs.

The welfare cost of not taking aggregate mortality risk into account is dramatically smaller when the consumer is allowed to update her life-cycle savings plan on the basis of the most recent point forecasts. It then ranges between just 0.04% and 0.06% of consumption. This is a remarkably small welfare cost. In terms of expected lifetime utility, it is not important for the consumer to take the uncertainty related to aggregate mortality into account. It suffices that she periodically updates her beliefs about future mortalities based on the most recent point estimates and reconsiders her savings plan accordingly.

It is perhaps worth noting that the relationship between the welfare cost of not having rational expectations and the risk aversion is non-monotonic. This is probably related to the fact that given our utility function, a high risk aversion means also a low intertemporal elasticity of substitution. A risk-averse consumer reacts to aggregate mortality risk by saving more in the earlier years (the so called precautionary savings motive; Kimball, 1990). On the other hand, even when consumers fail to take aggregate mortality risk into account, consumers with higher risk aversion, and hence a low elasticity of intertemporal substitution, save more because they want a smoother consumption profile in old age,

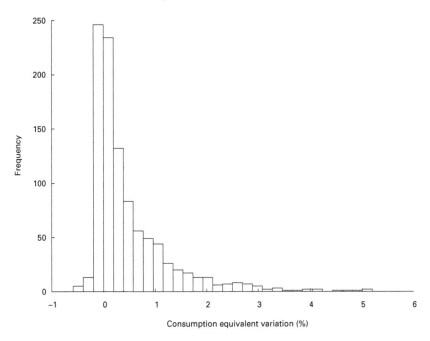

Figure 11.2. Welfare costs of using period 1 point forecast vs rational expectations.

when the survival probabilities are low. In other words, consumers with a high risk aversion parameter act as if they had a strong precautionary savings motive, even when they do not take the risk into account at all. An interesting extension of this analysis would be to consider a more general utility function where we can separate risk aversion and the intertemporal elasticity of substitution.

So far, we have discussed the expected or *average* welfare loss from not taking aggregate mortality risk fully into account. Figure 11.2 displays the *distribution* of welfare losses resulting from making savings decisions based on the period 1 point forecast rather than rational expectations. Here we assume $\sigma = 3$. The figure shows clearly that even though for most aggregate mortality paths the welfare difference is relatively small, in some cases having rational expectations would have improved welfare substantially. The largest welfare gains are equivalent to about 5 per cent in consumption in every period.

Figure 11.2 also shows that there is a probability of approximately 25 per cent that the low information solution is better than the rational expectations solution (the welfare 'cost' is negative). This is to be expected

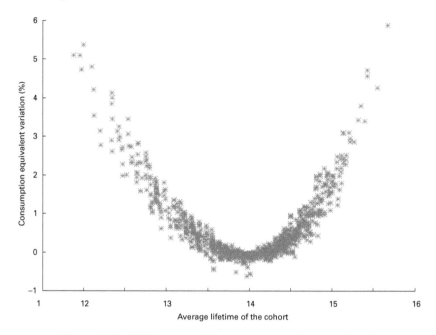

Figure 11.3. Welfare costs of constant expectations vs rational expectations as a function of average lifetime.

for a range of mortality paths that are near to what we expect based on the point forecast, because adjustment to random changes in early years sometimes leads to erroneous adjustments regarding saving for later life. However, we also see that in all cases the gain is 0.6 per cent, or less. (This result is not an absolute bound, of course, as it depends on the sample size used in simulation. However, it is clear that the probability of greater gains is less than 1 per cent.)

Figure 11.3 shows how the welfare cost stemming from using only the period 1 point forecast rather than having rational expectations is related to the average lifetime of a cohort. As one would expect, the welfare cost is highest in the cases where average lifetime is very different from the expected one (which is about 14.1 model periods).

Figure 11.4 displays the distribution of welfare costs resulting from using updated point forecasts rather than having rational expectations. The distribution is very different from that in figure 11.2. Even the largest welfare costs are now rather small, around 0.6 per cent, and the distribution is rather symmetric.

Figure 11.5 shows how this welfare cost is related to the average lifetime of a cohort. Just as in the low information case, the updating method

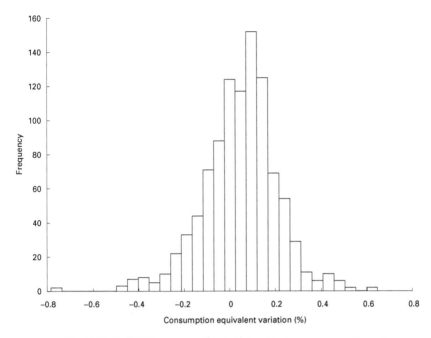

Figure 11.4. Welfare costs of updated point forecasts vs rational expectations.

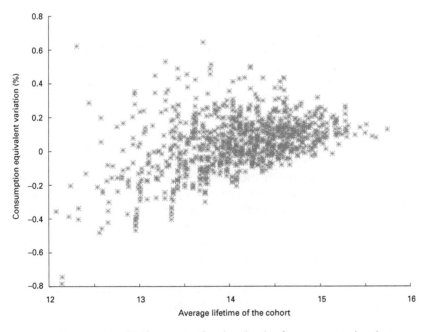

Figure 11.5. Welfare costs of updated point forecasts vs rational expectations as a function of average lifetime.

Table 11.3. *The welfare gain of having perfect foresight vs rational expectations.*

Risk aversion, σ	1	3	5
Welfare gain	0.16%	0.19%	0.16%

is better than rational expectations in (the rather unlikely) high mortality cases. For low mortality cases the reverse is true. In cases of expected mortality both approaches can dominate, but rational expectations sometimes produce fairly substantial gains over the updating method.

Perfect foresight vs rational expectations

A number of studies (e.g. Fehr and Habermann, this volume, chap. 7; Lassila and Valkonen, this volume, chap. 5) consider the implications of demographic uncertainty using numerical general equilibrium models. However, as discussed earlier most of these analyses assume perfect foresight on future demographics. Therefore, it is of interest to try to see how important, or problematic, this assumption is. To analyse this issue, we compare the consumer's savings problem with rational expectations to the one in which the consumer has access to a 'crystal ball' that tells the future aggregate mortality rates precisely, but does not reveal her own lifetime.

Table 11.3 displays the average welfare gain from having perfect foresight rather than simply rational expectations. The welfare gain deriving from perfect foresight is perhaps surprisingly small: it ranges from 0.16 per cent to 0.19 per cent in terms of consumption. One can argue that the normative solution to decision problems of the type we consider is obtained via rational expectations. Hence, the welfare costs computed here are measures of the welfare cost of aggregate mortality risk. Since this cost is small, the perfect-foresight assumption appears to be a reasonable proxy for rational expectations in this context.

Figure 11.6 shows the distribution of welfare gains resulting from having perfect foresight rather than rational expectations. Comparing Figures 11.2 and 11.6 shows that while using only the initial point forecast may lead to substantial welfare losses (around 5 per cent in consumption), having perfect foresight instead of rational expectations never increases welfare substantially (the gain in consumption is typically less than 2.5 per cent).

Figure 11.7 shows how the welfare gain of having perfect foresight over rational expectations is related to the average lifetime of a cohort. Again,

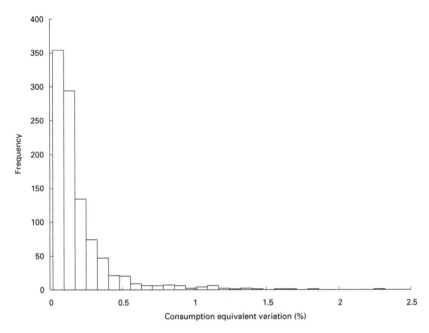

Figure 11.6. Welfare gains of perfect foresight vs rational expectations.

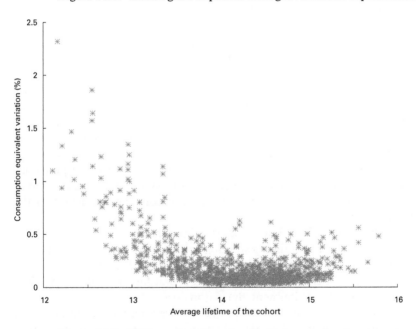

Figure 11.7. Welfare gains of perfect foresight vs rational expectations as a function of average lifetime.

the welfare gain is highest in cases where aggregate mortality is very high. However, the link between average lifetime and welfare gain is relatively weak.

Bracketing rational expectations

A consumer who has access to a 'crystal ball' is never worse off than those with less information. This has to hold, even pathwise. Similarly, the rational-expectations solution must always yield a higher *average utility* than that obtainable in the low information settings. Thus, the forecast-updating solution and the perfect-foresight solution can be used to bracket the rational-expectations solution. The result can be read from Tables 11.2 and 11.3. Depending on the level of risk aversion, the rational-expectations solution is in a band of width ≤ 0.25 per cent above the updating solution, when average utility is used as the measure.

Although this goes a long way towards understanding the nature of the rational-expectations solution, it is clear that other types of utility (or loss) functions may weigh sub-sets of the data in a manner that is different from the one we use. For example, Alho, Lassila and Valkonen (2006) consider combinations of pension contribution rates and replacement rates that might be viewed as politically acceptable (or they belong to the *viable region*) in the sense that if contribution rates became too high, the workers would refuse to pay them, or if replacement rates became too low, higher pensions would be demanded by the elderly. This directs attention to the joint distribution of the contribution rates and replacement rates, not just to their expected values.

Thus, it is also of interest to see how well the updating solution and the crystal-ball solution can bracket the rational-expectations solution for different levels of life expectancy, for example. It would be too much to ask for a pathwise bound, but we can look for bounds for conditional expectations. In the model at hand the relevant determinant seems to be the average lifetime of the cohort, so in Figure 11.8 we display non-parametric estimates[6] of average gain of the crystal-ball solution, and of the updating solution, over rational expectations, as a function of the average lifetimes.

The finding is that for low average lifetimes the gap between the crystal-ball solution and the updating solution is wider than the average gap, near the expected average lifetimes it is narrower, and for high average lifetimes it grows again. Perhaps one implication is that for mortality paths close to the expected development the rational-expectations solution can be bracketed quite closely with the perfect-foresight and updating solutions. Note, however, that for low life expectancies, even forecast updating produces utilities that are higher than those given by the rational-expectations

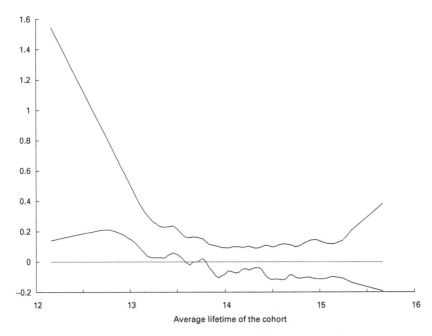

Figure 11.8. Average welfare gains of perfect foresight vs rational expectations (upper curve), and average welfare gains of using updated point forecasts vs rational expectations (lower curve) as a function of average lifetime.

solution. The reason appears to be the precautionary savings motive. Both the consumer with rational expectations and the consumer believing in updated point forecasts save, on average, too much in cases where longevity is low. However, the consumer with rational expectations saves more than the one following the forecast updating procedure because the former takes uncertainty into account with additional precautionary savings.

Conclusions

We have analysed the importance of aggregate mortality risk using a standard life-cycle model with a consumption–savings decision under different informational settings. We draw three types of conclusion.

Regarding the effect of different informational assumptions our main findings are as follows. First, the expected welfare cost of aggregate mortality risk is small for a consumer who knows the probability law and takes it rationally into account. That is, her expected lifetime utility would increase only a little had she access to a crystal ball that reveals future mortality rates without error. Second, a consumer who does not take the uncertainty related to future mortality into account at all, but makes her savings decisions based on the most recent point forecasts alone, loses very little compared to a consumer who takes the predictive distribution of future mortalities rationally into account. This is probably due to the fact that idiosyncratic uncertainty dominates an individual's longevity. (In contrast, aggregate uncertainty dominates the uncertainty of a pension institution, for example.) Third, a consumer who makes all her savings decisions based on the point forecast available at the beginning of her adult life, suffers substantial welfare losses for extreme mortality paths relative to a consumer having rational expectations. Intuitively, these results are all related to the fact that the consumer's information about her life expectancy improves over time. By adjusting her savings decisions as new information arrives, she can get relatively close to the perfect-foresight solution even if she does not take the uncertainty into account.

An important numerical finding is that the forecast updating formulation produces utilities that are perhaps surprisingly close to the rational-expectations solution. This suggests that a promising direction of future research is to develop computational tools that allow the forecast-updating approach to be implemented in the OLG settings used in pension analyses. One step in this extension has already been taken by the development of a computer program FPATH[7] that computes numerical approximations to future population forecasts that are conditional on population development up to their respective jump-off times.

An observation that arises from our having considered different informational assumptions in a stochastic setting is that there is merit in considering the whole distribution of utility outcomes, in addition to expected utility. This can reveal patterns of utility gains that are not easily detected by intuition alone. In a similar vein, we note that rational-expectations solutions can sometimes be bracketed by seemingly crude formulations, e.g. here when the perfect-foresight and the forecast-updating formulations for mortality outcomes are not too far removed from the expected one.

Finally, an important task for future research is to extend the present analysis to one that includes an unfunded pension system. As shown by Lassila and Valkonen (this volume, chap. 5) and Weale (this volume, chap. 4), demographic uncertainty makes the sustainability of public pension systems very uncertain. Although our numerical estimates suggest that consumers' welfare losses that are due to not taking into account aggregate uncertainty in mortality are not very large, the 'viability' issues we mentioned suggest that the possibility of structural change should be considered. Thus, the ultimate utility depends on the design of the pension system. If the system includes transparent rules that specify how the benefits and contributions are adjusted with changes in demographics, individuals can prepare for structural change by adjusting their savings plans correspondingly. However, unfunded (pay-as-you-go) pension systems typically do not include such rules, and pressures for structural change may suddenly mount to the point at which cost pressures are deemed politically unacceptable. Thus, in practice, failing to take demographic uncertainty into account (via additional precautionary saving) may result in much larger welfare losses for the consumer than the loss we have considered.

NOTES

1 For a recent study in the EU context, see http://ec.europa.eu/employment_ social/social_situation/docs/lot1_projections_finalreport_en.pdf
2 These correspond to a life expectancy at birth of about 78 years, which is the average life expectancy for females in Europe in 2000 (United Nations, 2002). Thus, the model can serve as an approximation of the combined male–female life expectancy for *cohorts* born now. From Table 2.3 we find that the UPE assumption of the combined life expectancy in 2049 is about 86.5 years for the EEA+ region. This area has a higher life expectancy than Europe as a whole.
3 Under the scaled model of error and its parameterizations discussed by Alho, Cruijsen and Keilman (this volume, chap. 3) the situation would be more complicated. For the random walk model of age-specific fertility the state variable would include a vector with as many components as there are child-bearing ages, say 30. For mortality the whole past history for males and females would have to be added (comprising at time t of, say, $t \times 2 \times 101$ components). The same number would have to be added for migration. Moreover, to the extent that any future optimizations in OLG models depend on actual population numbers, we might, in principle, need to add the full population history as well. Thus, even though the present formulation leads to a numerical optimization problem, it is far more transparent than the other models considered in this volume.
4 In practice we solve this problem separately for each sequence $\{Y_t\}_{t=1}^{T}$ in our simulations.
5 In the case where the consumer learns only the period 1 point forecast, the consumption path is independent of the aggregate mortality path.
6 Estimates were obtained by the LOWESS smoother of Cleveland (1981).
7 For a description, see http://joyx.joensuu.fi/ēk/pep/fpath.pdf.

REFERENCES

Alho, J. M. and Määttänen, N. (2006). 'Aggregate Mortality Risk and the Value of Annuities', Discussion Paper no. 1005, Research Institute of the Finnish Economy, Helsinki.

Alho, J. M., Lassila, J. and Valkonen, T. (2006). 'Demographic Uncertainty and Evaluation of Sustainability of Pension Systems', in *Pension Reform*, ed. R. Holzmann and E. Palmer. Washington, DC: The World Bank, pp. 95–112.

Alho, J. M. and Spencer B. D. (2005). *Statistical Demography and Forecasting*. New York: Springer.

Alho, J. and Vanne R. (2006). 'On Predictive Distributions of Public Net Liabilities'. *International Journal of Forecasting*, 22: 725–33.

Blake, D. and Burrows, W. (2001). 'Survivor Bonds: Helping to Hedge Mortality Risk'. *Journal of Risk and Insurance*, 68: 339–48.

Cleveland, W. S. (1981). 'LOWESS: a Program for Smoothing Scatterplots by Robust Locally Weighted Regression'. *American Statistician*, 35: 54.

Diamond, P. (2001). 'Comment', in *Demographic Change and Fiscal Policy*, ed. A. J. Auerbach and R. D. Lee. Cambridge: Cambridge University Press, pp. 93–7.

Filar, J. and Vrieze, K. (1997). *Competitive Markov Decision Processes*. New York: Springer.

Friedberg, L. and Webb, A. (2005). 'Life is Cheap', Working Paper no. 2005–13, Center for Retirement Research, Boston College.

Kimball, M. S. (1990). 'Precautionary Saving in the Small and in the Large', *Econometrica*, 58: 53–73.

Lee, R. D. and Carter, L. R. (1992). 'Modeling and Forecasting the Time Series of U.S. Mortality'. *Journal of the American Statistical Association*, 87: 659–71.

National Research Council (2000). *Beyond Six Billion*. Panel on Population Projections. Washington, DC: National Academy Press.

United Nations (2002). *World Population Prospects*, vol. I. New York: United Nations.

12 Uncertain demographics, longevity adjustment of the retirement age and intergenerational risk-sharing

Svend E. Hougaard Jensen and Ole Hagen Jørgensen

Introduction

It is well known that changes in the age structure of the population can have dramatic consequences for public finances. For example, under a pay-as-you-go (PAYG) scheme, changing demographics may lead to substantial swings in either taxes or welfare services. If neither of these outcomes is politically acceptable, the issue arises as to how a welfare system can be maintained which is not only fiscally sustainable, but which also offers a fair distribution profile across different generations.

To address this challenge, several countries are now operating a medium-term fiscal strategy of public debt reduction. This should help countries avoid substantial cuts in existing welfare arrangements, yet without having to raise taxes when the projected increase in the demographic dependency ratio becomes more severe. By developing the capacity to absorb demographic changes with stable taxes, a country would not only enjoy the efficiency gains associated with tax-smoothing (Barro, 1979), but also be better protected against adverse intergenerational distribution effects.[1]

Provided that the underlying shock – in this case a rise in the demographic dependency burden – is of a non-permanent kind, a saving (or pre-funding) strategy can be seen as a sensible way of smoothing a fiscal adjustment. Therefore, the question of whether the projected increase in the demographic dependency burden constitutes a temporary or a permanent shock is an important one. While changing demographics may originate from shocks to fertility, mortality and/or migration, it seems as if it is changes in mortality which tend to generate the most significant effects on the dependency ratio (Andersen, Jensen and Pedersen, 2008). Basically, this is because changes in future life expectancy impact almost

An earlier version of this chapter was presented at conferences in London, Copenhagen and Kittilä. We are grateful to Torben M. Andersen, Martin Flodén, Martin Kyed and Martin Weale for helpful comments.

exclusively on the retired part of the population, whereas changes in fertility and migration affect individuals in all phases of life. This observation clearly assigns a critical role to changes in life expectancy.

On account of advances within medical science, changes in life styles and more flexible working conditions, for example, the projected increases in longevity may well be of a more permanent nature. If this is the case, the rise in the (old-age) dependency ratio could continue over a much longer period than typically envisaged, and a smoothing policy is not what is necessary. Also, evidence suggests that the required amount of pre-funding is very sensitive to changes in key economic variables, especially the interest rate and the rate of productivity growth, and this lack of robustness implies that there may be a need for frequent changes in benefits and/or contribution rules. However, this would not be consistent with the main objective of keeping these rules stable across different generations.

With existing age limits on eligibility for early retirement and pensions, a longer lifetime will clearly lead to an increase in the proportion of life where an individual is a net recipient of welfare arrangements. However, since one would expect an increase in the life expectancy of future generations to be associated with higher levels of welfare, the question could be raised of whether current generations should contribute to the financing thereof, as a pre-funding strategy would imply. Rather, an obvious alternative to pre-funding would be to let benefits and/or contribution rules depend on changes in life expectancy. For example, by letting the age limits for retirement and pension follow expected lifetime, it is indeed possible to condition both benefits and contributions on expected lifetime.

Ideally, by introducing such a scheme the age limits become systematically linked to the generation to which an individual belongs. Since current demographic projections imply that future generations can expect longer lifetimes, it follows that those age limits would be higher for younger than for older generations. Generations expecting to live longer would therefore be active in the labour market longer, and a better balance would be ensured between the number of years a person is a net contributor and a net recipient, respectively. Adjustments to the system should be made at intervals – say, every ten years. When adjustments to changes in projections of expected lifetime are made well in advance of the pension age, it follows that the risk arising from unanticipated changes is smoothed over current and future generations.

In order to establish how a policy rule of longevity adjustment would affect intergenerational welfare distribution, as well as some broader macro-economic effects, we need a formal model with overlapping generations, optimizing individual behaviour and demographic shocks. We have in this chapter formulated such an analytical framework by adapting, and then extending, a model first suggested by Bohn (1998, 2001). We first describe the basic structure of that model. In the subsequent section, some macro-economic responses to demographic shocks are derived. The policy reform of longevity adjustment is then introduced. The focus here is on the potential of this initiative, compared to tax policy adjustments, for redistributing welfare across generations. The final section summarizes our conclusions and offers some suggestions for future research.

The model

This section presents the basics of our analytical framework, which is a model with overlapping generations (OLG) in the spirit of Diamond (1965), extended with stochastic features in line with Bohn (2001). We first outline the demographic details, then household behaviour, and finally resources and the pension system.

Demographics

Individuals live for three periods: as children, as workers and as retired persons, respectively. The number of children born in period t is denoted by N_t^c, where $N_t^c = b_t N_t^w$, and where $b_t > 0$ is the birth rate, and N_t^w is the number of workers living in period t. Adults work during period t (inelastic labour supply), and they are retired during period $t + 1$. All individuals in each cohort are assumed to be identical.

An increase in the birth rate clearly expands the labour force: the higher b_t, the more children are born and the larger is next period's labour force. But the size of the labour force is also determined by the probability of surviving from childhood into the working period, μ_{1t}, as well as by the length of the working period, χ_t. If χ_t increases, for instance, the children now entering as adults into the working period must work for a longer period of time, and therefore the *effective* growth rate of the labour force increases. Thus, the effective growth rate of the labour force is given by $N_{t+1}^w / N_t^w = \mu_{1t+1} \chi_{t+1} b_t$. If the probability of survival is 1, and with a standard working period normalized at 1 (i.e. $\mu_{1t} = \chi_t = 1$), the growth rate of the labour force is b_t.

There is also a probability of surviving from the working period into the retirement period, μ_{2t}. Both survival rates, μ_{1t} and μ_{2t}, and the total lifetime, ϕ_t, comprise an expected term and an unexpected term. Specifically, $\mu_{1t} = \mu_{1t-1}^e \mu_{1t}^u$; $\mu_{2t} = \mu_{2t-1}^e \mu_{2t}^u$; and $\phi_t = \phi_{t-1}^e \phi_t^u$ where $\mu_{1t}, \mu_{2t} \in (0, 1)$ and $\phi_t \in (0, 2)$. The survival probabilities at the individual level are assumed to equal the aggregate survival rate, and their stochastic terms, together with the stochastic components of ϕ_{t-1}^e, ϕ_t^u, b_t and χ_t, are assumed to be identically and independently distributed.

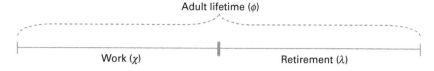

Figure 12.1. Adult lifetime, work and retirement.

The total adult lifetime equals the sum of the length of the working period and the retirement period. Thus, individuals initially have a total lifetime endowment, and if the length of the working period increases, then the length of the retirement period must decrease proportionally, as Figure 12.1 illustrates.

Formally, the length of the retirement period, λ, is residually determined from $\lambda_t = \phi_t \mu_{2t} - \chi_{t-1} = \phi_{t-1}^e \phi_t^u \mu_{2t-1}^e \mu_{2t}^u - \chi_{t-1}$, and is seen to be conditional on survival into old age, where $\chi_t, \lambda_t \in (0, 1)$. Increases in the *total* lifetime could also be envisaged. Clearly, if the length of the working period is unchanged, an increase in total lifetime falls entirely on the length of life in the retirement period.

Individual optimization and household behaviour

Parents make decisions about consumption on behalf of themselves and their children. With homothetic preferences, the utility of generation t in the working period (as parents) has this specification:

$$U_t^1 = \frac{1}{1-\eta} \chi_t \left[\rho^w \left(C_t^w \right)^{1-\eta} + b_t \rho_{c(b_t)} \left(C_t^c \right)^{1-\eta} \right] \tag{1}$$

where C_t^w is parents' consumption, C_t^c is children's consumption, ρ^w and $\rho_{c(b_t)}$ are weights, and $\eta > 0$ is the inverse elasticity of intertemporal substitution.[2] Also, the length of the working period, χ_t, is assumed to enter positively, and is included in a fashion similar to how Bohn (2001) incorporates the length of retirement period in second-period utility.[3] The factor $b_t \rho_{c(b_t)}$ is likely to be non-decreasing in the number of children, and is assumed to be positive but less than ρ^w. There is no specific functional form imposed on $\rho_{c(b_t)}$, since in later derivations it will only appear *relative* to ρ^w in the time preference for consumption over periods 1 and 2. The consumption constraint for generation t in their working period is simply $C_t^1 = C_t^w + b_t C_t^c$.

After maximizing utility in period 1 subject to the consumption restriction, the optimal level of first-period consumption, C_t^1, is derived.

Subsequently the indirect period 1 utility function can be derived:[4]

$$U_t^1\left(C_t^1\right) = \frac{1}{1-\eta}\left[\chi_t \rho_{1(b_t)}\left(C_t^1\right)^{1-\eta}\right] \tag{2}$$

Surviving retired persons are assumed to leave no bequests. In the retirement period, utility is given by:

$$U_{t+1}^2\left(C_{t+1}^2\right) = \frac{1}{1-\eta}\left[\lambda_{t+1}\left(C_{t+1}^2\right)^{1-\eta}\right] \tag{3}$$

The aggregate intertemporal utility function for the household is an additive composite of the indirect utilities in the two periods and may be written as:

$$U_t = U_t^1\left(C_t^1\right) + \rho_2 U_{t+1}^2\left(C_{t+1}^2\right) \tag{4}$$

where $\rho_2 > -1$ is the discount rate of old-age consumption. Upon inserting (2) and (3) in (4), we get:

$$U_t = \frac{1}{1-\eta}\left[\chi_t \rho_{1(b_t)}\left(C_t^1\right)^{1-\eta} + \left(\phi_{t+1}\mu_{2t+1} - \chi_t\right)\rho_2\left(C_{t+1}^2\right)^{1-\eta}\right] \tag{5}$$

Finally, consumption in the two periods can be written as:

$$\chi_t C_t^1 = W_t\left(1-\theta_t\right) - S_t \tag{6}$$

and

$$C_{t+1}^2 = \left[\frac{R_{t+1}}{\phi_{t+1}\mu_{2t+1} - \chi_t}\right]S_t + \beta_{t+1}W_{t+1} \tag{7}$$

where W_t, β_t, S_t and R_t denote, respectively, wages, the replacement rate, savings and the return to capital.

Resources and social security

Output is produced with capital and labour, according to the following Cobb-Douglas technology:

$$Y_t = K_t^\alpha\left(A_t N_t^w\right)^{1-\alpha} \tag{8}$$

where K_t is capital, A_t is productivity and α is the capital share. Productivity follows a stochastic trend, governed by $A_t = \left(1 + a_t\right)A_{t-1}$, where a_t is the growth rate (identically and independently distributed). Each individual supplies one unit of labour. The resource constraint of the economy is then:

$$Y_t + \left(1-\delta\right)K_t = \chi_t N_t^w C_t^1 + \left(\phi_t \mu_{2t} - \chi_{t-1}\right)N_{t-1}^w C_t^2 + K_{t+1} \tag{9}$$

where δ is the rate of depreciation of the capital stock. Individuals' savings will be next period's capital stock, i.e.

$$K_{t+1} = N_t^w S_t \tag{10}$$

The public sector operates a PAYG social security system:

$$\lambda_t N_{t-1}^w \beta_t W_t = \theta_t W_t N_t^w \tag{11}$$

where $\beta(\theta)$ denotes the benefit (contribution) rate. Equation (11) may feature both defined-benefit (DB) and defined-contribution (DC) schemes. For example, in a DB system the replacement rate is fixed, and the contribution rate varies. Solving for the endogenous contribution rate in a DB system, and using the equations $\lambda_t = \phi_t \mu_{2t} - \chi_{t-1}$ and $N_t^w/N_{t-1}^w = 1 + n_t^w$, yields

$$\theta_t = \beta_t \left[\frac{\phi_t \mu_{2t} - \chi_{t-1}}{1 + n_t^w} \right] \tag{12}$$

Evidently, with the replacement rate held fixed, an increase in the population growth rate and an increase in the retirement age leads to a lower contribution rate. Similarly, an increase in the length of the retirement period and an increase in the probability of surviving into the retirement period call for a higher contribution rate.

Finally, it should be mentioned that in order to obtain a solution on the balanced-growth path we state the model in effective units of labour such that, for example, $(C^1/A)_t \equiv c_t^1$; $(C^2/A)_t \equiv c_t^2$; $(W/A)_t \equiv w_t$; $K_t/(A_{t-1}N_{t-1}^w) \equiv k_{t-1}$; and $y_t = [k_{t-1}/((1 + a_t)(1 + n_t^w))]^\alpha$.

This completes the presentation of the baseline OLG model.

Equilibrium and responses to shocks

Before introducing the policy reform framework, this section offers some illustrations of how the OLG model works when the existing pension system is designed either as DC or DB, and when various shocks hit the economy. As a starting point, we briefly outline the solution technique.

The solution technique

The model is first transformed into log-deviations from the steady state, and then the method of undetermined coefficients is used to obtain an analytical solution for the recursive equilibrium. Adopting this analytical approach, the non-linear OLG model is replaced by a log-linearized approximate OLG model with variables stated in terms of percentage deviations from the steady state.[5]

The log-linearized law of motion of any endogenous variable, $\widehat{x}_t$, as a function of the endogenous state variable, $\widehat{k}_{t-1}$, and any exogenous state variable, $\widehat{z}_t$, may be conjectured as follows:

$$\widehat{x}_t = \pi_{xk}\widehat{k}_{t-1} + \sum_{z \in Z} \pi_{xz}\widehat{z}_t \tag{13}$$

where

$$\widehat{x}_t = \left\{ \widehat{k}_t, \widehat{c}_t^1, \widehat{c}_t^2, \widehat{w}_t, \widehat{R}_t, \widehat{\theta}_t \right\}$$

and

$$Z = \left\{ \widehat{\chi}_{t-1}, \widehat{\chi}_t, \widehat{a}_t, \widehat{b}_{t-1}, \widehat{b}_t, \widehat{\mu}_{1t-1}^e, \widehat{\mu}_{1t}^e, \widehat{\mu}_{1t}^u, \widehat{\phi}_{t-1}^e, \widehat{\phi}_t^e, \widehat{\phi}_t^u, \widehat{\mu}_{2t-1}^e, \right.$$
$$\left. \widehat{\mu}_{2t}^e, \widehat{\mu}_{2t}^u \right\}$$

where π_{xk} and π_{xz} denote, respectively, the elasticity of $\widehat{x}$ with respect to the endogenous state variable, $\widehat{k}$, and the elasticity of $\widehat{x}$ with respect to the exogenous state variables, $\widehat{z}$. For example, the linear recursive equilibrium law of motion for the capital stock can be written as:

$$\widehat{k}_t = \pi_{kk}\widehat{k}_{t-1} + \pi_{k\chi 1}\widehat{\chi}_{t-1} + \pi_{k\chi}\widehat{\chi}_t + \pi_{ka}\widehat{a}_t + \pi_{kb1}\widehat{b}_{t-1}$$
$$+ \pi_{kb}\widehat{b}_t + \pi_{k\mu 1e1}\widehat{\mu}_{1t-1}^e + \pi_{k\mu 1e}\widehat{\mu}_{1t}^e + \pi_{k\mu 1u}\widehat{\mu}_{1t}^u + \pi_{k\phi e1}\widehat{\phi}_{t-1}^e$$
$$+ \pi_{k\phi e}\widehat{\phi}_t^e + \pi_{k\phi u}\widehat{\phi}_t^u + \pi_{k\mu 2e1}\widehat{\mu}_{2t-1}^e + \pi_{k\mu 2e}\widehat{\mu}_{2t}^e + \pi_{k\mu 2u}\widehat{\mu}_{2t}^u.$$

The model is log-linearized around the steady state and solved using the method of undetermined coefficients. The equations which characterize the equilibrium of the model are the following:

$$0 = \Lambda_1\widehat{k}_{t-1} - \Lambda_5\widehat{k}_t - \Lambda_3\widehat{c}_t^1 - \Lambda_4\widehat{c}_t^2 + \Lambda_4\widehat{\chi}_{t-1} - \Lambda_{14}\widehat{\chi}_t - \Lambda_1\widehat{a}_t$$
$$- \Lambda_2\widehat{\mu}_{1t-1}^e - \Lambda_2\widehat{\mu}_{1t}^u - \Lambda_2\widehat{b}_{t-1} - \Lambda_4\widehat{\phi}_{t-1}^e - \Lambda_4\widehat{\phi}_t^u$$
$$- \Lambda_4\widehat{\mu}_{2t-1}^e - \Lambda_4\widehat{\mu}_{2t}^u \tag{14}$$

$$0 = -\Lambda_7\widehat{c}_{t+1}^2 + \Lambda_9\widehat{w}_{t+1} + \Lambda_{12}\widehat{R}_{t+1} + \Lambda_{12}\widehat{w}_t + \Lambda_{12}\widehat{\chi}_t - \Lambda_8\widehat{\theta}_t$$
$$- \Lambda_{12}\widehat{a}_t - \Lambda_{12}\widehat{\phi}_t^e - \Lambda_{12}\widehat{\phi}_{t+1}^u - \Lambda_{12}\widehat{\mu}_{2t}^u - \Lambda_{12}\widehat{\mu}_{2t+1}^u \tag{15}$$

$$0 = \widehat{R}_{t+1} + \Lambda_6\widehat{c}_t^1 - \Lambda_6\widehat{c}_{t+1}^2 - \pi_{\rho_1(b)}\widehat{b}_t \tag{16}$$

$$\widehat{R}_t = -\Lambda_{10}\widehat{k}_{t-1} + \Lambda_{10}\widehat{a}_t + \Lambda_{10}\widehat{\mu}_{1t-1}^e + \Lambda_{10}\widehat{\mu}_{1t}^u$$
$$+ \Lambda_{10}\widehat{b}_{t-1} + \Lambda_{10}\widehat{\chi}_t \tag{17}$$

$$\widehat{w}_t = \Lambda_{11}\widehat{k}_{t-1} - \Lambda_{11}\widehat{a}_t - \Lambda_{11}\widehat{\mu}_{1t-1}^e - \Lambda_{11}\widehat{\mu}_{1t}^u$$
$$- \Lambda_{11}\widehat{b}_{t-1} - \Lambda_{11}\widehat{\chi}_t \tag{18}$$

$$\widehat{\theta}_t = \widehat{\phi}_{t-1}^e + \widehat{\phi}_t^u + \widehat{\mu}_{2t-1}^e + \widehat{\mu}_{2t}^u - \widehat{\chi}_{t-1} - \widehat{\chi}_t - \widehat{\mu}_{1t-1}^e$$
$$- \widehat{\mu}_{1t}^u - \widehat{b}_{t-1} \tag{19}$$

where (14) is the resource constraint; (15) is second-period consumption; (16) is the Euler equation; (17) is the return to capital; (18) is the wage

Table 12.1. *Calibration of the model.*

Parameter	Calibration	Interpretation
α	1/3	Capital share in output
δ	1	Rate of depreciation of capital
β	0.3(0.1379)	Replacement rate (payroll taxes)
a	0.35	Productivity growth rate
$1/\eta$	1/3	Elasticity of intertemporal substitution
s	0.2	Savings rate
ϕ	1.3	Length of adult life
χ	0.8	Length of working period
λ	n.a.	Length of retirement period (residual)
b	0.1	Growth rate of the number of children
μ_1	0.95	Probability of surviving into working period
μ_2	1	Probability of surviving into retirement period
$\pi_{\rho_{1(b)}}$	0	Elasticity of the weight of first-period consumption in utility with respect to current birth rate

rate; and (19) is the pension contribution rate. The Λ's denote the relevant coefficients, which comprise combinations of steady-state variables.[6]

The next step is to present (14) to (19) in accord with (13) where the elasticities in the law of motion appear explicitly. It turns out that the analytical elasticities have fairly complex expressions, and to facilitate the interpretation we therefore also report numerical elasticities. This involves calibrating the model using what we believe are realistic parameter values, as shown in Table 12.1, and simulating the model using a Matlab routine (available upon request from the authors of this chapter).

Economic effects of demographic shocks

As to the effects of demographic shocks on key economic variables, we focus on shocks to fertility, $\widehat{b}$, and to longevity, $\widehat{\phi}$, as well as to the retirement age, $\widehat{\chi}$.[7] The relevant economic effects include consumption possibilities for workers, $\widehat{c}^1$, and retired persons, $\widehat{c}^2$, respectively, and the capital stock, $\widehat{k}$.

A shock to the birth rate A fall in the size of the working-age population, as currently experienced by several OECD countries (UN, 2004), may originate from a negative shock to the birth rate in an earlier period. The effects of a shock to the lagged birth rate, $\widehat{b}_{t-1}$, may be stated in terms of the relevant analytical and numerical elasticities; see

Table 12.2. *Economic effects of a fertility shock.*

Policy coeff.	DB	DC	
$\pi_{\theta b1}$	1	0	Analytical elasticity
Effect on:			
π_{c2b1}	0.3659	0.5057	$\dfrac{(\Lambda_8\pi_{\theta b1} - \Lambda_{12}\pi_{wb1})\,(\Lambda_3\Lambda_{13}\pi_{Rk} - \Lambda_3\pi_{c2k} - \Lambda_5)}{(\Lambda_9\pi_{wk} - \Lambda_7\pi_{c2k} + \Lambda_{12}\pi_{Rk})\,\Lambda_4} - \dfrac{\Lambda_2}{\Lambda_4}$
π_{c1b1}	−0.1018	−0.1981	$(\pi_{c2k} - \Lambda_{13}\pi_{Rk})\,\pi_{kb1}$
π_{kb1}	−0.1421	−0.2764	$\dfrac{\Lambda_4\pi_{c2b1} + \Lambda_2}{\Lambda_3\Lambda_{13}\pi_{Rk} - \Lambda_3\pi_{c2k} - \Lambda_5}$

Table 12.2. Note that we are assuming a negative shock, so the elasticities in Table 12.2 must be interpreted with the opposite sign.

The following insights may be reported. First, the difference between DB and DC systems is captured by the elasticity of the contribution rate with respect to a lower birth rate: in the pure DC system, $\pi_{\theta b1}$ is zero by definition, while in the DB system it is equal to 1.

Second, a lower workforce has a negative effect on the consumption possibilities of retired persons ($\pi_{c2b1} = -0.3659$). The reason is that retired persons receive two types of income: interest earnings on capital, and pension benefits. Since the latter are fixed in a DB system, the only source of change to the consumption of this group stems from interest fluctuations which generate changes in rent earnings on the capital stock owned by them. This shows that the endogenous response of factor prices plays a critical role: when the number of workers falls, there is a rise in the capital–labour ratio, and the real rate of return to capital falls. Hence, the capital income accruing to retired persons will fall.

Third, the effect on workers' consumption possibilities, π_{c1b1}, is more complicated. On the one hand, with a fall in the number of workers, each worker has to pay more taxes to finance the fixed benefits to retired persons, which impacts negatively on the consumption of workers. On the other hand, workers get higher wages because of the higher capital–labour ratio. The net effect is thus ambiguous. With the parameter values in Table 12.1, the 'factor price effect' is seen to dominate the 'fiscal effect'. In fact, we can state the necessary condition under which the factor price effect dominates the fiscal effect. By log-linearizing workers' income, $c_t^1 = w_t\,(1 - \theta_t)/\chi_t$, around the steady state, we get $\widehat{c}_t^1 = \widehat{w}_t - \frac{\theta}{1-\theta}\widehat{\theta}_t - \widehat{\chi}_t$, and we can then insert the law of motion, where the elasticities have already been derived, for wages and contributions (see equations (18) and (19)) to get $\widehat{c}_t^{\,1} = \left[-\alpha\widehat{b}_{t-1}\right] - \frac{\theta}{1-\theta}\left[-\widehat{b}_{t-1}\right] - \widehat{\chi}_t$. Focusing on a shock to lagged

Table 12.3. *Economic effects of a longevity shock.*

Policy coeff. $\pi_{\theta\phi e}$	DB n.a.	DC n.a.	Analytical elasticity
Effect on:			
$\pi_{c2\phi e}$	0	0	n.a.
$\pi_{c1\phi e}$	-0.2225	-0.2587	$\pi_{c2\phi e1} - \Lambda_{13}\pi_{R\phi e1} + (\pi_{c2k} - \Lambda_{13}\pi_{Rk})\,\pi_{k\phi e}$
$\pi_{k\phi e}$	0.8900	1.0346	$\dfrac{\Lambda_3\pi_{c2\phi e1} - \Lambda_3\Lambda_{13}\pi_{R\phi e1} + \Lambda_4\pi_{c2\phi e}}{\Lambda_3\Lambda_{13}\pi_{Rk} - \Lambda_3\pi_{c2k} - \Lambda_5}$

fertility of -1 per cent, we obtain: $\widehat{c_t}^{\,1} = \alpha - \frac{\theta}{1-\theta}$. So, provided that $\alpha >$ $\frac{\theta}{1-\theta}$ the factor price effect dominates the fiscal effect.[8]

If the pension system is of the DC type, wages still increase because of the higher capital–labour ratio, yielding a positive effect on their consumption. Workers pay fixed contributions to pensions, so there is no negative 'fiscal effect' and the impact on consumption is unambiguously positive. However, the total amount available to retired persons is lower, and the replacement rate falls, which naturally reduces the consumption of retired persons. The interest earnings will still fall, on account of the lower return on capital caused by the higher capital–labour ratio. Thus, retired persons will lose in terms of both their types of income. There is a stronger transfer of risk between generations in the DB system than in the DC system, as reflected by the fact that the difference between π_{c1b1} and π_{c2b1} is smaller in a DB than in a DC system; see Table 12.2.

A shock to expected future longevity A shock of this kind will not impact on the consumption of current retired persons, because the capital–labour ratio does not change. Since the contribution rate is not a function of the expected future longevity (only of the current longevity, $\widehat{\phi}^e_{t-1}$), taxes cannot be used as a policy instrument to reallocate risk in relation to this shock.[9] Current workers, however, anticipate a longer lifetime as retired persons. They would therefore begin to save more, by giving up current consumption ($\pi_{c1\phi e} = -0.2225$), and the capital stock would increase ($\pi_{k\phi e} = 0.8900$); see Table 12.3.

In the DB system the increase in the expected future longevity will require higher contributions in the future, while in the DC system contributions will not vary and current workers will have to save more, since the risk is not shared with future workers. Concequently, the DC system will again magnify the results of the DB system.

Table 12.4. *Economic effects of delayed retirement.*

Policy coeff.	DB	DC	
$\pi_{\theta\chi}$	-1	0	Analytical elasticity
Effect on:			
$\pi_{c2\chi}$	0.3659	0.5057	$\dfrac{\left(\Lambda_8\pi_{\theta\chi} - \Lambda_{12}\pi_{w\chi}\right)\left(\Lambda_3\Lambda_{13}\pi_{Rk} - \Lambda_3\pi_{c2k} - \Lambda_5\right)}{\left(\Lambda_9\pi_{wk} - \Lambda_7\pi_{c2k} + \Lambda_{12}\pi_{Rk}\right)\Lambda_4} - \dfrac{\Lambda_2}{\Lambda_4}$
$\pi_{c1\chi}$	0.1207	0.0606	$\pi_{c2\chi1} - \Lambda_{13}\pi_{R\chi1} + \left(\pi_{c2k} - \Lambda_{13}\pi_{Rk}\right)\pi_{k\chi}$
$\pi_{k\chi}$	-1.0321	-1.3111	$\dfrac{\Lambda_3\pi_{c2\chi1} - \Lambda_3\Lambda_{13}\pi_{R\chi1} + \Lambda_4\pi_{c2\chi} + \Lambda_2}{\Lambda_3\Lambda_{13}\pi_{Rk} - \Lambda_3\pi_{c2k} - \Lambda_5}$

A shock to the retirement age A positive shock to the retirement age means that an individual must work for a longer time, and the length of the retirement period is residually lowered. Like a shock to lagged fertility, this affects the labour force and hence the capital–labour ratio. With a shorter retirement period, the need for savings would fall, and a higher level of consumption is available to workers. However, consumption in the now longer working period would now be spread over more sub-periods. In a DB system, the net effect on savings is negative ($\pi_{k\chi} = -1.0345$); see Table 12.4.

The capital–labour ratio falls since the labour force has increased. This produces lower wages and a higher return on savings, as reflected in greater consumption available to retired persons ($\pi_{c2\chi} = 0.3659$). Lower wages would also in itself cause a fall in workers' consumption. However, each worker now needs to pay less contributions to the DB pension system, which points to increased workers' consumption. With the chosen parameter values, the net effect is positive ($\pi_{c1\chi} = 0.1207$). Clearly, with fixed contributions, as in a DC system, retired persons gain even more. This is so because of the higher return on the capital stock, but also because contributions are fixed and there are more sub-periods for taxation ($\pi_{c2\chi} = 0.5057$). And since the workers pay contributions over a longer period, their gains are smaller in the DC system than in the DB system.

While several other types of shocks could be studied, there is already enough material to make the point that within a very *passive* policy framework, such as a public pension system operating on a period-by-period basis, demographic shocks may lead to highly unequal distributions of consumption possibilities across generations. For that reason it is worth considering an alternative more *active* policy adjustment in order to achieve more equitable outcomes following demographic shocks. This is the aim of the next section.

Evaluating alternative policy rules

Performance criteria

When studying the effects of demographic shocks we have seen that two main forces are operating: first, the (endogenous) factor price effect and, second, the fiscal effect originating from the pension system. The latter constitutes the (passive) policy rule which plays a major role in how the welfare effects of demographic shocks are distributed across generations. In general, it was found that the fiscal effects were not sufficient to counteract the factor price effects and, consequently, workers and retired persons were exposed differently to the demographic shocks.[10]

In order to evaluate the social desirability of the results obtained in the previous section, we would want to compare those results to a socially optimal allocation derived from a social welfare function. If the optimal allocation differs from the allocation found in the previous section, we may need to consider redistributional policies. This immediately raises the question as to how the social welfare function should be formulated.

Specifically, we assume that aggregate social welfare can be measured as:

$$W_t = E\left\{\sum_{t=-1}^{\infty} \Phi_t N_t^w U_t\right\} = \left\{\Phi_{t-1} N_{t-1}^w U_{t-1} + \Phi_t N_t^w U_t\right\} \qquad (20)$$

where Φ is the weight on the utility of a given generation. The problem of the policy-maker is now to maximize (20), subject to the resource constraint in (9) and the lifetime utility function, as given by (5). Assuming that all generations are weighted equally ($\Phi_{t-1} = \Phi_t$), the efficiency condition (in log-deviations from the steady state) may be stated as follows:

$$\widehat{c}_t^1 = \widehat{c}_t^2 + \left(\pi_{\rho 1(b)}/\eta\right)\widehat{b}_t \qquad (21)$$

where the factor $\rho_{1(\widehat{b}_t)}$ is assumed to be log-linearized as $\pi_{\rho 1(b)}\widehat{b}_t$, and where $\pi_{\rho 1(b)}$ is the elasticity of the weight of first-period consumption in utility with respect to the current birth rate.[11] If there is no shock to the current birth rate, (21) states that the condition for an *efficient risk-sharing* (Bohn, 2001) is that the percentage change in the consumption of workers equals the percentage change in the consumption of retired persons. The key implication of a policy reform is thus a redistribution of income. If the equilibrium generated by a passive policy rule in the presence of demographic shocks is characterized by unequal changes in different generations' consumption possibilities, then the government should 'correct' this outcome, by redistributing income from workers to retired persons (or vice versa) up to the point where both generations bear the burden (or share the gains) of shocks in equal proportions.

Intergenerational redistribution could be achieved either through changes in the contribution rate (or the benefit rate) of the pension system, or through structural (or labour market) reforms by changes in the retirement age. The potential of the latter has only been explored to a very limited extent compared to the former. Yet, from a policy perspective, it would be of interest to consider an alternative way of coping with demographic changes than through adjustments to the contribution and/or benefit *rates* of the public PAYG pension system. More promising, however, might be reforms which affect the *number* of retired persons and workers, or the lifetime labour supply of each worker, through the introduction of a link between longevity changes and the retirement age.

The shock we consider is a 'composite shock', taking the form of a negative shock to lagged fertility and a positive shock to expected future longevity. Our motivation for focusing on these shocks is their empirical relevance: the fall in the lagged fertility rate reminds us of the so-called 'baby bust' phenomenon in the 1970s and 1980s, and an expectation of increased longevity has become common among social and medical scientists. Indeed, because of changes in life style and advances in medical science, people are expected to live longer in the future (United Nations, 2003).

Results

Taxation as a policy instrument Basically, the idea is to solve for the response of the contribution rate which ensures an efficient allocation of risk for the composite shock in accord with (21). Since taxes cannot respond to a shock to $\widehat{\phi}_t^e$, but only to $\widehat{b}_{t-1}$, we choose to denote the efficient response of taxes for the composite shock by $\pi_{\theta b 1}^*$. Leaving out the details of the derivation, we find:

$$\pi_{\theta b 1}^* = \frac{\pi_{c2\phi e} - \pi_{c1\phi e}}{\Omega_7 - \Omega_9} \widehat{\phi}_t^e / \widehat{b}_{t-1} + \frac{\Omega_8 - \Omega_{10}}{\Omega_7 - \Omega_9} \pi_{wb1} - \frac{\Omega_{11}}{\Omega_7 - \Omega_9} \quad (22)$$

where the Ω's comprise steady-state variables and other elasticities.[12] With the parameter values reported in Table 12.1, the numerical elasticity of the contribution rate with respect to the composite amounts to $\pi_{\theta b 1}^* = -2.04$. Recall that the empirically relevant shock to lagged fertility is negative, and to expected future longevity is positive. Thus, optimal risk-sharing implies an increase in the tax rate of about 2 per cent.

It would be interesting to compare the effects obtained with a passive rule to the results obtained with an active response. With the above parameter values, we get $\widehat{c}_t^1 = \pi_{c1b1}\widehat{b}_{t-1} + \pi_{c1\phi e}\widehat{\phi}_t^e = -0.12$ and $\widehat{c}_t^2 = \pi_{c2b1}\widehat{b}_{t-1} + \pi_{c2\phi e}\widehat{\phi}_t^e = -0.37$. In words, workers' consumption stands to decrease by 0.12 per cent while that of retired persons is expected to decrease by 0.37 per cent. The pension contribution rate is designed to respond automatically to 1 per cent shocks by increasing proportionally by 1 per cent, but this is not enough to ensure equal sharing of the risks associated with the shocks. As shown, we find that the tax rate must increase by about 2 percentage points, in order to transfer enough income from workers to retirees to achieve efficient risk-sharing across generations. When this active fiscal policy is adopted both generations bear the burdens in exactly equal proportions by a decrease in consumption of about 0.22 per cent for both workers and retired persons (i.e. $\widehat{c}_t^1 = \widehat{c}_t^2 = -0.22$). Thus, when the contribution rate is used to guarantee an efficient risk-sharing, there is a *net* welfare loss on the part of both generations. Against that, it would be of interest to see if a better outcome could be achieved, and this is the objective of the remainder of the chapter.

Retirement age as a policy instrument   From an analytical perspective, it is not straightforward how a change in the retirement age should be conceptualized.[13] An increase in the working period can, in principle, be thought of in two different ways. Workers could simply choose to work more years for some exogenous reason(s), or, alternatively, it could be the result of a government policy designed such that the age limit for eligibility to pension benefits of a representative worker is postponed. In the latter case we would assume that people are induced to work for this extra sub-period of what in any case is 'working life'. In this analysis it is assumed that people do not want to cover their expenses out of savings in this extra sub-period, which previously was part of the retirement period. Instead, they decide to work this extra sub-period until they become recipients of ordinary pension benefits.

Within the formal framework set out above, this discussion is captured by the parameter $\widehat{\chi}_t$, which denotes 'the change in the length of the working period from its steady-state value'. For example, one can think of $\widehat{\chi}_t$ as an exogenous shock to the supply of labour, such as a change in people's perception of work, which is not derived from the model structure. It is also possible to think of $\widehat{\chi}_t$ as a policy variable which the policy-maker can change as part of, say, a labour market reform.

In the following, we adopt the practice of treating $\widehat{\chi}_t$ as an exogenous variable and allowing it to be used as a policy parameter. We then impose the condition for efficient risk-sharing (21) on the recursive equilibrium law of motion for the consumption of workers and retired persons, respectively. Solving for the optimal length of the working period in accord with (21), $\widehat{\chi}_t^*$, yields

$$\widehat{\chi}_t^* = \omega_1 \widehat{b}_{t-1} + \omega_2 \widehat{\phi}_t^e \tag{23}$$

where the coefficients ω_1 and ω_2 comprise steady-state variables and other elasticities. Assuming the shocks to be -1 per cent for lagged fertility and $+1$ per cent for expected future longevity, this will lead to an efficient policy response of an increase in the retirement age of *exactly* 1 per cent. In fact, the two shocks generate dynamics which offset each other. Using the parameter values of Table 12.1, a numerical analysis shows that retired persons are affected by -0.3659 from $\widehat{b}_{t-1}$; by 0 from $\widehat{\phi}_t^e$; and by 0.3659 from $\widehat{\chi}_t$. Similarly, workers experience a response of 0.1018 from $\widehat{b}_{t-1}$; -0.2225 from $\widehat{\phi}_t^e$; and 0.1207 from $\widehat{\chi}_t$. Note that both retired persons and workers experience the combination of three shocks, but the net effect is zero for both generations. Importantly, this assumes a policy response of 1 per cent for $\widehat{\chi}_t$. This could also be regarded from the perspective of an efficient policy response of $\widehat{\chi}_t$. For a shock only to $\widehat{b}_{t-1}$ then $\widehat{\chi}_t = 1.9074$, and for a shock only to $\widehat{\phi}_t^e$, $\widehat{\chi}_t = -0.9074$. By adding these effects, we get exactly the result corresponding to $\widehat{\chi}_t = 1$ per cent.

The intuition behind this result is as follows: a negative shock to $\widehat{b}_{t-1}$ will reduce the current labour force, and a positive shock to $\widehat{\chi}_t$ will offset this reduction. The other feature of the shock concerns the retirement period. A positive shock to $\widehat{\chi}_t$ will lead to a lower expected retirement period, while a positive $\widehat{\phi}_t^e$ will offset it. This is because the length of the retirement period is modelled to be residually determined from changes in the length of the working period and the total length of life ($\lambda_{t+1} = \phi_{t+1}\mu_{2t+1} - \chi_t$). As such, a policy response of $\widehat{\chi}_t = 1$ per cent will offset all effects stemming from the two demographic shocks.

This result indicates that the retirement age is a better policy instrument than the contribution rate. Indeed, the utility effect from employing taxes would generate a utility loss for both generations of ($\widehat{c}_t^1 = \widehat{c}_t^2 = -0.2207$, given that $\pi_{\theta b1}^* = 2.0388$). When employing the retirement age as a policy instrument there will not be any utility loss for either generation ($\widehat{c}_t^1 = \widehat{c}_t^2 = 0$, given that $\widehat{\chi}_t = 1$ per cent). This result, among other assumptions, is based on the choice of modelling, incorporating with equal weights in utility both the length of the working period and the length of the retirement period for each generation (χ_t and λ_{t+1}).

Finally, we have found that this result is robust over both a DB and a DC PAYG regime, and also in a model without any pension system. Different combinations of shocks could be analysed, but the empirically most relevant shock is the one covered in this section. While much more academic work is needed in this area, it seems reasonable to suggest that an indexation scheme for retirement age relative to expected longevity, in order to ensure intergenerationally efficient risk-sharing, would be a sensible policy adjustment.

Conclusions

Based on a stochastic OLG model, this chapter has shown how various demographic shocks may affect the intergenerational distribution of welfare. It has also discussed how policy rules may be designed in order to achieve outcomes which are more equitable compared to those obtained within a passive policy framework.

The novelty of this chapter is a study of longevity adjustment of the retirement age as an instrument to generate efficient risk-sharing in an economy faced by demographic shocks. We find that a rise in the retirement age following an increase in expected longevity may leave both workers and retired persons better off. However, this is not the case within an alternative setting where taxes on wage incomes are adjusted to share risks efficiently across generations. So, the retirement age outperforms taxes as a policy instrument.

While we are convinced that the analytical framework used in this chapter offers a fruitful starting point for studying an important policy area, we are also aware of several limitations and potential extensions that we want to address in future research.

First, the supply of labour is assumed exogenous in our analysis, and an obvious extension would be to introduce endogenous labour supply decisions by households. While this would raise a number of technical complexities, important insights could be obtained into the effects of a higher retirement age on labour supply. For example, would an increase in labour supply at the extensive margin be offset by a fall in the endogenous labour supply at the intensive margin? In any case, appropriate policy measures would need to take into account the endogeneity of labour supply.

Second, it is also feasible to endogenize other variables and solve for additional dynamics, which are absent in this analysis. Future research could include endogenous human capital formation (through education, for example), and endogenous fertility decisions in order to address the reasons behind the negative shock to fertility in the 1970s and 1980s.

Third, while the present analysis is stated in terms of a closed economy, it would be of interest to consider an open economy perspective. For example, in the case of a small open economy, one would need to specify the structure of the OLG model differently and incorporate an exogenously determined interest rate.

Fourth, in relation to the probability distributions of the exogenous state variables, one could specify detailed distributions instead of the i.i.d. specification which we follow. As such, a more accurate picture of the stochastic properties of the demographics could be obtained.

Finally, to study the welfare effects of demographic shocks on the sustainability of public finances, a more detailed government sector could be incorporated into the model. Some, if not all, of the above extensions we have in mind for our future research in this area.

NOTES

1 However, uncertainty is inherent in demographic projections, and experience has shown that they may be prone to radical variations, even within relatively short periods of time.

2 This specification of the utility function is quite standard. If the (inverse) elasticity of intertemporal substitution is larger than 1, then utility decreases if consumption increases. If $\eta = 1$, equation (1) simplifies to the log-utility function, $U_t = \chi_t [\rho^w \ln C_t^w + b_t \rho_{c(b_t)} \ln C_t^c]$, in which case an increase in consumption yields an increase in utility. The construction of the utility function with $\eta > 1$ is mainly intended to highlight the risk aversion motive.

3 Auerbach and Hassett (2001, 2002) also incorporate the length of the retirement period.

4 The term $\rho_{1(b_t)} = \rho^w [1 + (\rho_{c(b_t)}/\rho^w)^{1/\eta} b_t]^{1-\eta} + b_t \rho_{c(b_t)} (\rho_{c(b_t)}/\rho^w)^{(1-\eta)/\eta}$ denotes the weight on first-period consumption in the first-period indirect utility.

5 The method is inspired by Campbell (1994), Uhlig (1999) and Bohn (1998, 2001, 2003), and it has become standard practice in the context of real business-cycle (RBC) models. However, in relation to stochastic OLG models this technique has, to our knowledge, not been clearly documented elsewhere.

6 Further details on the specific derivations made in this chapter using the method of undetermined coefficients are in a separate note which is available upon request. For a more general presentation of solution techniques relevant to stochastic OLG models, the reader is referred to Jørgensen (2006).

7 Much attention is devoted to the length of the retirement period, λ, which is derived residually ($\lambda_t = \phi_t \mu_{2t} - \chi_{t-1}$). Since we calibrate χ with 0.8, ϕ with 1.3 and μ_2 with 1, λ becomes 0.5.

8 The value of θ is derived through calibration for $\beta = 0.3$ such that $\frac{\theta}{1-\theta} = 0.16$. With a value of $\alpha = 1/3$, the pension system must be relatively large (with contribution rates above 30%) before this result is overturned.

9 However, the retirement age, $\hat{\chi}_t$, could be used, as we will discuss in the next section.

10 From the specification of the pension system in (11) it is clear that the contribution rate, θ, will change if the lagged fertility rate, b_1, changes. The magnitude of this change will be in equal proportion to the size of the shock to lagged fertility, and this is accounted for in the equivalent log-linearized equation (19) in terms of $\pi_{\theta b1}$. Therefore, the automatic (passive) change in contributions, and thus in the 'fiscal effect', $\left(\frac{\theta}{1-\theta}\right)$, of $\hat{b}_{t-1} = \pi_{\theta b1} = 1$ per cent. We have shown that the 'factor price effect' dominates the 'fiscal effect' for a reasonable size of the pension system ($\beta = 0.3$ and thus $\theta = 0.1379$). This is the key fiscal mechanism that has the potential to redistribute income across generations living in the same period. As a result, the higher (more active) is $\pi_{\theta b1}$, the stronger is the fiscal effect, and the more likely is it that the fiscal effect will offset the factor price effects – and hence that risks will be shared more equally across generations.

11 The derivation of this optimality condition is documented in a separate note, which is available upon request.

12 The details are again documented in a separate note (available upon request).

13 Cutler (2001), in his comment on Bohn (2001), suggests an extension of Bohn's model to incorporate the length of the working period.

REFERENCES

Alho, J., Jensen, S. E. H., Lassila, J. and Valkonen, T. (2003). 'Controlling the Effects of Demographic Risks: The Role of Pension Indexation Schemes'. *Journal of Pension Economics and Finance*, 4: 139–53.

Andersen, T. M., Jensen, S. E. H. and Pedersen, L. H. (2008). 'The Welfare State and Strategies Towards Fiscal Sustainability in Denmark', in *Sustainability of Public Debt*, ed. R. Neck and J. Sturm. Cambridge, MA: MIT Press.

Auerbach, A. J. and Hassett, K. (2001). 'Uncertainty and the Design of Long-run Fiscal Policy', in *Demographic Change and Fiscal Policy*, ed. A. J. Auerbach and R. D. Lee. Cambridge: Cambridge University Press, pp. 73–92.

(2002). *Optimal Long-run Fiscal Policy: Constraints, Preferences and the Resolution of Uncertainty*. Working Paper no. 7036, Boston: NBER.

Barro, R. (1979). 'On the Determination of Public Debt'. *Journal of Political Economy*, 87: 940–71.

Bohn, H. (1998). 'Risk Sharing in a Stochastic Overlapping Generations Economy'. Department of Economics, University of California at Santa Barbara.

(2001). 'Social Security and Demographic Uncertainty: The Risk-Sharing Properties of Alternative Policies', in *Risk Aspects of Investment-Based Social Security Reform*, ed. J. Campbell and M. Feldstein. Chicago: University of Chicago Press, pp. 203–41.

(2003). 'Intergenerational Risk Sharing and Fiscal Policy'. Department of Economics, University of California at Santa Barbara.

Campbell, J. (1994). 'Inspecting the Mechanism: An Analytical Approach to the Stochastic Growth Model'. *Journal of Monetary Economics*, 33: 463–506.

Cutler, D. (2001). 'Social Security and Demographic Uncertainty: The Risk Sharing Properties of Alternative Policies: A Comment', in *Risk Aspects of*

Investment-Based Social Security Reform, ed. J. Campbell and M. Feldstein. Chicago: University of Chicago Press, p. 245.

Diamond, P. (1965). 'National Debt in a Neoclassical Growth Model'. *American Economic Review*, 55: 1126–50.

Jørgensen, O. H. (2006). 'A General Procedure for Solving Stochastic Overlapping Generations Models'. Centre for Economic and Business Research, Copenhagen. Available at www.cebr.dk/oj.

Uhlig, H. (1999). 'A Toolkit for Analysing Nonlinear Dynamic Stochastic Models Easily', in *Computational Methods for the Study of Dynamic Economies*, ed. R. Marimon and A. Scott. Oxford: Oxford University Press, pp. 30–61.

United Nations (2003). *World Population in 2300*. New York: United Nations.

13   A general equilibrium analysis of annuity rates in the presence of aggregate mortality risk

Justin van de Ven and Martin Weale

Introduction

A life annuity provides an income stream for an individual's lifetime, thereby insuring them against the risk of unanticipated longevity. Annuities – whether provided by government implicitly through a public pension system, or purchased privately in an open market – consequently play an important role in financial planning for retirement throughout the developed world. Nevertheless, few studies have explored the workings of the annuities market, which is distinguished by its intertemporal nature and relation to demographic risk. This chapter therefore uses an overlapping-generations model to consider how the market-clearing annuity rate is affected by uncertainty regarding individual life span.

An annuity is defined by its annuity rate. This is the amount paid out to an annuitant, as a percentage of the purchase price of the annuity, while the annuitant is alive, with payment ceasing on the death of the annuitant. Because life spans are finite, fair annuity rates are typically higher than interest rates and for populations facing substantial immediate mortality risk (old people) they are considerably higher. Annuity rates offered on the UK market have fallen substantially over the last twenty-five years, from a high of 16 per cent for 65-year-old males in 1981, to 7 per cent in 2006.[1] This long-term trend has been attributed to two principal factors. First, mortality rates have also fallen considerably over the same period – a 65-year-old male was estimated to have a life expectancy of 13.0 years in 1981, compared with 17.1 years in 2006.[2] Second, the yield on long-term government debt has declined over the period, from 9.33 per cent in 1986 to 3.84 per cent in 2006.[3] Given existing interest and mortality rate profiles, Murthi Orszag and Orszag (1999), Finkelstein and Poterba

We should like to thank participants at the DEMWEL conference, Kittilä, March 2006, and especially Martin Flodén and Nico Keilman, for valuable comments. The usual disclaimer applies.

(2002) and Cannon and Tonks (2003) report that the annuity rates provided by UK markets are approximately actuarially fair. Similar findings are also reported by Mitchell *et al.* (1999) for the USA.

An evaluation of actuarial fairness provides an indication of the extent to which annuity markets provide value for money to consumers. It is important to note, however, that the evaluation of actuarial fairness is far from straightforward. The analysis reported by Finkelstein and Poterba (2002), for example, suggests that the nominal annuities of 65-year-old males in the UK are approximately 10 per cent below the actuarially fair level when based on the survival probabilities of the total population, but are very close to being actuarially fair after adjusting individual mortality to reflect the size of the annuity actually purchased.[4] This highlights the difficulties associated with identifying the appropriate mortality rates to use for analysis. Furthermore, insurance companies may earn substantial profits despite paying premiums that are actuarially fair, if they earn a higher rate of return on capital than the yields on long-term debt which are commonly used to calculate an annuity's 'money's worth' (James and Song, 2001). Indeed, if potential consumers of annuities consider a rate of return on capital that exceeds the yield on long-term debt, then the annuity yields offered by the market are likely to be less than actuarially fair, and this may go some way to explaining the 'annuity puzzle'.[5]

A further issue is raised by the inherent uncertainty that characterizes the market for annuities. Specifically, although uncertainty is associated with any forecast, in the United Kingdom there is a widespread view that the decline in mortality rates among the elderly over the last fifteen years has taken actuaries by surprise. As noted by the Pensions Commission in its Second Report, 'in the early 1980s public pension policy and private pension provision decisions were based on the assumption that average male life expectancy at 65 in 2010 would be 15.1 years: the best estimate is now 20.1 years' (Pensions Commission, 2005, p. 90). Obviously the mere fact that life expectancy is believed to have risen does not itself imply that forecasts of life expectancy are particularly uncertain, but the point is that most actuarial calculations involve forecasts of future mortality and, like all forecasts, these must be uncertain.

Given the uncertainty associated with mortality projections, it seems reasonable to suppose that a charge will be levied by providers of annuities in return for adopting cohort-specific mortality risk. This chapter focuses on the extent to which cohort-specific risk is likely to depress annuity rates in a perfectly competitive market where both consumers and investors are characterized by risk-averse preferences.

Very little analysis has been conducted to identify the effects of mortality risk on annuity rates. One exception is the study by Friedberg and

Webb (2005), which considers the use of longevity bonds as a method of hedging longevity risk. Longevity bonds are loan stocks that provide a yield which is proportional to the longevity of a cohort. Friedberg and Webb focus on a stock issued by the European Investment Bank that relates payments to the survival rate of the UK male cohort aged 65 in 2003. They assess the empirical magnitude of the risk associated with this loan, and use the Consumption Capital Asset Pricing Model (CCAPM) (Mehra and Prescott, 2003) to identify the associated risk premium. On the basis of this analysis, Friedberg and Webb find that the longevity bond should trade at a discount of two basis points, which is less than the twenty-basis-point discount that was observed in the market. Friedberg and Webb suggest that the discount associated with the longevity bond was influenced by risk-averse annuity providers purchasing bonds to hedge themselves against aggregate mortality risk.

It is not clear, however, that the CCAPM is a suitable tool for calculating the risk premium of longevity bonds. Specifically, the CCAPM is based upon the assumption of a consumer with an infinite life, which is at odds with the fact that the very reason for introducing a longevity bond is that people live for a finite period.[6] Since the investment decision becomes more complex when mortality constraints and periods of retirement are taken into consideration, it seems important to take these explicitly into account in pricing annuities in the context of mortality risk, which is the focus of this chapter.

The next section describes the overlapping-generations model that we use to consider the effects of aggregate longevity uncertainty on annuity rates, and draws out some of the analytical results. A brief account of the numerical solution to the problem follows, and results of alternative simulations are then presented. The chapter concludes with directions for further research.

The model

We consider the question of how the annuity price is affected by mortality risk using a two-period overlapping-generations model. The first period of life is of unit length, while the length of the second period is uncertain. Each generation receives unit labour income in the first period of its life. It can choose to invest some of this income by selling annuities to the current old population.[7] Annuities are transacted at the start of each period at a fixed price, and the repayment on them is proportional to the life-span of the older generation. Thus the annuity contracts sold by the young to the old are subject to aggregate mortality risk. Just as the young choose how much of their wealth to invest in annuities, so too the old decide to what extent they wish to annuitize the wealth that they hold at the start of their second period. A market-clearing price is established for annuities where the marginal willingness of the young to take on risk is balanced with the desire of the old to protect themselves from it. Given risk-averse preferences, the market-clearing annuity rate is consequently expected to be discounted, compared to the rate that would prevail in the absence of aggregate mortality risk.

On average the sellers of the annuities make a profit as compensation for the risk that they run in providing a guarantee to old people. While we consider only representative individuals from each generation, we assume that uninsured individuals are subject to the same mortality risk that is borne by sellers of annuities. Thus there is the assumption that uninsured individuals diversify their individual-specific mortality risk as far as is possible within their cohort, for example by investing their wealth in a tontine[8] – an annuity where each cohort carries its own aggregate mortality risk. The results would be rather different if they did not have this option and that is a topic to be explored in future work.

We denote by $c_{y,i}$ consumption of generation i when young, and by $c_{o,i}$ consumption of generation i when old. w_i is the amount of wealth held by generation i at the start of period 2. t_i is the life span in the second period with $E(t_i) = t_o$ for all generations, i. π_i is the rate at which generation i can purchase an annuity when old. In exchange for an annuity purchase of one pound, an annuitant receives a payment of π_i/t_o pounds per unit of time in retirement. ϕ_i is the proportion of wealth that old people in generation i use to purchase annuities. ϕ_i' is the proportion of old people's wealth in generation i which young people in generation $i + 1$ are prepared to annuitize. $\phi_i = \phi_i'$ is therefore the equilibrium condition.

To simplify discussion, we assume that the interest rate is zero, and that the discount factor is unity. Thus the lifetime utility of a representative individual from generation i (hereafter referred to simply as generation i), measured from the start of their life, is:

$$U_{y,i} = U(c_{y,i}) + t_i U(c_{o,i}/t_i) \tag{1}$$

The wealth of generation i at the start of their old age is given by the amount that it saved from period 1, $1 - c_{y,i}$ plus the profit that it makes on the annuities it has sold to generation $i - 1$:

$$w_i = \left(1 - c_{y,i} + \phi_{i-1}' w_{i-1}\left[1 - \pi_{i-1}\frac{t_{i-1}}{t_o}\right]\right) \tag{2}$$

The total amount it consumes when old depends on the proportion of wealth that it annuitizes, given by ϕ_i and its life span, t_i:

$$c_{0,i} = \phi_i w_i \frac{\pi_i t_i}{t_0} + (1 - \phi_i) w_i$$

$$= \left(1 - c_{y,i} + \phi'_{i-1} w_{i-1} \left[1 - \pi_{i-1}\frac{t_{i-1}}{t_o}\right]\right)\left(\frac{\pi_i t_i}{t_0}\phi_i + 1 - \phi_i\right) \quad (3)$$

Thus lifetime utility is:

$$U_{y,i} = U(c_{y,i}) + t_i U \left\{\left(1 - c_{y,i} + \phi'_{i-1} w_{i-1}\left[1 - \pi_{i-1}\frac{t_{i-1}}{t_o}\right]\right)\right.$$
$$\left. \times \left(\frac{\pi_i \phi_i}{t_0} + \frac{(1 - \phi_i)}{t_i}\right)\right\} \quad (4)$$

Young people in generation i are considered to optimize by choosing their consumption, $c_{y,i}$, and how much of their non-consumed wealth to invest in annuities, ϕ'_{i-1}. Old people in generation $i - 1$, by contrast, select how much of their wealth to spend on annuities, ϕ_{i-1}, to maximize expected utility in their second period:

$$U_{o,i-1} = t_{i-1} U \left\{w_{i-1}\left(\frac{\pi_{i-1}}{t_0}\phi_{i-1} + \frac{1 - \phi_{i-1}}{t_{i-1}}\right)\right\} \quad (5)$$

We assume that $\mathrm{Var}(t_i) = \sigma^2$ for all i, and also that the life spans of successive generations are independent of each other (leaving for future study the case where they are correlated).

Equation (5) indicates that the demand for annuities by generation i when old depends upon their wealth, w_i, which in turn depends upon the longevity of the immediately preceding generation $i - 1$ (equation 2). Hence, the market-clearing annuity price paid by generation i, π_i, is uncertain when the generation is young. Although no analytical solution exists to the intertemporal utility maximization problem for the young generation, the problem can be solved numerically by backward induction. It is useful, however, to simplify the problem here by assuming that $\pi_i = \pi$ for all i, which enables convenient expressions to be derived for the expected utility of young and old generations. This simplification – which is returned to in the Conclusions – is likely to be of second-order importance with regard to the implied relationship between longevity uncertainty and annuity rates, and helps to clarify the current discussion. A rigorous consideration of the intertemporal utility maximization problem described above remains an issue for further research.

We solve the problem numerically, using second-order Taylor expansions to calculate expected utility in the light of uncertainty about t_i and

t_{i-1}. Looking first at the expected value of $U_{o,i-1}$:

$$
E(U_{o,i-1}) = t_0 U\left\{\frac{w_{i-1}}{t_0}\left(\pi\phi_{i-1} + 1 - \phi_{i-1}\right)\right\}
$$
$$
+ \frac{\sigma^2}{2}\frac{\partial^2}{\partial t_{i-1}^2} t_{i-1} U\left\{w_{i-1}\left(\frac{\pi}{t_0}\phi_{i-1} + \frac{1-\phi_{i-1}}{t_{i-1}}\right)\right\}\Bigg|_{t_o}
$$
$$
= t_0 U\left\{\frac{w_{i-1}}{t_0}\left(\pi\phi_{i-1} + 1 - \phi_{i-1}\right)\right\}
$$
$$
+ \frac{\sigma^2 (1-\phi_{i-1})^2 w_{i-1}^2}{2t_o^3} U''\left\{\frac{w_{i-1}}{t_0}\left(\pi\phi_{i-1} + 1 - \phi_{i-1}\right)\right\}
$$

In the standard way, the expected utility of old people is influenced by the variance of their life span, with the impact depending only on the extent to which they are not annuitized.

For young people at the start of period 1 there are two sources of uncertainty. To the extent that they sell annuities, they are affected by the uncertainty about the mortality of the old people to whom the annuities are sold. And they are also affected by uncertainty about their own life duration, to the extent that they are not insured. These two terms are shown in the third and fourth terms of the following sum:

$$
E\left(U_{y,i}\right) = U(c_{y,i})
$$
$$
+ t_0 U\left\{\left(1 - c_{y,i} + \phi'_{i-1} w_{i-1}\left[1 - \pi\right]\right)\left(\frac{\pi\phi_i + 1 - \phi_i}{t_0}\right)\right\}
$$
$$
+ \frac{\sigma^2}{2}\left(\frac{\pi w_{i-1}\phi'_{i-1}}{t_0^2}\right)^2 (\pi\phi_i + 1 - \phi_i)^2 t_0
$$
$$
\times U''\left\{\left(1 - c_{y,i} + \phi'_{i-1} w_{i-1}\left[1 - \pi\right]\right)\left(\frac{\pi\phi_i + 1 - \phi_i}{t_0}\right)\right\}
$$
$$
+ \frac{\sigma^2 (1-\phi_i)^2 \left(1 - c_{y,i} + \phi'_{i-1} w_{i-1}\left[1 - \pi\right]\right)^2}{2}\frac{}{t_0^3}
$$
$$
\times U''\left\{\left(1 - c_{y,i} + \phi'_{i-1} w_{i-1}\left[1 - \pi\right]\right)\left(\frac{\pi\phi_i + 1 - \phi_i}{t_0}\right)\right\}
$$

We work with a constant elasticity of substitution utility function, $U(x) = \Gamma + \frac{x^{1-\gamma}}{1-\gamma}$ and $U''(x) = -\gamma x^{-1-\gamma}$ with $\gamma \neq 1$. Γ is selected to ensure that, for any value of γ, second-period utility is increasing in life span. Hence, the model excludes suicide as a solution to longevity.

The structure of the model can be seen clearly in Figure 13.1, which shows, for $\gamma = 3$, $t_i = t_{i-1} = t_0 = 0.6$ and $\sigma^2 = 0.01, 0.04$, the positions

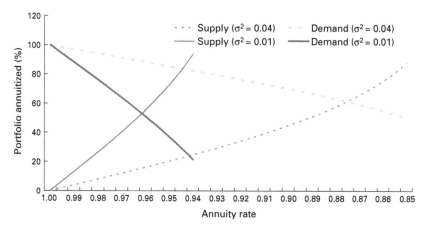

Figure 13.1. Supply and demand for annuities ($\gamma = 0.3; \sigma^2 = 0.01$, 0.04).

of the demand and supply curves for annuities.[9] Figure 13.1 indicates that demand falls and supply rises as the annuity rate falls below the actuarially fair rate. When uncertainty is set such that $\sigma^2 = 0.01$ it can be seen that the demand for annuities by old people falls off fairly steeply as the annuity rate declines. The willingness of young people to supply annuities rises almost as steeply, and the equilibrium price is given by the intersection of the supply and demand curves. With higher uncertainty, both the demand and supply curves flatten out, resulting in a substantially lower market-clearing annuity rate. Higher risk aversion has a similar effect on the market-clearing annuity prices as higher risk for a given risk aversion parameter – as aversion to risk rises the impact of the risk discount on willingness both to provide and to buy annuities declines.

With higher risk aversion and also with greater uncertainty the two curves flatten out, so that the equilibrium price is reduced.

Model solution

The model does not have an analytical solution and we therefore solve numerically for the three choice variables described by the utility maximization problem (the amount that the individuals choose to consume when young, the proportion of old people's wealth that the young are prepared to annuitize and the proportion of wealth which old people would like to annuitize), for an arbitrarily chosen annuity rate. The annuity rate is then adjusted to clear the annuity market. The model is programmed in Matlab and makes use of the optimizing routines available there.

The assumption of a constant elasticity of substitution utility function means that, given values for the parameters of the model, the proportion of wealth that old people would like to annuitize depends only on the annuity rate and is independent of their wealth. For a starting price, we find the proportion of wealth that old people would like to annuitize (ϕ_i). With an exogenous value for the actual wealth-holding of old people, w_i, we then find the optimal values of the three decision variables of young people ($c_{y,i+1}, \phi'_i, \phi_{i+1}$). We then calculate the new value of old age wealth implied by these and also reduce π by an amount proportional to $\phi'_i - \phi_i$. The process continues until ϕ'_i, ϕ_i and ϕ_{i+1} converge. It should be noted that, although w_i is influenced by the optimization choices, it is exogenous to the optimization decision of the young. This reflects the fact that the wealth of generation i in old age is not a choice variable of generation $i + 1$.

Results

The only structural assumption of the model is that $t = 0.6$. We present results for two values of σ^2, 0.04 and 0.01, corresponding to standard deviations of t of 0.2 and 0.1 respectively. We also look at a range of values of γ including $\gamma = 1.01$ so as to avoid having to respecify the model for the situation where $\gamma = 1$, given logarithmic utility.

The results reported in Table 13.1 are consistent with intuition in so far as it can be formed about a market-clearing process. The annuity rate, π, is decreasing in γ, the coefficient of relative risk aversion, and annuity rates are low when there is high uncertainty about future life spans $\left(\sigma^2 = 0.04\right)$. For very low levels of risk aversion the annuity rate rises towards 1 (the actuarially fair rate) as would be expected.

The amount of first-period consumption is also decreasing with the degree of risk aversion. This does not represent an income effect, because the expected effect of annuity transactions on lifetime income is zero; if annuity rates are low, someone expects to make a good profit on the annuities which they sell when young, but at the same time, does not expect to do very well on the annuities that they buy when old. Since the model is solved in a steady state these two effects must cancel out each other. Rather it reflects the fact that, with high levels of risk aversion, young people are more concerned about the uncertainty in their consumption when old; thus they undertake precautionary saving at high levels of risk aversion. The extent of annuitization, given by ϕ, increases with risk aversion, and with the extent of uncertainty in mortality rates. This suggests that demand reacts more strongly to these factors than does supply.

Table 13.1. *Effects of aggregate mortality risk on the annuity market.*

	γ	π	c	ϕ
$\sigma^2 = 0.01$	6.0	0.933	0.618	0.572
	5.0	0.942	0.619	0.557
	4.0	0.951	0.620	0.543
	3.0	0.962	0.622	0.530
	2.0	0.973	0.623	0.519
	1.0	0.986	0.625	0.509
	0.5	0.993	0.626	0.504
	0.1	0.999	0.626	0.501
$\sigma^2 = 0.04$	6.0	0.833	0.602	0.732
	5.0	0.840	0.606	0.693
	4.0	0.853	0.609	0.653
	3.0	0.875	0.614	0.613
	2.0	0.906	0.619	0.573
	1.0	0.948	0.625	0.534
	0.5	0.973	0.628	0.516
	0.1	0.994	0.631	0.503

The results may be contrasted with what would emerge if the sale of an annuity were a simple bet by a risk-averse individual – in other words what might happen if we settled for a partial solution and were not concerned about finding the market-clearing annuity rate. We would then use the standard formula for pricing a bet by an individual with relative risk aversion γ; the rate would be given as $\pi = 1 - \gamma\sigma^2/2$. It is straightforward to see that this gives annuity rates that are higher than those shown in Table 13.1; the consumption risk faced by the young when selling annuities is greater than that implied by the simple model and so the price is driven up considerably.

Conclusions

A general equilibrium framework is needed to assess the risk discount which is likely to be applied to annuity rates to reflect the fact that sellers of annuities cannot protect themselves from aggregate mortality risk. We have studied a framework in which annuities are supplied by young people to old people and the risk discount is established at a level which clears the market. Our analysis, set out in the context of representative members of young and old cohorts, assumes that old people have the choice between buying an annuity, which protects them completely from mortality risk, and investing in a tontine, which protects them from most mortality risk but which leaves them exposed to the aggregate mortality risk faced by the cohort to which they belong. Subject to these conditions, we find that moderate rates of aggregate mortality risk are likely to imply that market-clearing annuity rates are between 1 per cent and 7 per cent below actuarially fair rates, depending upon the extent of risk aversion.

The model set out here is obviously stylized. It does, however, focus on the fact that annuities must be supplied by someone, and that the suppliers have to be people of working age. Thus the terms on which they supply annuities are crucial. While it is possible that some of the aggregate mortality risk described here could be smoothed by intergenerational transfers – either through government finances or private bequests – it is unlikely that these channels will fully insure any one generation. And in the absence of contracts with unborn generations, people of working age have no guarantee that they will have access to an annuity market when they reach retirement. Furthermore, it is unlikely that alternative investment media would have a major impact on the results unless the returns on such media are closely correlated with mortality shocks. These issues suggest that aggregate mortality risk may have an important influence on market-clearing annuity rates, as described here.

A number of issues would seem to warrant further research. One is the assumption that there is no individual-specific risk. In the absence of tontines, the demand for annuities by old people in the current context would be raised appreciably and the risk discount on the annuity rate would also be increased as young people demanded greater reward for the extra risk that they carried. Furthermore, the analysis reported here is time-inconsistent, in the sense that it abstracts from the temporal variation in the market-clearing annuity rate that is implied by aggregate mortality risk.

To understand the potential implications of this second restriction, it is useful to consider a specific example. If the current older generation lives unexpectedly long, then the current younger generation has unexpectedly little wealth when it reaches old age. This means that, even though its desired purchase of annuities as a proportion of second-period wealth maintains its standard relationship to the annuity rate, nevertheless, the total amount that it wishes to spend on annuities will be low. In consequence, even if the mortality risks are serially uncorrelated, the market-clearing annuity rate at which young people will purchase annuities is likely to be slightly higher than it would be if the current old people had died as expected. Thus the realization is likely to be more favourable to the currently young than might seem the case if one focused on the effects of mortality shocks alone. The annuity rate which the currently young will face when old is negatively correlated with the life span of the currently old and this negative correlation will increase the willingness of the currently young to sell annuities as compared to the earlier results. Such an effect can be seen as an example of Le Chatelier's principle – that nature tends to reverse a change. However, it also points to a mechanism whereby the cost of meeting unexpected variations in life span is spread, at least to some extent, beyond the cohort which experiences the shock and the younger cohort which has sold them annuities.

Incorporation of this effect can be obtained by numerical solution of the intertemporal Bellman equation via backward induction. It will then be possible to explore how far the annuity market offers a means for spreading these demographic shocks across future generations. In the mean time the results in Figure 13.1 can be seen as setting lower limits to annuity rates in the face of mortality risk.

NOTES

1 The UK annuities market is one of the largest in the world, and therefore provides a useful reference point for discussion.
2 See Government Actuary's Department website: www.gad.gov.uk.
3 Yields quoted for 20 year 0 coupon gilts; see www.statistics.gov.au.
4 This is because annuitants tend to live longer than the wider population, and because longevity also tends to increase with the size of the annuity purchased. In similar and slightly earlier work, Murthi, Orszag and Orszag (1999) suggest that roughly two-thirds of the apparent difference between actual and fair annuity rates (based on aggregate mortality tables) can be accounted for by adverse selection.
5 Yaari (1965) showed that risk-averse consumers will choose to annuitize all of their wealth when subject to an uncertain length of life and actuarially fair annuity rates. Nevertheless, the private market for annuities tends to be thin in the absence of compulsion (e.g. Brown *et al.*, 2001). Brown (2001) considers the effects of choosing alternative interest rates for analysis, and Murthi, Orszag and Orszag (1999) and Poterba (2001) consider possible explanations for the annuity puzzle.
6 The influence of finite lives in the current context is partly mitigated by the role of individual bequests in intergenerational transmission of wealth, and by the fact that governments provide the majority of annuities in many countries around the world.
7 The lifetime labour incomes of adjacent cohorts has an impact on the market-clearing annuity price. In the current context we assume that each generation receives the same labour income. If, however, younger generations earned higher labour incomes than older generations, then the supply of annuities would, *ceteris paribus*, be higher, and the market-clearing annuity rate more favourable to purchasers of annuities. The effect of this correlation remains an issue for further research.

8 Named after Lorenzo Tonti who set up such a scheme for Louis XIV around 1653.

9 The assumption that $t_i = t_{i-1} = t_0$ implies that, although individuals take into consideration the uncertainty of life spans, the out-turns are equivalent to *ex ante* point estimates.

REFERENCES

Brown, J. R. (2001). 'Private Pensions, Mortality Risk, and the Decision to Annuitize'. *Journal of Public Economics*, 82: 29–62.

Brown, J. R., Mitchell, O. S., Poterba, J. M. and Warshawsky, M. J. (2001). *The Role of Annuity Markets in Financing Retirement*. Cambridge, MA: MIT Press.

Cannon, E. and Tonks, I. (2003). 'UK Annuity Rates and Pension Replacement Ratios 1957–2002'. Discussion Paper no. 8, UBS Pensions Research Programme, London School of Economics.

Finkelstein, A. and Poterba, J. (2002). 'Selection Effects in the Market for Individual Annuities: New Evidence from the United Kingdom'. *Economic Journal*, 112: 28–50.

Friedberg, L. and Webb, A. (2005). 'Life is Cheap: Using Mortality Bonds to Hedge Aggregate Mortality Risk'. Working Paper no. 2005-13, Centre for Retirement Research, Boston College.

James, E. and Song, X. (2001). 'Annuity Markets around the World: Money's Worth and Risk Intermediation'. Working Paper no. 16/01, CeRP.

Mehra, R. and Prescott, E. (2003). 'The Equity Premium in Restrospect', in *Handbook of the Economics of Finance*, ed. G. Constantinides, M. Harris and R. Stulz. JAI Press, pp. 887–936.

Mitchell, O. S., Poterba, J. M., Warshawsky, M. J. and Brown, J. R. (1999). 'New Evidence on the Money's Worth of Individual Annuities'. *American Economic Review*, 89: 1299–1318.

Murthi, M., Orszag, J. M. and Orszag, P. R. (1999). 'The Value for Money of Annuities in the UK: Theory, Experience and Policy', Discussion Paper, Birkbeck College, University of London.

Pensions Commission (2005). *A New Pensions Settlement for the Twenty-First Century*, Norwich: TSO.

Poterba, J. M. (2001). 'Annuity Markets and Retirement Security'. *Fiscal Studies*, 22: 249–79.

Yaari, M. (1965). 'Uncertain Life-time, Life Insurance and the Theory of the Consumer'. *Review of Economic Studies*, 32: 137–50.

The economics of demographic uncertainty

Martin Flodén

Introduction

It is well documented that future demographic development is uncertain and difficult to predict (see, for example, Keilman, Cruijsen and Alho, this volume, chap. 2; and Alho, Cruijsen and Keilman, this volume, chap. 3). This uncertainty may have important implications both for individual decisions and for economic policy. Several contributions to this volume examine how macro-economic aggregates or public finances are affected by alternative demographic developments under the assumption that these demographic developments are perfectly predicted and anticipated by economic decision-makers. The final three chapters in this part of the book (chaps. 11–13) differ in that they explicitly model the demographic uncertainty and allow agents to react and take precautionary measures in response to this uncertainty.

A number of important economic topics can only be studied if uncertainty is explicitly modelled. The three chapters take a step in the right direction and contribute by introducing demographic uncertainty to the analysis of some specific questions. Alho and Määttänen analyse how households respond to the demographic uncertainty in a partial equilibrium setting. Van de Ven and Weale analyse how different generations can share demographic risks on private markets, whereas Jensen and Jørgensen analyse how economic policy may improve risk-sharing, and to some extent how economic policy may be affected by demographic shocks. These contributions also raise a number of issues that need further study, and they indicate that integrating different elements of their analysis could be important.

Household behaviour and welfare

The first issue I want to address is how demographic uncertainty affects behaviour (as analysed by Alho and Määttänen) and welfare and the value of insurance (as analysed by van de Ven and Weale). In particular, it is

270

worth noting that the analysis from settings with income uncertainty is not directly applicable in this setting.[1]

Let me use a simplistic analytical framework to illustrate this. Consider an endowment economy where households live for a maximum of two periods. Young households have exogenous income y which can be consumed (c_1) or saved (s). A stochastic fraction ρ of households survive to the second period where they consume (c_2) what was saved in the first period. There is an annuity market so that those who survive share the savings of those who did not survive. Households then maximize expected lifetime utility by solving

$$\max \mathrm{E}\{u(c_1) + \beta\rho u(c_2)\} \tag{1}$$

subject to

$$c_1 + s = y \text{ and } c_2 = s/\rho$$

where β is the discount factor and E is the expectation operator.[2] Note that second-period consumption for the survivors is stochastic if the aggregate survival probability is stochastic.

The solution to the household's problem is characterized by the Euler equation $u'(c_1) = \beta\mathrm{E}[u'(c_2)]$. Assume that utility belongs to the standard constant relative risk aversion class of functions, $u(c) = c^{1-\mu}/(1-\mu)$, and let $\bar{\rho}$ and σ denote the mean and variance of ρ. A second-order expansion of $u'(c_2)$ around $\bar{\rho}$ implies that the Euler equation can be approximated as

$$u'(c_1) \approx \beta u'\left(\frac{s}{\bar{\rho}}\right)\left[1 + \frac{\sigma^2\mu(\mu-1)}{2\bar{\rho}^2}\right] \tag{2}$$

In the analysis of behaviour under income uncertainty, Kimball (1990) demonstrates that this utility function implies precautionary behaviour for any risk aversion $\mu > 0$, i.e. higher income uncertainty implies higher saving and less consumption in the first period. From (2) we see that higher demographic uncertainty ($\sigma\uparrow$) raises s only if $\mu > 1$. If utility is logarithmic ($\mu = 1$), behaviour does not change in response to changed uncertainty. This result helps explain Alho and Määttänen's finding that households may not lose much by ignoring uncertainty. The optimal response may actually be to behave as if survival probabilities were non-stochastic.

The analysis of welfare consequences of demographic uncertainty is also different from the standard analysis under income uncertainty. The stochastic variable has a direct impact on utility in the second period, $\beta\rho u(c_2)$. Note that income uncertainty in the second period only affects c_2. Welfare falls when second-period consumption becomes more volatile if the instantaneous utility function, u, is concave. Mortality risk has somewhat different implications since it affects not only consumption but also the effective discount rate, $\alpha\rho$.

Consider, for example, annuities that reduce the volatility of second-period consumption. The difference between income and mortality risk affects the interpretation of what these annuities do. If the instantaneous utility function is concave in consumption then $\beta\rho u(c_2)$ is concave in ρ, and households would benefit if the demographic uncertainty could be reduced. The annuities, however, cannot reduce the demographic uncertainty but only its impact on consumption. If annuities succeed in holding c_2 constant, welfare will increase but households will face *more risk* since $\beta\rho u(c_2)$ will become more volatile.[3] These annuities reduce the convexity but not the volatility of $\beta\rho u(c_2)$.

This analysis does not only affect the interpretation of what annuities do, but also indicates that the optimal insurance typically does not imply constant consumption. Since the annuities only can affect one of the two channels through which demographic uncertainty affects utility, it is typically not optimal to fully eliminate volatility in that channel. An optimal insurance will instead let the outcome in the channel that can be affected (consumption) counteract the outcome in the other channel, which implies that consumption will vary with the aggregate survival rate.

The scope for insurance

The other issue I want to address is the scope for insurance. In particular, I want to focus on two questions. First, what insurance can be provided by private markets and what is the role of the government? Second, how are the possibilities of insuring affected by the nature of the stochastic process for demographic development?

Consider an economy that is populated by overlapping generations of households behaving as in the analytical framework presented above. Since households live for a maximum of two periods, and since all households in a generation face identical risks, there will be no market for insurance. Different generations have lives that overlap a maximum of one period and consequently cannot engage in intertemporal trade. What if we consider a more realistic setting where life spans are greater than two periods? Insurance markets can then arise, but as argued by Bohn (2005), the scope for private insurance is still limited since much of the uncertainty for a middle-aged generation will be resolved before it can start trading with younger generations. Providing insurance against these long-run risks is therefore best handled by governments that can also engage in trade with generations that have still not been born.

Consider again the analytical framework presented above, but assume that the government runs a pay-as-you-go defined-benefit pension system. It promises a pension p to all survivors, and it finances this payment by taxing the young. Suppose that aggregate longevity turns out to be unusually high. The government may now reduce the pension p and/or raise tax payments by the young, but it may also let future generations contribute. For example, the government can hold p fixed, raise tax payments of the currently young, but also promise higher pensions for the currently young so that they are compensated for their tax payments. Therefore, the government can, in principle, achieve a better outcome than private markets.

But the scope for government insurance may also be limited. The discussion above implicitly assumes that the demographic shock is temporary, so that longevity increases for today's old but not (or to a lesser extent) for future generations. If longevity increases for today's old and all future generations, the strategy described above would require pension payments that increase from generation to generation to compensate for tax payments that also increase, and such strategies will not be feasible in dynamically efficient economies. In general, it will be difficult, even for a benevolent government, to insure against shocks that affect all present and future generations.

This is how demographic uncertainty has often been modelled in economic studies, including those in this volume by Jensen and Jørgensen and van de Ven and Weale. More realistically, however, longevity does not fluctuate around a constant mean but increases stochastically over time, as in Alho and Määttänen's study. Analysing such non-stationary processes is much more complicated, and new methodological developments will be necessary before such processes can be incorporated in general equilibrium models with private or public insurance.

Conclusions

To summarize, I have argued that the impact of demographic uncertainty on welfare and behaviour differs from the impact of income uncertainty, and that there is a need for further theoretical analysis of these issues. It is unlikely that insurance against aggregate demographic uncertainty can be provided by the market, but governments can possibly do so. Furthermore, and maybe more importantly, existing government programmes such as pension systems will unavoidably be affected by different demographic outcomes. Future research should explicitly model demographic uncertainty to analyse how public finances are affected when demographic development is not perfectly anticipated. Examples of other related questions that need further study are: what are the conditions for dynamic efficiency when aggregate demographic developments are uncertain? Can the government (in a dynamically efficient economy) issue debt that with a high probability raises welfare for all future generations? Can the government repay the debt and fulfil pension obligations under all demographic developments?[4]

NOTES

1 Pratt (1964) analyses the effects of income uncertainty on welfare, and Kimball (1990) analyses the effects on behaviour.
2 For some questions it may be important to guarantee that higher longevity raises welfare. Lifetime utility can then be specified as $u(c_1) + \beta \rho u(c_2) + (1 - \rho) D$ where D is a sufficiently large negative number.
3 To see this, note that fluctuations in ρ have two opposing effects on $\beta \rho u(c_2)$ in the absence of annuities. A higher ρ raises the number of survivors, a positive welfare effect, but also reduces each survivor's consumption, a negative welfare effect. By stabilizing consumption, annuities remove the second effect but leave the first effect unmoderated.
4 In settings with stochastic income or production, Zilcha (1991) and Blanchard and Weil (2001) analyse dynamic efficiency, and Ball, Elmendorf and Mankiw (1998) examine debt strategies.

REFERENCES

Ball, L., Elmendorf, W. and Mankiw, N. G. (1998). 'The Deficit Gamble'. *Journal of Money, Credit and Banking*, 30: 699–720.
Blanchard, O. and Weil, P. (2001). 'Dynamic Efficiency, the Riskless Rate, and Debt Ponzi Games under Uncertainty'. *Advances in Macroeconomics* 1: article 3.
Bohn, H. (2005). 'Who Bears What Risk? An Intergenerational Perspective'. University of California at Santa Barbara.
Kimball, M. S. (1990). 'Precautionary Saving in the Small and in the Large'. *Econometrica*, 58: 53–73.
Pratt, J. W. (1964). 'Risk aversion in the small and in the large'. *Econometrica*, 32: 122–36.
Zilcha, I. (1991). 'Characterizing Efficiency in Stochastic Overlapping Generations Models'. *Journal of Economic Theory*, 55: 1–16.

Index

For EU product safety concerns, contact us at Calle de José Abascal, 56–1°,
28003 Madrid, Spain or eugpsr@cambridge.org.

www.ingramcontent.com/pod-product-compliance
Ingram Content Group UK Ltd.
Pitfield, Milton Keynes, MK11 3LW, UK
UKHW012157180425
457623UK00018B/243